Challenges in a Changing World

Clingendael Views on Global and Regional Issues

Challenges in a Changing World

Clingendael Views on Global and Regional Issues

On the occasion of the twenty-fifth anniversary of the Netherlands Institute of International Relations 'Clingendael'

edited by

Jaap de Zwaan
Edwin Bakker
Sico van der Meer

T·M·C· Asser Press
The Hague

Published by T·M·C·Asser press
P.O. Box 16163, 2500 BD The Hague, The Netherlands
<www.asserpress.nl>

T·M·C·Asser press' English language books are distributed exclusively by:

Cambridge University Press, The Edinburgh Building, Shaftesbury Road,
Cambridge CB2 2RU, UK,
or
for customers in the USA, Canada and Mexico:
Cambridge University Press, 100 Brook Hill Drive, West Nyack, NY 10994-2133, USA
<www.cambridge.org>

Language editing: Peter Morris
Final editing: Peter Schregardus
Layout: Oasis Productions

ISBN 978-90-6704-297-0

FOREWORD

In 2008 the Netherlands Institute of International Relations 'Clingendael' is celebrating its 25th anniversary. Congratulations!

In the Netherlands the Institute is well known as a relevant partner in the public debate on foreign affairs policy. But also abroad the prestige of Clingendael as a think-tank and a diplomatic academy, where hundreds of foreign diplomats have been trained over the years, is fully recognized and appreciated.

This book includes a series of articles written by Clingendael staff members on a wide variety of policy domains. The selection of topics illustrates the considerable expertise and knowledge that Clingendael possesses in so many fields relating to foreign policy.

'Reflecting the World' is the motto of Clingendael's activities during its anniversary year 2008. Consequently, this book aspires to offer the reader a series of reflections on the new challenges and developments the world is experiencing in this rather turbulent period of time.

The reader finds the different dimensions of the process of globalization well represented in this thought-provoking book. In that context attention is in particular paid to issues like: the new upcoming global players and economies; the new security challenges and threats like climate change and energy; the role of international organizations like the United Nations and NATO; the importance of regional cooperation; the responsibilities in this respect of the European Union; and the Dutch interests in all these areas. In so doing all four main domains of specialization at Clingendael – European studies, Security, Diplomacy and Energy – are well represented.

For all these reasons, this book is highly recommended to politicians, policy makers, academics and all those who may be interested in the fast-track developments of our modern world.

On behalf of all members of the Governing Board I wish the Institute and its staff members lots of success in the next period of 25 years!

The Hague, December 2008

Bernard R. Bot
Chairman of the Board of Governors
of the Clingendael Institute

Summary of Contents

Contents

About the Authors

Louise Anten
Louise Anten MA is Head of the Conflict Research Unit of the Clingendael Security and Conflict Programme.

Edwin Bakker
Dr Edwin Bakker is Head of the Clingendael Security and Conflict Programme.

Bernard Bot
Dr Bernard R. Bot is Chairman of the Board of Governors of the Clingendael Institute. From 2003 to 2007 he was Minister of Foreign Affairs of the Netherlands.

Willy Bruggeman
Professor Dr Willy Bruggeman is President of the Belgian Federal Police Board and Professor of Police Science at the Benelux University Centre. He was Deputy Director of Europol from 1993 to 2003.

Ko Colijn
Professor Dr Ko Colijn is a Senior Research Fellow in the Clingendael Security and Conflict Programme and Professor of International Relations at the Erasmus University Rotterdam.

Lucia van Geuns
Lucia van Geuns MSc is Deputy Head of the Clingendael International Energy Programme.

Bibi van Ginkel
Bibi van Ginkel LLM is a Senior Research Fellow in the Clingendael Security and Conflict Programme.

Marcel de Haas
Lieutenant-Colonel Dr Marcel de Haas (Royal Netherlands Army) is a Senior Research Fellow in the Clingendael Security and Conflict Programme.

Peter van Ham
Dr Peter van Ham is Director of Global Governance Research in the Clingendael Diplomatic Studies Programme.

Stijn van den Heuvel
Stijn van den Heuvel MSc is a Researcher in the Clingendael International Energy Programme.

Kees Homan
Major-General (retired) Kees Homan LLM, MA (Royal Netherlands Marine Corps) is a Senior Advisor in the Clingendael Security and Conflict Programme.

Warner ten Kate
Warner ten Kate MA is a Researcher in the Clingendael International Energy Programme.

Willem van Kemenade
Willem van Kemenade MA is a Senior Visiting Fellow in the Clingendael Diplomatic Studies Programme.

Mendeltje van Keulen
Dr Mendeltje van Keulen is a Senior Fellow in the Clingendael European Studies Programme.

Sico van der Meer
Sico van der Meer MA is a Research Fellow in the Clingendael Security and Conflict Programme.

Paul Meerts
Paul Meerts MA is Advisor to the Director of the Clingendael Institute.

Emma van der Meulen
Emma van der Meulen BA was an Intern in Clingendael Asia Studies in 2008. She is studying at the Graduate Institute of International Studies in Geneva, Switzerland.

Alfred Pijpers
Dr Alfred Pijpers is a Senior Research Fellow in the Clingendael European Studies Programme.

Willem Post
Willem Post MA is a Senior Visiting Fellow in the Clingendael Diplomatic Studies Programme.

Frans Paul van der Putten
Dr Frans Paul van der Putten is a Research Fellow in Clingendael Asia Studies.

Louise van Schaik
Louise van Schaik MA is a Fellow in the Clingendael European Studies Programme.

Stephan Slingerland
Dr Stephan Slingerland is a Senior Researcher in the Clingendael International Energy Programme.

Roos Toxopeus
Roos Toxopeus MA is a Fellow in the Clingendael Security and Conflict Programme.

Jaap de Zwaan
Professor Dr Jaap W. de Zwaan is Director of the Clingendael Institute and Professor of the Law of the European Union at the Law School, Erasmus University Rotterdam.

More detailed information about the authors can be found on the website of the Clingendael Institute: <www.clingendael.nl>

Reflecting the World: Impressions from a Dutch Perspective

Jaap de Zwaan

Introduction

This chapter[1] provides an analysis of the changes the world has experienced – and still is experiencing – as a consequence of the process of globalization and internationalization.[2] The developments vary from changes in the balance of power at the world level to new threats and challenges related to our security. The question will be discussed whether the present system of global governance – the reference here is in particular to the role of international organizations and, in Europe, of the European Union – is able to cope with these new challenges. In this context the following question will additionally be raised: which adaptations are to be preferred in the light of the Dutch interests at stake?

In a way the present analysis reflects the main issues and developments on the Clingendael research agenda for the near future.

A multipolar world

The world is rapidly changing. New economies are rising, such as Brazil, Russia, India and China, the so-called BRICs. Will they become new superpowers? So much is clear, the situation characterized by the existence of only one superpower – the United States – as we have experienced during the last twenty years, after the collapse of the Soviet Union, might come to an end in the coming decade(s). Russia, with its enormous energy reserves, seems to be on its

---

[1] The title of this contribution 'Reflecting the World' represents the motto covering all activities which Clingendael has organized in 2008, the year of its 25th anniversary.

[2] Extensive discussions exist on globalization and its impact, with many advocates and (modest) opponents such as Jagdish N. Bhagwati, *In Defence of Globalization* (Oxford University Press, 2004), or Joseph Stiglitz, *Globalization and its Discontents* (Penguin Group, 2002).

J. de Zwaan, E. Bakker and S. van der Meer (eds.), Challenges in a Changing World

way to regaining the status of a major player at the world level. China, with its population of over 1.3 billion and its booming economy, has the ambition to become a new superpower.[3]

Russia

However, nothing can be taken for granted in this discussion. The Russian economy, for example, is not developing in a balanced manner. The impetus these days is, put in a one-sided manner, the energy sector, whereas reforms in other sectors are lacking. Indeed, the Russian economy is in desperate need of new technologies and innovations. Moreover, demographic developments indicate that the Russian population might shrink from about 150 million inhabitants today to less than 100 million in two decades from now. Uncertainties too exist as to the political reforms taking place in Russia. More generally speaking, the question is whether Russia will become a stable, credible and responsible partner for the Western world in world politics. So far there is no indication that a lot has changed since the arrival of the new President, Medvedev. In the context of foreign policy, however, the invasion of Georgia in August 2008 is certainly a disturbing event.[4]

China

China, for its part, tries to present itself to the world as a new and stable superpower. The fact that the country has managed to organize the recent Beijing Olympic Games in a perfect manner is a point of reference in this context. However, as to the standards of human and fundamental rights, still a lot has to improve. Moreover, the energy needs of the country are huge and – given current gas and oil prices – extremely expensive. Because of the urgency of the matter China, to mention only one aspect, is trying to cover its needs through cooperation with oil producing countries, independent of the democratic standards of the countries concerned (e.g., Sudan in Africa).[5] It demonstrates the lack of importance that the Chinese authorities themselves attach to human rights.

---

[3] Mahbubani discusses the probability of a power shift not exclusively to China but to the East as a whole: Kishore Mahbubani, *The New Asian Hemisphere, the irresistible shift of global power to the East* (New York, Public Affairs 2008).

[4] On Russia's foreign and security policy see also the contribution by Marcel de Haas in this book. See for an impression of the personality of the new President, Medvedev, an article by the same author in the *Internationale Spectator*, the monthly journal of the Clingendael Institute: 'Dmitri Medvedev: een liberaal in het Kremlin', No. 3 (March 2008) pp. 170-171.

[5] See on this practice also: Sara van Hoeymissen, 'China, niet-inmenging als PR-troef onder druk', 62 *Internationale Spectator*, No. 6 (June 2008) pp. 331-336.

Moreover, economic growth does not necessarily imply prosperity for all citizens. Indeed, China is a vast country and the economic reforms, started by Deng Xiaoping, are more particularly concentrated in the eastern part of the country. This means that tremendous efforts – both economic and financial – have to be made in order to overcome the backwardness of other parts of China. Another vital element in this discussion concerns the stability at the fringes of the country. The signs of unrest in border areas such as Tibet and Xinjiang can only be interpreted as a threat to China's unity.[6]

Other countries

Similar questions can be raised as to the economic developments in countries like India and Brazil. In many upcoming countries severe poverty still exists. And, to the extent that economic progress is made, inter alia, enormous income differences are apparent.[7] Will India and Brazil for example be able to develop their economies in such a way that the totality of their peoples can profit therefrom? And will they manage to maintain political stability and the rule of law? These are important questions with no clear answers. The same holds true for several other upcoming countries, such as Mexico, South Africa, and Indonesia.[8]

Western world

And what about the *United States* and Europe? The former has been a constant factor in world politics since the Second World War and has been among the founding fathers of many international organizations and standards. As an extremely wealthy and militarily powerful country the United States will certainly remain an important player at world level. This being said, the way the United States has participated in international cooperation over the last few years, especially since the terrorist attacks of 11 September 2001, has given rise to concerns. The US-led invasion of Iraq in 2003 was not supported by a UN Security

---

[6] On the role of China see also the contribution by Willem van Kemenade in this book. The contribution in this book by Frans-Paul van der Putten and Emma van der Meulen concerns the relationship between China and Europe. A number of other articles with regard to topical developments in China are to be found in 62 *Internationale Spectator*, No. 3 (March 2008) pp. 127-159. See on the tendencies of separatism in China also: Henk Schulte Nordholt & Sander Tideman,, 'Tibet en China: seperatisme of culturele autonomie', 62 *Internationale Spectator*, No. 7/8 (July-August 2008) pp. 418-421.

[7] For a discussion on different ways to realize long-term sustainable economic growth and poverty reduction, see: Deepak Nayyar, José Antoni Ocampo, Joseph Stiglitz (among others), *Stability with Growth: Macroeconomics, Liberalization and Development* (Oxford, 2006).

[8] Ibid.

Council resolution; the United States did not ratify the Kyoto Protocol; and it did not become a party to the Statute of the International Criminal Court, to mention only three examples. In all these cases the United States apparently did not want to join in projects developed by specialized and competent international organizations which might restrict US foreign and defence policies. To some extent this attitude reflects the status of the United States as the sole superpower over the last two decades. Whether the politics of the United States and its attitude with regard to international organizations will change after the Bush administration, has to be awaited.[9] We will probably know more after the presidential elections of November 2008.

For Europe, particularly the *European Union*, a crucial stage in the process of integration is approaching. An economic giant, but a political dwarf, that is the saying.[10] Therefore, if Europe wants to be taken seriously by major players at the world level, it has to produce some 'hard' power in the areas of foreign and security policy.[11] For the moment, however, Europe is not able to act as an entity and to speak with one voice in those areas. The Iraq crisis and the way this dossier was handled during the discussions at the level of the United Nations in 2002/2003 was certainly a sad example in this respect. France as well as Germany as the acting chairman of the UN Security Council at that time, took completely opposite positions – compared to the one adopted by the United Kingdom – with respect to the issue of the invasion of Iraq. The Georgian crisis in the summer of 2008 is another example. A division became apparent between 'old' Member States, such as Germany and France, which did not want to suspend cooperation and relations with Russia, and a number of 'new' Member States of Central Europe, who were in favour of sanctions to be imposed on Russia. Also the fact that the Lisbon Treaty will not enter into force shortly, as a consequence of the negative outcome of the Irish referendum of 12 June 2008, will result in a negative drawback.

So, many uncertainties do exist. This being said, the two sides of the Atlantic will need each other, also in the future.[12] Both sides of the pond share the same

---

[9] On the future position of the United States in a world full of 'global political awakening', see: Zbigniew Brzezinski and Brent Scowcroft, two former National Security Advisors, *Amercia and the World: Conversations on the Future of American Policy* (Basic Books, 2008).

[10] The EU has often been described as a 'soft power', the ability to persuade using the attractiveness of political ideas, culture and policies: Joseph Nye, *Soft Power: The Means to Success in World Politics* (Public Affairs, 2004).

[11] See also the speech of the Dutch Minister of Foreign Affairs, Maxime Verhagen, of 1 September 2008 ('Veranderende wereld, vaste waarden: Nederlands buitenlands beleid in de 21^{e} eeuw') at Leyden University, 62 *Internationale Spectator*, No. 10 (October 2008) pp. 507-512. On the necessity for some EU hard power see also the contribution of Peter van Ham in this book.

[12] On the relationship between the US and Europe see also the contribution of Willem Post in this book.

'Western' norms and values with regard to democracy and human rights. They also share many economic interests, are part of the same important worldwide economic organizations, such as the World Trade Organization (hereafter, WTO),[13] and both have to deal with potential new strong economic powers (e.g., the BRICs). In addition, Europe and America also need each other in the security field and have common interests in security organizations such as NATO and the OSCE.[14]

Threats and challenges

Apart from geopolitical tendencies in a developing multipolar world, existing and new threats to our security have to be countered. For decades the world has been suffering from conflicts originating from a number of politically unstable regions: the Middle East, South Asia, the Korean peninsula and Central Africa, to mention the most important ones.

The *Middle East* – the reference here is to the Israeli-Palestine conflict in the first place – is still the place of origin of some of the most worrisome threats to world peace. Notwithstanding the fact that efforts have been periodically undertaken to solve the underlying problems, and to strive, for example, for the foundation of a Palestine state, so far no real solutions have been found. On the contrary, whereas in view of the complexity of the problems the United States seems to have lost its ambition to strive for a general settlement of the conflict at short notice, the positions of the interested local parties have hardened in the last ten years or so. In the meantime the regional scope of the conflict in the Middle East has increased. In this context the political situation in the Lebanon and the delicate problems related to Iran, with its nuclear programme,[15] can be referred to. In this way the possession and eventual use of nuclear weapons has become a particularly dangerous dimension of the dossier.

The nuclear issue is also present in the file *North Korea*. Fortunately, recently developments have become apparent according to which the North Korean authorities are prepared to dismantle their nuclear capacity. Let us hope that it will shortly be possible to welcome this country, or a reunited Korean peninsula, into the sphere of civilized countries.[16]

---

[13] The eventual WTO membership of the Russian Federation is a connected element in this context.

[14] Organization for Security and Cooperation in Europe.

[15] On Iran's nuclear programme see also the contribution by Alfred Pijpers in this book. See on the option of sanctions against Iran: Sico van der Meer,, 'Economische sancties tegen Iran: successen en tegenvallers', 62 *Internationale Spectator*, No. 9 (September 2008) pp. 451-453.

[16] On the issue of 'rogue states' see also the contribution by Sico van der Meer in this book.

Poverty and an unequal distribution of wealth traditionally also represent a constant threat to stability in many parts of the world. They are closely related to several serious problems: hunger, social unrest, bad systems of governance, the phenomenon of failed and fragile states,[17] massive migration and organized crime, to mention but a few. These kinds of threats can easily give rise to severe conflicts within countries or between states. The African continent – obvious examples are countries like Zimbabwe and Liberia – unfortunately still has a bad reputation in this respect.

Other threats are connected to *international crime*, acts of terrorism to be mentioned in the first place.[18] Since the attacks on the United States on 11 September 2001 the 'war on terror' has become the number one priority subject-matter on Western security agendas.[19] In fact, '9/11' is directly linked to the attack on Al Qaida and the Taliban regime in Afghanistan and – at least according to the Bush administration – to the invasion of Iraq in 2003. The situation in Iraq has been extremely damaging for the ordinary citizens of that country for a long time, but now seems to be improving somewhat. Nonetheless, the geographical scope of the 'war on terror' has broadened and, for example, has seriously infected Pakistan. In conjunction with the internal political developments in Pakistan – we can mention the assassination of the former Prime Minister Benazir Bhutto in the first place – the South Asian region in fact has only become more unstable. In this context it is only a tiny reassurance that, at the moment of writing this chapter, at least major incidents like the ones in the United States in 2001, Madrid in 2004 and London in 2005 have not occurred for some time. Outside the West, however, terrorists have continued to hit hard, for example in the Muslim world, resulting in thousands of casualties.

Peace missions

Since the end of the Cold War, an increasing number of international peace missions have been organized in reaction to violence within and between countries, especially in the Balkans, in Africa and in Asia.[20] There they try to pre-

---

[17] On fragile states see also the contribution by Louise Anten in this book.

[18] Thomas Friedman wrote when describing the impact of 9/11, 'History just took a right turn into a blind alley': in *Longitudes and Attitudes: Exploring the World After September 11* (Farrar, Straus & Giroux, 2002).

[19] On the judicial protection aspect of terrorism see also the contribution by Bibi van Ginkel in this book.

[20] This post-Cold War optimism was reflected in Francis Fukuyama's often cited *The End of History and The Last Man* (Free Press, 1992) but also in the UN *Agenda for Peace* (June 1992), an initiative by the former UN Secretary-General Boutros-Boutros Ghali, that lays out the UN objectives and ambitions for more preventive diplomacy, peacemaking, peacekeeping and peacebuilding.

vent more violence and to ease the situation. The United Nations, NATO, the European Union, other regional organizations like the African Union and individual countries – the Netherlands being one of them – have gained many experiences, fortunate and less fortunate ones, in the course of such missions.[21] One of the reasons why the Dutch are heavily involved in these missions is due to the fact that the Netherlands is strongly committed to upholding international stability and developing the international legal order – as laid down in its Constitution – and that it has the ambition to participate in several missions at the same time.[22] To that end the military in the Netherlands have been well organized and modernized during the last few decades.

The military activities in places such as Iraq, Afghanistan, Congo, and Chad, involve new tasks and responsibilities for the military. For example, civil tasks – assistance to local people, the development of reconstruction projects and educational work – have to be performed. Such reconstruction projects are provided – and financed – mainly by international organizations and the Western world. However, in an emerging multipolar world it seems fair that also others, for instance, new major world players – Brazil, Russia, India, and China – take their responsibility in this process.

New threats and developments

Apart from the traditional threats, a number of relatively new ones, all representing a new dimension of worldwide security, have gained in importance during the last decades. To mention a few: climate change, environmental degradation and energy scarcity.[23] Related problems include limited water supplies and the rise of food prices, natural disasters and world diseases (such as SARS). Also the current so-called banking ('credit') crisis can be regarded as an example of a new worldwide threat. Indeed, what appeared to be a temporary and local – American – incident has in the course of time adopted a strong international dimension. Meanwhile the crisis also affects European banks, Fortis in Belgium and the Netherlands to mention one, as well as stock markets around the globe.

All these new threats are global in nature and should, for that reason, be tackled at the world level. Bilateral cooperation between states will no longer

---

[21] A number of articles concerning experiences with regard to reconstruction after conflict projects are to be found in: 62 *Internationale Spectator*, No. 4 (April 2008) pp. 191-217.

[22] See also the contribution by Edwin Bakker and Kees Homan in this book.

[23] On the energy issue see also the contributions by Lucia van Geuns and Warner ten Kate; as well as by Stephan Slingerland and Stijn van den Heuvel in this book. A number of other articles concerning climate change, environmental protection and energy security are to be found in: 62 *Internationale Spectator*, No. 5 (May 2008) pp. 257-299.

suffice. A more global approach has to be developed. Only through models of international cooperation can suitable answers be found.

The role of international organizations

Over the last, say, fifty years trust has more particularly been extended to forms of multilateral cooperation within the framework of international organizations in order to secure peace and stability in the world. As a reaction to the horrifying experiences in Europe during the First and Second World Wars, for example the League of Nations and, later, the United Nations were founded.

United Nations

Practice shows, however, that the UN is not able to properly fulfil its mission to secure pace and stability worldwide. Indeed, for the last few years it has been difficult to find an example of a concrete UN success in preventing or managing a conflict.

Certainly the ever-growing number of UN member states – in the 1960s and the 1990s – and the differences of opinion between them have played an important role in this process. Also the right of veto granted to the permanent members of the Security Council is a serious hindrance for the UN to do its job. Apart from the fact that the present group of five states possessing such a right of veto – the United States, Russia, China, the United Kingdom and France – does not reflect the new balance of power at the world level, practice shows that permanent members often invoke specific interests to block decision making in the Security Council. Thus, instead of contributing to peace and stability, the UN often stands in the way of realizing its own objectives. The discussion in the Security Council of July 2008 in the context of which China and Russia vetoed proposals to impose sanctions on President Mugabe and other political leaders of Zimbabwe is a recent example of this practice. The impossibility of developing an appropriate approach to end the crisis in the Caucasus – the conflict in Georgia – in August 2008 is another.

Thus, far-reaching reforms have to be introduced with regard to the functioning of the organs of the United Nations, the Security Council in the first place. The risk being that if the organization will not be able to function properly, it will lose its authority and be phased out as the most suitable framework to secure peace and security at the world level. Most probably, however, political reality will prevent these reforms from being realized.[24]

[24] The need for UN reforms and the position of former secretary-general of the UN, Kofi Annan, with respect to those reforms, has been amply discussed in the volumes 2004 and 2005 of

Human rights

The protection of human and fundamental rights is another example to demonstrate the limits of the impact that international organizations can have.[25] On the one hand, important legally-binding instruments have been concluded at the world level – at the United Nations – and at the regional level – for instance, at the Council of Europe – to ensure the protection of these rights. However, such norms and standards have to be implemented, applied and enforced at the national level. Now, practice shows that either the system of judicial protection developed by the organization concerned is defective or that judgments of international courts are not executed properly. The way in which, for example, the Russian Federation implements the judgments of the European Court of Human Rights in Strasbourg is a sad example in this respect.[26]

The multipolar world

The fact that the balance of power at the world level is gradually shifting may also have a negative effect on the functioning of international organizations. Indeed, because of the emergence of new global players a certain 're-nationalization' tendency may become apparent.[27] In such a scenario the ambitions of big global players (like the United States, China and Russia) or groups of states (like the European Union) may have far more impact than the activities of organizations operating worldwide. The way in which the United States and India have managed to get their nuclear deal accepted by the Non-Suppliers Group despite the fact that it undermines the Non-Proliferation Treaty, may be regarded as an example of this tendency.

---

the *Internationale Spectator*, the monthly journal of Institute Clingendael: Dick Leurdijk, 'Kofi Annans pleidooi voor radicale hervormingen van de VN', 58 *Internationale Spectator*, No. 2 (February 2004) pp. 84-89; Dick Leurdijk & Geert Steeghs, 'Rapport over radicale hervormingen VN loopt stuk op 101 tamme aanbevelingen', 59 *Internationale Spectator*, No. 2 (February 2005) pp. 63-68; Jan Wouters & Tom Ruys, 'Hervorming van de Veiligheidsraad, op zoek naar Europees perspectief', 59 *Internationale Spectator*, No. 6 (June 2005) pp. 295-298; and Peter Baehr,, 'Ingrijpende hervorming Verenigde Naties opnieuw mislukt', 59 *Internationale Spectator*, No. 11 (November 2005) pp. 586-590.

[25] Human Rights have in some ways become the dominant language of the public good since the Universal Declaration of Human Rights (1948): Michael Ignatieff, *The Rights Revolution* (Viking, 2000).

[26] Another frustrating example concerns the refusal by Russia to ratify Protocol no. 14 of the Council of Europe aiming to make the procedures of the European Court in Strasbourg more efficient.

[27] Robert Kagan discusses this change in geopolitics in: *Return of History and the End of Dreams* (Toronto, 2008).

Regional cooperation

Despite a certain 're-nationalization' tendency, the existence of models of multilateral cooperation remains vital to manage the global problems of today. We simply cannot do without international organizations.[28] The same is true for the establishment, in the form of treaties or otherwise, of standards and norms regarding peace and security.

This being said, it may be that the surveillance of respect for internationally accepted norms and standards can better be secured by reliable organizations at the regional level. In most cases regional organizations are in a position to structure the working of their institutions more efficiently than organizations operating worldwide. As a rule, they also possess adequate systems to control the implementation, in practice, of any decisions adopted, suitable mechanisms of judicial protection for the ordinary citizen included. The existence of the Council of Europe and the 'authority' of the European Convention for the Protection of Human Rights and Fundamental Freedoms of 1950 can be referred to as an illustration of this finding.

Frameworks like the European Union, ASEAN,[29] Mercosur,[30] the African Union, NAFTA,[31] CIS[32] and SCO[33] are, although different in nature and organization, examples of structures aiming to create (more) stability at the regional level. The recent establishment, on 13 July 2008 at the initiative of the French President Sarkozy, of a Mediterranean Union as a framework for cooperation between the Member States of the European Union and a number of states in Northern Africa and the Middle East, once more reflects the belief in structures of regional cooperation.

The European Union

For the Netherlands undoubtedly the European Union is the most logical vehicle to secure peace, stability and prosperity on our continent. Because of the

[28] The Dutch former Minister of Foreign Affairs and the present Chairman of the Clingendael Governing Board, Bernard Bot, stated in 2006 that because of the defects in the functioning of international organizations the Netherlands had to practise its membership of such organizations in a 'realistic' manner: 'Met overtuiging en berekening: van zuiver naar realistisch multilateralisme', 60 *Internationale Spectator*, No. 11 (November 2006) pp. 547-551. On the role of institutions with regard to international security see also the contribution by Ko Colijn in this book.

[29] Association of Southeast Asian Nations, founded in 1967.

[30] 'Mercado Común del Sur' or Southern Common Market, founded in 1991.

[31] North American Free Trade Agreement, entered into force in 1994.

[32] Commonwealth of Independent States, founded in 1991.

[33] Shanghai Cooperation Organization, founded in 2001.

international orientation of our country over the centuries – e.g., as to foreign policy and trade – the Union is a unique framework to be part of. It is unique because of the aim of the organization to contribute to a real integration of the economies and societies of its Member States, while keeping their national identities intact.[34] The Union is also unique because the organization is equipped with a number of institutions, legally binding instruments and procedures to make EU cooperation really effective. In that context the Union, for example, is provided with an adequate system of judicial protection, accessible not only for Member States and institutions but also for individuals. A vital element of that system concerns the possibility of cooperation between the EU Court of Justice in Luxembourg and national courts and tribunals.[35] All these elements illustrate the so-called supranational character of the cooperation in the framework of the European Union.

The EU cooperation is structured around its primary objective to establish an open market consisting – in 2008 – of 27 Member States. This concept –the internal market – is characterized by the principle of free movement and competition. Over the years the Union has gradually been conferred with other important responsibilities not only in the economic domain but also in the fields of foreign policy and defence as well as justice and home affairs.[36] In doing so, a complete and coherent package of responsibilities and activities has been developed.

The question, however, is whether the Union – at the beginning of the 21st century – is sufficiently prepared to face the present and new challenges referred to above. More in particular the reference here is to the emerging multipolar world. What will be the place and the impact of Europe in a world system where the balance of power is seriously shifting and which will be determined not only – as has been the case since the collapse of the Soviet Union – by the United States but also by countries like Russia and China and, possibly also, India and Brazil?

Here doubts do exist. On the one hand, the content of the European Union Treaty has been amended regularly in the light of new international tendencies and developments. Over time also the democratic character of the EU cooperation has been improved[37] and the decision-making process made more effi-

---

[34] According to Art. 6(3) of the EU Treaty the Union shall respect the national identities of its Member States.

[35] The so-called preliminary rulings procedure of Art. 234 EC Treaty.

[36] On the (external dimension of the) role of the European Police Office (Europol) see also the contribution by Roos Toxopeus and Willy Bruggeman in this book.

[37] The reference here is to the involvement of the European Parliament in the legislative process.

cient.[38] On the other hand, it can be argued that, today, not sufficient instruments and procedures are available to face future challenges related, more particularly, to the subject-matters of asylum and immigration; climate change and energy; as well as foreign policy and defence.

This finding is certainly true now that the successor of the Constitutional Treaty, the so-called Lisbon Treaty, will not shortly enter into force due to the Irish 'no'.[39] Indeed, unlike the Lisbon Treaty, the present text of the EU Treaty lacks, for example, a suitable framework in the area of asylum and immigration policy. The existing legal bases in these domains are simply outdated. Also an adequate policy programme does not exist. In this context the Hague Programme, adopted at the highest political level – the European Council – in 2004, can no longer serve as a roadmap. Furthermore and contrary to the Lisbon Treaty, in the present treaty text references to energy and climate change are lacking. This means that the Union will encounter difficulties once it tries to develop common approaches in these areas. This finding may also have foreign policy implications. The difficulties involved in establishing a common position with regard to Russia as a vital energy supplier for many Member States of the EU is only one example.

Also with regard to the common foreign and security policy (hereafter, CFSP) and the common security and defence policy (hereafter, CSDP) at present insufficient instruments are available to develop really effective common approaches. More particularly in these domains it has become high time for Europe to speak with a single voice. The shaping of a new relationship with Russia, i.e., the framework to be developed now that the Partnership and Cooperation Agreement of 1997 has expired, is an example where Europe should act in common.[40]

In this context it is regrettable to note that even the Lisbon Treaty does not provide for substantially amended rules and procedures regarding CFSP decision making. Indeed, only the creation of the function of a High Representative of the Union for Foreign Affairs and Security Policy[41] obviously is no guaran-

---

[38] The reference here is to the possibility of adopting decisions by (qualified) majority.

[39] See on the Treaty of Lisbon: Mendeltje van Keulen, Bas Limonard & Jan Rood, '*Nederland, de Europese Unie en het Verdrag van Lissabon*', paper of the Clingendael European Studies Programme (CESP). The Dutch position in the negotiations for the Treaty of Lisbon has been discussed by two of the fore mentioned three authors: Bas Limonard & Jan Rood, 'Uitzicht op einde impasse, van Europese Grondwet naar Hervormingsverdrag', 61 *Internationale Spectator*, No. 9 (September 2007) pp. 403-408.

[40] Obviously, the recent events in Georgia, including the recognition by Russia of the independence of two Georgian provinces, South Ossetia and Abchazia, may have serious consequences for the EU-Russian relationship. The European Council decided in its extraordinary session of 1 September 2008 to postpone the negotiations on a new relationship with Russia.

[41] The new Art. 9E(1) of the EU Treaty (Art. 1(19) of the Treaty of Lisbon).

tee that such a policy will be developed. Furthermore, the provision included in the Lisbon Treaty that once the High Representative presents a proposal at the request of the European Council, then the Council can decide by a qualified majority on this proposal[42] does not alter the fact that unanimity has been maintained as a general rule for CFSP decision making. And, as for CSDP, the most interesting innovations concern the introduction of forms of enhanced cooperation, such as the concepts of the 'coalition of the willing' and 'permanent structured cooperation'.[43] Thus, although the Lisbon Treaty provides for some improvements to the EU mechanisms of foreign policy and defence, even if that treaty would soon enter into force the Union would not have suitable tools available to enable it to act effectively in these areas.[44]

Therefore, certainly without the Lisbon Treaty, but even if the Lisbon Treaty would enter into force, in crucial areas insufficient tools and instruments are available to enable the European Union to act credibly in the international arena. Because of these missed opportunities, it is improbable that the Union can act as a global player in the multipolar world of the future. Will the economic giant remain a political dwarf? In the new international environment a positive answer to that question would be a sad one, given the need for more political power for the EU. In fact that finding is unacceptable as Europe needs to have a say in world politics.[45]

The Dutch interest

How must the Dutch interest be assessed in all this? So much was already clear that adequate answers to the challenges discussed in this chapter can no longer be provided exclusively at the national level. It is equally obvious that the geographic size and international orientation of our country – its open economy, traditional trade relations, history and culture – necessitate that we fully participate in all relevant international fora.

Economically we are tied to the integration model of the European Union, a framework that has been very beneficial for our country and its individual citizens. Our military are part of and build on the framework of NATO and play an active role in several peace missions abroad.

42 The text of a new Art. 15 ter of the EU Treaty (Art. 1(34) of the Treaty of Lisbon).

43 The new Art. 28A(5) respectively (6) of the EU Treaty (Art. 1(49) of the Treaty of Lisbon).

44 On certain aspects of the EU foreign policy see also the contribution by Louise van Schaik in this book.

45 See on this subject also: Jaap de Zwaan, 'De Europese Unie, uitgebreid en hervormd, ook voorbereid op de toekomst?', 62 *Internationale Spectator*, No. 1 (January 2008) pp. 19-25.

Effective multilateral cooperation is therefore vital for our country. Cooperation in the NATO framework requires a good and stable relationship with the United States, both today and in the future. Let us hope that the new presidential administration, which will take office in January 2009, will reinvest in multilateral cooperation as well as in its ties with its European partners.

As to the European Union, our membership of that organization makes us dependent on the political will of 26 other Member States with regard to the question whether or not Europe can make further progress in facing the new threats and challenges. In view of the existing shortcomings of the EU cooperation, it may be wise to reflect on ways and means to make the process of European integration still more effective. Forms of enhanced or differentiated cooperation, i.e., models of EU cooperation in which not necessarily all Member States participate,[46] have to be seriously discussed and thought through.

In this discussion the citizens of all EU Member States have to be involved too. Without the support of the ordinary citizen Europe cannot advance and will lack a sufficient degree of legitimacy.[47] Here we touch upon the responsibility of politicians, civil society and – certainly also – the media.

Final remarks

The world is rapidly changing. Complicated and truly global policy matters and new challenges will determine our future agenda. International cooperation with regard to these new issues and challenges has to be organized in a more effective way, and be accompanied by suitable modalities to guarantee the full application, implementation and enforcement of decisions made.

Against this background, it is clear that Dutch interests are best served by intensive European cooperation in all cross-boundary policy sectors. However, in order to become a real global player, the European Union should better organize the external dimension of its activities. More particularly Europe has to start to gather capacities to be able to practise not only 'soft' power, but also some 'hard' power in the areas of foreign policy and defence. The alternative being that Europe will be 'marginalized' by other key players, such as China and Russia. Such a result would obviously not contribute to the stability and prosperity of our continent or the world at large.

[46] The Economic and Monetary Union (EMU) and aliens policy (border control, visa, asylum and immigration policy) can be referred to as examples of differentiated cooperation which already exist. The reference here is also to the principle of enhanced cooperation embedded in Title VII of the EU Treaty.

[47] On the EU legitimacy issue see also the contribution by Mendeltje van Keulen in this book. Of that same author see also: Mendeltje van Keulen & Jan Rood, 'Ook een Iers ja lost het probleem van de EU niet op', 62 *Internationale Spectator*, No. 9 (September 2008) pp. 454-455.

Reflecting on the Purpose, Past and Present of the Clingendael Institute

Paul Meerts

Introduction

The 25th anniversary of the Netherlands Institute of International Relations 'Clingendael' is not only an excellent occasion for a celebration, but also a moment to look back at things. How did the Institute evolve in those 25 years? What were key developments and achievements and how did this come about? This chapter will reflect on these questions, looking back into Clingendael's history. In the final section, it also takes the opportunity to look ahead to see what is in store for the coming years. First, however, we will look at the more distant past of the history of the location of the Institute.

Valley between the Inland Dunes

The Netherlands Institute of International Relations has been named after its housing: the Clingendael mansion and its surrounding park to the North of the city of The Hague. Clingendael is old Dutch for Valley (= Dael) between the Inland Dunes (Cling). In 1544 the area and its farmhouse was mentioned for the first time.[1] The development into a country estate started in 1591 and between 1632 and 1634 a country house was built as a twin to the small palace owned by the famous Dutch politician and poet Christiaan Huygens on the eastern outskirts of the city. At the start of the nineteenth century an adept of Napoleon Bonaparte inherited the park and house, thereby thoroughly changing its appearance. The ninetieth century saw a change from pro-French to pro-British inhabitants, with members of the Bloomsbury Group – among them the famous diplomat and thinker Harold Nicolson – holding sway.

[1] Frans Micklinghoff, *Monumentaal Groen in Wassenaar* (The Hague, Euromedia MPP 1990) pp. 59-82.

J. de Zwaan, E. Bakker and S. van der Meer (eds.), Challenges in a Changing World

One of the most dramatic periods in the history of the place occurred between 1940 and 1945 when Clingendael was home to the *Reichskommissar* for the occupied Netherlands, the Austrian Nazi leader Arthur Seyss-Inquart. After the Second World War the original owners returned, but soon sold the park and house to the municipality of the city of The Hague, although they are formally located on the territory of the neighbouring village of Wassenaar. The house remained empty for a while after which squatters took over. This raised the question about who was going to make use of the marvellous mansion and its surroundings. This discussion took place at the same time as a discussion on how to integrate four different institutes in the area of security studies and international relations. This resulted in the idea to use the location for an academic policy-oriented institute dealing with international affairs and the training of diplomats, somewhat comparable with Chatham House in the United Kingdom, the Stiftung Wissenschaft und Politik in Germany, or the Diplomatische Akademie in Austria.

Merger

On 3 January 1983 the Netherlands Institute of International Relations 'Clingendael' emerged out of the four organisations dealing with international politics from different angles.[2] The oldest, and also the smallest, came into being just after the First World War: the Netherlands Society for International Legal Order (VIRO). After the Second World War this tiny organisation joined hands with the small Dutch Public Relations Office for the United Nations (VVN). Next in chronological order came the Netherlands Society for International Relations (NGIZ), created just after the Second World War and accompanied in the late 1960s by the Course on International Relations (LBB) for training the young attachés of the Dutch Ministry of Foreign Affairs, navy officers and postgraduate students. The Society merged its institute into Clingendael, but is still flourishing as an independent group of interested people whose secretariat is based at Clingendael. As is the indirect successor of the UN public relations office, the Netherlands Society for the United Nations (NVVN). Next in the chronological line is the Defence Study Centre (DSC), created in the 1950s, organising courses on international security. And finally – as a fourth component – the Netherlands Institute for Peace Issues (NIVV), which came into being in the 1960s, focussing mainly on peace research.

---

[2] Hans van den Broek, 'Foreword', in A. van Staden et al., eds., *Cannons and Canons* (Assen, Van Gorcum 2003) p. 1.

Organizational structure

As the NIVV was the biggest among the merger organisations, its director, Prof. Henk Neuman, became Clingendael's director for its first eight years (1983-1990), heading a staff of 42 people. The merging parties were rearranged into three departments: Research, Education and Public Relations. The libraries merged into one and the *Internationale Spectator* (IS) – journal of the NGIZ since 1946 – became the Institute's monthly publication.

Under the second director of Clingendael, Prof. Joris Voorhoeve, the Institute gradually expanded its activities, thereby helped by the fall of the Berlin Wall. This event opened up Central and Eastern Europe, as well as Central Asia, to the Institute. It resulted in scores of diplomatic courses financed by the Dutch Ministry of Foreign Affairs. The Institute continued to grow after Voorhoeve – who became Minister of Defence in 1994 – was succeeded by Prof. Alfred van Staden who was director from 1995 to 2005. In this period, three new initiatives were added to the Institute: the Conflict Research Unit (CRU) that studies post-conflict reconstruction, the Clingendael International Energy Programme (CIEP), which mainly focuses on gas and oil issues, and the Clingendael Centre for Strategic Studies (CCSS), a business portal for joint commercial projects between Clingendael and the Netherlands Organisation for Applied Scientific Research (TNO). The CRU is funded by the Development Cooperation General Directorate of the Ministry of Foreign Affairs. Under Van Staden, Clingendael transformed the Research and Education Departments into three Programmes where research and training are no longer separated: the Clingendael Diplomatic Studies Programme (CDSP), the Clingendael European Studies Programme (CESP) and the Clingendael Security and Conflict Programme (CSCP).

In 2005 Prof. Jaap de Zwaan became the fourth director of the Clingendael Institute. He found an Institute which had more than doubled in staff and turnover since 1983. Under his leadership Clingendael has reorganized its management systems. Clingendael also launched another long-term strategic initiative, the Clingendael Asian Studies (CAS), uniting the efforts of all programmes concerning the Far East, notably China. Under Jaap de Zwaan, the Institute is celebrating its 25th anniversary in 2008, with conferences, a jubilee book, and many other events. One of them was a special issue of the *Internationale Spectator* in which the current chairman of the board, Dr Bernard Bot, gave his view on Clingendael's future.[3]

Dr Bot is the fifth President of the board of the Clingendael Institute. His predecessors are Hans van den Broek, Ruud Lubbers, Schelto Patijn, and Baron

---

[3] Bernard Bot, 'Clingendael, denken, doen en durven', 62 *Internationale Spectator,* No. 1 (2008) pp. 1-2.

Van Lynden. Despite the fact that many of the directors and the chairmen of the board had been leading figures in government or governmental organisations – including former ministers of foreign affairs and a former prime minister – they always made sure that Clingendael remained an independent institute.

The Clingendael Institute is also assisted by an advisory council. The CAROO ('Clingendael Adviesraad voor Opleidingen en Onderzoek') issues opinions with regard to Clingendael's research and training programmes.

Independent think-tank

Many countries throughout the world have independent policy-oriented academic institutes or societies that fulfil tasks the governments themselves feel they cannot and should not take on board themselves.[4] Unlike governmental organisations, independent think-tanks are not troubled by partisan politics, protocol and procedure. They are much freer to produce critical reports and studies, to comment on and interpret news by media appearances, to train diplomats from other countries, or to play a role in Second Track-Diplomacy freeways. Clingendael has always used its independent position to play an active role in these fields and has not shied away form clashing opinions. This is why the Institute does not have a 'Clingendael opinion' on the international issues on which it focuses. Its staff members have individual opinions based on their research activities. This may seem a hazardous position, but does not prove to be too challenging or complicated in practice. Only on a few occasions have problems arisen. Like in the case of the (in)famous Clingendael Report on the opinions of Dutch schoolchildren on Germany – *de facto* a report from Leiden University under Clingendael's responsibility. It raised many eyebrows and led to much discussion as the data of the research indicated a very negative attitude in the Netherlands towards Germans and Germany.

The Institute's independence and the freedom of its individual researchers created ample opportunities to contribute to the Dutch and international media through interviews and op-eds. Moreover, it contributed to the positive reputation of Clingendael, both at home and abroad.

That the Clingendael Institute would develop in this direction was not clear from the beginning in 1983, as the four merging parties each had a different level of experience in research, training or contacts with the media. In fact, the four organisations differed quite a lot from each other.

---

[4] *Instituut Clingendael, de eerste vijf jaar* (The Hague, NIIB Clingendael, 1988) p. 1.

Research

Only one of the constituent parties of Clingendael, the Netherlands Institute for Peace Issues (NIVV), in a less literate translation: the Netherlands Institute for Peace Research, brought substantial research know-how to the new Netherlands Institute of International Relations. As a consequence, the ranks of the Research Department of Clingendael were mainly filled with persons form the NIVV. Its culture of serious qualitative analysis on peace and security issues became Clingendael's standard for research and publications. As the NIVV had done before the merger, Clingendael commented on these and other issues of international relations in an academic though policy-relevant way. Its products were focused on academics and non-academics alike. Studies, seminars and other products needed to be of value to diplomats and civil servants at ministries, and, if possible, to influence the framing and thinking of politicians and other policy makers. The issues dominating the 1980s were very much security oriented. European integration only came seriously into play in the 1990s, while diplomacy had to wait until the new Programme structure in the new millennium gave it a chance to flourish as one of the leading focuses of research.

Publications

At the beginning the output of Clingendael's research had been channelled into so-called Clingendael Cahiers, in later eras differently named, but *de facto* surviving to this day. A problem has always been the marketing of these in-house productions. This is why the management stimulated Clingendael researchers to publish in other sources as well: books, journals and newspapers. The *Internationale Spectator* had its own – interesting – niche in this arena of outlets for the Institute's findings. Of course it published many articles written by Clingendael 'staff. But as a monthly in the Dutch language, it could not bridge the gap to the English-speaking international community. Moreover, it fulfilled a much broader task as *the* platform for international relations analysis in the Netherlands. On average more outsiders than Clingendaelers filled its columns, mainly from the Netherlands and Belgium. This was reflected in the Dutch/ Flemish composition of its editorial board of which the directors of Clingendael acted as Editors-in-chief. Only in recent years did the *Discussion Papers in Diplomacy* and *The Hague Journal of Diplomacy* (HJD) successfully fill the gap by catering for an international audience. But again: these periodicals take mainly non-Clingendael academics on board, as does the recent book series *Diplomatic Studies*. As the different Programmes take more and more responsibility for their own publications in the English language, series like the

Clingendael Diplomacy Papers and *Clingendael Security Papers* are being created, covering a substantial part of Clingendael's research output. Another important outlet is the research symposia which have been organised from the very beginning, building platforms for insiders and outsiders alike, often resulting in up-to-date topical publications.

Exchanges

Clingendael has never been a stand-alone place, it has always been connected to both policy making and policy analysing organisations. It became a part of the European and Global academic networks at an early stage. It especially played a leading role in the European one (TEPSA, Trans European Policy Studies Association) and it wants to intensify its cooperation with other international networks and think-tanks. Staff members have been participating in international conferences from the very outset, and several of them worked in institutions outside the Netherlands on an exchange basis. Exchanges also took place between the Dutch Ministries of Foreign Affairs and Defence on the one hand, and Clingendael on the other. In addition there were close personal ties with other academic institutions. Quite a number of researchers at Clingendael held part-time positions at universities. Today, these personal links include ties with universities in several countries in and outside Europe.

Training

From the start in 1983, teaching and training have been one of the main two legs on which the Institute stands – research being the first leg. Clingendael inherited one major course which still survives today: the *Leergang Buitenlandse Betrekkingen* of the Netherlands Society for International Affairs (NGIZ). This course has been of particular importance as it has functioned as the model for most of the courses run by the different Clingendael Programmes. The *Leergang*, created in 1967 as a cradle for attachés of the Dutch Ministry of Foreign Affairs, as well as for mid-career navy officers, changed fundamentally, however, as in the mid-1990s the Ministry decided to withdraw its young diplomats from this curriculum. This also happened with the navy officers when the Ministry of Defence decided to merge the Dutch Defence Staff Schools into one Defence College – although Clingendael is now responsible for a module in the Higher Defence Course of this College. The *Leergang* nowadays caters for young post-graduate students wanting to enhance their insights and skills in international relations. Begun in the 1990s the model of the *Leergang* proliferated into a range of courses for diplomats from Central, Eastern and South Eastern Europe, as well as Central Asia and Mongolia. As years went by, courses for South African, Iranian, Yemeni, Indonesian, Iraqi, Sudanese and Moroccan diplomats added to the international pallet which made Clingendael famous as an institute for diplomatic training and education.

The Defence Study Centre (DSC) has been the other organisation involved in course work. Its programmes were much shorter and less interactive than the *Leergang* and focused much more on one issue, i.e., international security. However, they were connected to a series of conferences, which formed the basis of the seminars nowadays produced by Clingendael. Clingendael staff remained very much involved in the organisation and the teaching of the programmes of the Dutch Staff Colleges.

Not connected to the four merging institutions are a multitude of policy-oriented seminars for civil servants having to deal with 'Brussels'. The same is true for the contributions of Clingendael staff to many courses at institutions and organisations abroad, from the NATO Defence College to Diplomatic Academies and Universities all around the world. For instance, Clingendael staff organised and delivered negotiation seminars in ninety countries, mainly in Europe and Asia, but also in Africa and Latin America.

Clingendael Courses could never have survived, however, if professors and other staff from universities, practitioners from diverse Ministries, trainers from commercial companies and societal figure-heads would not have thrown their expertise into the Institute's curricula. Clingendael staff themselves, although teaching and training on a large scale, constitute only a minority of those instructing the participants in Clingendael's educational system. Clingendael is connected with sister institutes with whom it has been in close cooperation, for example in the Leiden-Clingendael Masters Programme and the Fourth Programme of the Bruges' College of Europe, both on International Relations and Diplomacy.

An important aspect of Clingendael's curricula has been the positive effect on research. On the one hand, because of the very substantial financial contributions which made possible the boom in Clingendael's staff in the early and late 1990s, but also because of students who supported the Institute's growth as interns and short-term staff.

Platform

After research and education, Clingendael's third main task is to act as a platform in Dutch society and abroad. All four preceding organisations performed such a function. As it was the main stay of the VIRO/VVN, the staff of this smallest Clingendael segment became the bearers of the public relations of the

Institute. However, their Public Relations Department soon faltered and its functions were taken over by the Departments of Research and Education. At the end of the 1990s some of its tasks were integrated in the newly constituted External Relations Office, nowadays the Office of External Affairs. Together with the Programmes, this office organises public meetings, providing a platform for government leaders and other prominent speakers, thereby servicing both the diplomatic community, the Dutch Ministries and the general public. It also publishes a biannual *Newsletter*.

Another platform section of Clingendael is its library. It functions as an important resource for staff and students, the general public and other libraries. Its staff helped to create libraries at Diplomatic Academies in the new Member States of the European Union. Underneath the Platform are the logistical units, creating the conditions under which the operational segments of Clingendael can carry out their work towards the outside world. The Internal Affairs Office and the Financial Administration are indispensable cornerstones of an Institute with over seventy staff, over seventy course members on a daily basis, not counting those who visit the library and attend the conferences.

A less well-known platform function is performed by the activities of the Institute and some of its members in international politics itself. Staff members represent the Institute in Advisory Boards of the Dutch government and foreign institutions. They sometimes act as advisors in crisis situations and chair peacemaking meetings. Things cannot always be seen from the outside, like the confidential talks on the establishment of a free-trade zone between some countries and authorities on the Western shores of the Middle East. The negotiations were successful, but did not produce an outcome because of the declining political situation in the Middle East. Philippine government officials and representatives of the communist resistance negotiated an agreement to start peace negotiations, which faltered after the downfall of the Soviet Union. The Chechen leadership came to the Peace Palace to discuss a rapprochement to the Russian Federation under the aegis of Clingendael and the Washington Conflict Management Group, with Russian parliamentarians as counterparts and the presidents of Tatarstan and Ingoushetia as mediators. Muslim and Christian Moluccan leaders came to the Institute to communicate with each other on putting an end to the atrocities in the Moluccans, invited by the Moluccans in the Netherlands. Clingendael director Voorhoeve and the Chairman of its Board Lubbers played a vital role in these Second-Track Diplomacy processes, as did members of the Clingendael staff.

Concluding remarks

Clingendael has been steadily growing in quality and quantity ever since its inception 25 years ago. In general, many things have changed. For instance, since a couple of years Clingendael is partner in the so-called 'Hague Academic Coalition' (HAC), which is a framework for cooperation between academic institutes having their seat in The Hague.[5] Through the organization of a number of joint activities the HAC aims at contributing to the world wide reputation of the city of The Hague as 'City of Peace, Security and Justice'. Clingendael's present Director, Jaap de Zwaan, is the acting chairman of the coalition.

With regard to Clingendael two things, however, have remained the same: the beauty and charm of the location, and the key characteristic of the people who work there. These 'Clingendaelers' share a passion for what is happening in the world, a desire to understand international events and developments, and the ambition to pass this knowledge on to a wide public. This characteristic has made Clingendael a place that likes to open its doors to many different people: scholars, trainers, diplomats, military personnel and many foreign guests. The mix of these people and their backgrounds have made Clingendael what it is today, a truly international and very special place; not only for those who work there or participate in its activities, but for all those who share a deep interest in what makes this world go round.

[5] The current members of the HAC, except for the Clingendael Institute, are the Carnegie Foundation, the Hague Institute for the Internationalisation of Law, the International Institute of Social Studies, Leiden University (Campus The Hague) and the T.M.C. Asser Institute for International and European Law.

BETWEEN FALSE PROMISES AND FAIR PRACTICE: INSTITUTIONS AND DEINSTITUTIONALIZATION IN THE FIELD OF INTERNATIONAL SECURITY*

Ko Colijn

INTRODUCTION

Does our security still benefit from institutions, or have their existence become irrelevant? Or even worse, could institutions possibly even be a barrier? This is a traditional question from international relations theory that continues to be asked, especially during transition periods witnessing redistributions of power, and where the usefulness of the existing inventory is to be evidenced once again. We only need to point to the reform debate on the United Nations and its Security Council that keeps dragging along, the question about NATO's *raison d'être* that is deepening in Afghanistan, the deadlock around the continuation, respectively ratification, of several important treaties restraining the proliferation of weapons of mass destruction, or the sluggish, but nonetheless undeniable genesis of (what is already known in the pending Lisbon Reform Treaty as) the Common Security and Defence Policy of the European Union.

The usefulness and necessity of security institutions belong without doubt to the wider discourse of (novel?) threats. The attempt to make a classification of threats against our security, not at all an easy task in the complex international relations after the fall of the Berlin Wall (1989), is further thwarted by the moving referent concept of 'security', that appears to have lost is unambiguous

* This chapter (the draft of which was completed in early May 2008) contains elements published by the author in *The Broker*, the bimonthly magazine of the Stichting International Development Publications, Leiden, 'Globale Dreigingen en de Nationale Veiligheid van Nederland', in G. Wismans, ed., *Crisisbeheersing Andermaal Belicht* (Den Haag, Ministerie van Binnenlandse Zaken en Koninkrijksrelaties/Directie Crisisbeheersing 2007) pp. 41-51; and *De Goede Instelling – op zoek naar mondiale veiligheid*, lecture on 8 June 2007 upon the acceptance of the post of Honorary Professor in international relations, in particular global security issues (on behalf of the Netherlands Society for International Affairs), at the Faculty of Social Sciences, Erasmus University, Rotterdam.

J. de Zwaan, E. Bakker and S. van der Meer (eds.), Challenges in a Changing World

meaning. Whoever wishes to outline future threat scenarios cannot assume automatically that the usual audiences – politicians, policy planners, interested readers, citizens – all mean the same by *insecurity*. A large diversity of perceived threats will result from this. Equally broad is the variety of policy scenarios that need to be taken into consideration, not to mention the true implications in terms of the policy agenda, policy planning and the allocation of resources, and the end-use policy solutions.

So how did the notion of security develop? Briefly summarized, the proposition can be made that the classical paradigm of interstate security is now accompanied by the holistic concept of global security and, conversely, the almost atomic but, even so, comprehensive idea of human security. The difference can somewhat be explained in a numerical comparison, where the 'old' interstate security system reaches out for harmony between 192 states, whereas global security refers to the principle of one single peaceful world society, and human security is about finding a solution for the security needs of six and a half billion people.

Excerpted from the report *A More Secure World: Our Shared Responsibilities* (2005), the UN High Level Panel on Threats, Challenges and Change came to the conclusion that a combination of 1) poverty, disease and environmental degradation; 2) interstate and intrastate conflicts; 3) the proliferation of chemical, biological, radiological and nuclear (CBRN) weapons; 4) terrorism; and 5) transnational organized crime in general have to be considered as the most threatening to the world order.[1] The broadening of the notion of security is shown from this list: only two, maybe three, out of five priorities (2, 3 and 4) would have shown up in similar lists only a few decades ago.

One could wonder how these global threats are particularly relevant for the Netherlands. In a report by the Advisory Council on International Affairs (AIV), from as far back as 1999, a shift from the classical territorial conflict to new threats, as mentioned above, to the Netherlands had already been observed.[2] But at that time the AIV rightly stated that the relevance of the various new security risks could not be put in a general ranking order. A top 10 can thus not be delivered. The actual relevance depends on (at least) five factors that will need to be weighed for every case:

1. The chance that a risk materializes (with respect to any specific country);
2. The damage that can then be inflicted upon that particular country;

---

1 United Nations, *A More Secure World – Our Shared responsibilities, Report of the Secretary-General's High-level Panel*, December 2004 <http:// www.un.org/secureworld>.

2 Advisory Council on International Affairs (AIV), Report 10, September 1999) <http:// www.aiv-advies.nl>.

3. The physical distance to that country;
4. The nature and availability of military resources to that country (in case of a military threat); and
5. Considerations of international solidarity.

Thus in 1999, the AIV concluded, by implication, that a large global security risk for the Netherlands would only have limited relevance, namely if the source of the threat were to manifest itself at a greater distance from our territory, it would cause little damage within the Netherlands, the Dutch defensibility would be sufficient, and the Netherlands could count on the support of other countries. The latter could be possible through durable and broad alliances (e.g., permanent multilateral institutions), or less durable coalitions (e.g., narrow and/or temporary coalitions of opportunity).

Although these conditions in general still matter in 2008, it is my conviction that in less than ten years gradually less protection has been (and will be) enjoyed, as the operation of these five immunizing factors has been further disintegrated. Why? The world has shrunk away even more, the physical, communicative and electronic means of bridging the dual dimension of time and distance between the Netherlands and possible threat sources have increased in size and potential, the logistical and economic interdependency (meaning the density of networks) of the Netherlands with the rest of the world, and therewith, its sensitivity and vulnerability for the disruption of those networks, have increased. And last but not least, the relative security guarantees that the Netherlands enjoyed from its allies and brothers-in-fate have become uncertain on balance because of rapid deinstitutionalization.

This chapter will focus on the latter institutional factor and more particularly on the presumed phenomenon of deinstitutionalization. First, the reader will be offered a sketch, and maybe a personal evaluation, of the usefulness and necessity of security institutions in general.

THE IMPORTANCE OF SECURITY INSTITUTIONS

Trivial as the suggestion that institutions are important may be, even in world politics the trivial is essential. For the purpose of this contribution, I define international security institutions (hereafter, ISIs) as enduring arrangements, in which participants seek to establish patterns of behaviour of members and/or potential opponents and/or reach certain security goals, notably by reducing their vulnerability to any threat of violence or coercion. The sociological baseline argument is that institutions are created because they offer net cooperative profit. The alternative, a chaotic collection of unilateral actions or *ad hoc* arrangements, would be a poor substitute for the routine and transparency that institutions offer. Especially in situations of crisis and threat, where everybody benefits from clear game rules and predictable behaviour, the latter tends to be considered as a major benefit. The institutional interest is only a minimum criterion, because elsewhere the institutions show extensive variation: they can be formal or informal, of a public or private character and the key to their success lies with their specific competence or actual power, and specifically through the degree of autonomy they exert. Even in that respect, a significant variety can be found.

Some collective goods, such as security or economic prosperity, can no longer be exclusively delivered at the level of national communities. Absent central authority at the supranational level as well, the collective will to deliver collective goods successfully can only manifest itself in case of intergovernmental unanimity rule. But that is a rare phenomenon. 'The world's economy is global, its politics are national. This, in a nutshell, is the dilemma of global governance.'[3] The same simple draft of the dilemma is true for security, probably the most primary global collective good. National states develop mechanisms and organizations for solving the security issue as good as they can. The United Nations – not united *above* but *as* sovereign nations, and for just that reason so vulnerable and easy to paralyze as a global decision-making institution – are the chief example of this. In the public imaging, the UN may not be the greatest success story. The *2005 Human Security Report* (HSR), to which I will come back below, nonetheless concludes that the UN organization has received far too little institutional praise for its useful behind-the-scenes efforts after the Cold War ended.[4] The outbreak of armed conflicts is breaking news; the dawning of peace is hardly so. But exactly that has occurred approximately 400 times since 1945 according to the HSR, of which a disproportionally large share has occurred since 1989, and to a great extent due to the patience and efforts of the UN. One can debate the question of whether that praise should indeed be accrued to the UN as an operational institution, or that its skyscraper has in fact not been more than a place to hang out for some 190+ national states. However questionable that minimalist view may be, the UN's mere existence as a platform can already be seen as 'value added' in finding solutions to world problems.

On a more abstract institutional level, the concept of 'multilateralism' deserves to be specifically mentioned. One could indeed call multilateralism an

---

[3] Martin Wolf, 'The dilemma of Global Governance', *Financial Times* (24 January 2007) p. 2.

[4] *The Human Security Report 2005* (hereafter, HSR), published for the Human Security Centre (University of British Columbia/Oxford University Press, 2005) <http://www.humansecurityreport.info/content/view/28/63/>.

abstract embodied in numerous organizations and procedures. The term often refers to a cooperative approach where finding solutions to world problems elevates from the level of sheer interstate, intergovernmental bargaining within (or without!) institutional settings. Mutuality, the 'reciproque' understanding of long-term interests and expectations are keywords of multilateralism, if not for idealistic reasons then for their sheer 'collective policy output'. Indeed, nation states are sometimes willing to give something up, and be submitted to a norm of reciprocity that leads to policy outcomes with a higher grade of legitimacy than to policy solutions that – sometimes with violence or the threat of violence – have been forced upon or laid down. While it is certainly not the case that multilateral solutions from the great powers' perspective can be perceived as altruistic, they are distinct from the unilateral – at times even forceful – solutions for global issues imposed by one or more superpowers, which may appear more effective and may have come about more rapidly but tend to be less legitimate and conceivably less sustainable.

The Bush administration (2001-2009) has been criticized for putting reciprocal multilateralism back to gear one in its foreign policy. In a sense, that criticism found confirmation in the fact that the US administration itself (supported by the Blair government) persistently added the 'effective' label to its professed multilateralism.[5] It can indeed be said that the complaint about the 'reciprocal' multilateralism as a slow, tedious and defective institution, found recognition in Dutch foreign policy, when sharply formulated in the pursuit of a '*realistic* multilateralism' by the end of 2006. We are past the era of the village idiot, as literally quoted by Minister of Foreign Affairs Bot. The Netherlands intended to pay more attention to its own interests, a 'bitter necessity in a world hollowed out by directories. If the big countries are systematically calling the shots, without too much regard of other countries, we are simply left with no other choice.'[6]

Not taking the little ones into consideration, giving preference to national interests: it is a diagnosis that reveals a normative perspective of accommodating multilateralism that diverges from that of the American-British definition which, from 'cold, hard necessity,' needs to be retaliated with a dose of self-interest. What conclusion can we draw here? The conclusion that institutions are not simply administrative-technical constructions that facilitate decision making on global security, but that they can be assessed, from standards of input and output legitimacy, or process and result, from different national per-

---

[5] US/UK Joint Statement on Multilateralism, *Effective Multilateralism to Build a Better World. Joint Statement by President George W.Bush and Prime Minister Tony Blair*, Office of the Press Secretary, November 20, 2003 <www.whitehouse.gov/news/releases/2003/11/20031120>.

[6] Bernard Bot (Minister for Foreign Affairs), *Speech marking the 60th anniversary of the International Spectator*. The Hague, Institute Clingendael, November 16th, 2006 <http://www.minbuza.nl/nl/actueel/speeches,2006/11/Toespraak-ter-gelegenheid-van-het-60-jarig-jubileu.html>.

spectives. Institutions can be seen as instrumental or less-instrumental, depending on a preferred mix of collective *and* certain national security interests within a given 'Kaplanian' systemic power context. Even more recent are those analyses that do not put the debate about the usefulness and instrumentality of institutions in the context of a unipolar, bipolar or multipolar system of power. When the world after the unipolar intermezzo of roughly 1990-2005 is moving in the direction of a system of non-polarity, speculations as to the 'instrumentality' of institutions in the agendas of polar powers become doubtful.[7] Indeed, according to Haass, a system of non-polarity 'lacks the more predictable fixed structures and relationships that tend to define worlds of unipolarity, bipolarity or multipolarity.' A non-polar world not only denies national hegemonic centre(s) of power but, moreover, experiences a great spreading of power due to the multiple emergence of non-state actors (both benign and malign NGOs, terrorist networks, militias, media outlets, large multinational corporations, regional and functional organizations. etc.). 'With so many actors possessing meaningful power and trying to assert influence, it will be more difficult *to build collective responses and make institutions work* [emphasis added].' The specific conclusion that Haass makes for the United States as the vulnerable hegemon is also found in the wider context: non-polarity will increase the number of threats and vulnerabilities. 'These threats can take the form of rogue states, terrorist groups, energy producers that choose to reduce their output, or central banks whose action or inaction can create conditions that affect the role and strength of the US dollar.'[8]

What is interesting about Haass' analysis is the further nuancing of the relationship between power politics and the intervening role of security institutions. Coming from the one-dimensional liberal-institutionalist debate that usually depicts a trade-off between institutional density and national power, the present discourse introduces the non-polarity future that displays the less-less scenario of dispersed national powers and institutional decline. The question is, of course, what consequences any such trend would have for global security.

False promises?

Any judgment on *de*-institutionalization as a source of *in*security has to be presented, of course, in the wider context of the general academic debate on institutional relevance for international politics. If, as the traditional realist consensus holds, the impact of institutions is limited or indeed non-existent, one would not

[7] Richard N.Haass, 'The Age of Nonpolarity – what will follow U.S. dominance', 87 *Foreign Affairs*, No. 3 (May/June 2008) pp. 44-57.

[8] Ibid., pp. 52, 56.

care for their erosion or even their absolute absence. Deinstitutionalization would be correspondingly less of a threat in a world where institutions actually function as the mere instruments of leading powers. It is the decline of leading powers that matters, not deinstitutionalization in the first place. Indeed, in his milestone article 'The False Promise of International Institutions', John Mearsheimer in 1994-1995 took up classic Waltzian thinking by leaving little doubt as to his scepticism concerning the relevance of institutions.[9] Mearsheimer's argument is based on a thorough analysis of realism, liberal-institutionalism and critical theory, respectively, neither of the three persuading him to abandon the conviction that institutions, or deinstitutionalization for that matter, are a factor to be taken seriously. 'What is most impressive about institutions, in fact, is how little independent effect they seem to have had on state behavior.'[10]

First, the most pronounced institution-sceptics are the (neo-)realists, of course. In their view, the fear of cheating and the famous relative gains threshold are sufficient factors to prevent states from entering into meaningful cooperation, let alone delegate their sovereign powers to independent institutions. This is all the more so in the high field of security politics. In one of its most extreme variants realist thinking, parallel to radical economic market theory, holds that sheer rivalry among states in an institutionless world may already serve as the Pareto-efficient road to 'peaceful equilibrium'. Flexible alliance formation, messing around, engaging in arms races, and even fierce conflict may not just be looked upon as a pathology of the competitive international state system, but may actually serve as the correctional mechanisms of that system as well in that they lead to dynamic anarchic peace. Rather absurd as it may sound, Edward Luttwak, having the bomb-to-Dayton campaign and operation *Allied Freedom* (the military intervention by NATO in the Kosovo crisis) in mind, in 1999 argued along these lines in a provocative but even so serious contribution to *Foreign Affairs*. In his view conflict resolution might be attained in the best and least harmful way along the adagium of *Give War a Chance.*[11] For all these reservations, it is still feasible to think of institutions performing a positive role on the realist stage of scepticism and mistrust. They may act as clearing houses of multiple relative gains dossiers in which governments become involved over time, become neutral referees in disputes thereon, or eventually open doors to sustainable practices of mostly technical and administrative cooperation. The

---

9 John J. Mearsheimer, 'The False Promise of International Institutions'. 19 *International Security*, No. 3 (Winter 1994/5) pp. 5-49.

10 Ibid., p. 47.

11 Edward N. Luttwak, 'Give War a Chance', 78 *Foreign Affairs* (July/August 1999) pp. 36-44. (Only by including 'war' as another species of institutions – which I do not – could one maintain that realists had their own version of the institutions-do-matter thesis).

very existence of institutions which administer give-and-take games in the longer run may tip the balance in favour of *negotiated* conflict-settlement systems rather than a system of imposed, let alone military solutions, or of no solutions at all.

Second, liberal-institutionalism follows neo-realism in that it accepts states to be still the main, and self-interested, cheating-wary actors, but its thinking does allow for a degree of institutional *policy* relevance. In particular, liberal-institutionalists conclude that the problem of cheating can be solved by positively addressing the pay-off conditions for individual states embarking on institutional cooperation. What is more, the overall transaction costs of inter-state bargaining will be significantly reduced by the long-term acceptance of institutional procedures and the exchange of information, eventually into building mutual trust, within a particular institution. However, Mearsheimer, et al., continue to criticize liberal-institutionalism for its neglect of the relative-gains dilemma, and its preoccupation with the political-economics field rather than the international security domain. Mearsheimer recollects that the experience with historical collective security projects that ought to be the prime examples of institutional cooperation (League of Nations, United Nations) is quite unfortunate. If collective security organizations are at all able to reach a quick and clean consensus on who is an aggressor and who is demonstrably not, the larger collective security systems may still turn out to be counterproductive, i.e., proliferate *in*security, in that they might even internationalize conflicts that used to be merely local. Watered-down versions of institutional collective security find no support from Mearsheimer either. Peacekeeping may be seen as its surrogate option, as it is sometimes called the budget version of collective security. But it only works on the margins, if at all, and definitely not at the big powers level and, moreover, in excluding the use of coercion, peacekeeping principally runs counter to the essential ingredients of a credible collective security assurance. Still more watered-down versions of peacekeeping like *concerting* hardly qualify for that category. Functioning as deliberate systems of 'partner swapping', they actually fall into the category of enduring power-balancing – arguably an interesting case of realism rather than stable institutionalism.

Third, critical theory opposes the idea of nation states driven by power and self-interest. Ideas and intellectual discourse have transforming power and move the world, or at least a part thereof, beyond the realist power struggle to post-anarchic, even genuine peace systems. Deutschian 'zones of peace', think of the European Union, serve as a case in point. Mearsheimer rejects critical theory as unwarranted optimism and 'wishful thinking' and by pointing at its inherent contradictories: while opposing the realist idea in claiming that ideas drive politics rather than structural factors, it at the same time acknowledges that ideas for their ultimate prevailing effect depend on the very structural factors it rejects in the first place. Furthermore, critical theory fails to prove in what direction – let alone the peaceful and communitarian – the post-realist world will develop.

Mearsheimer's analysis not only mattered from a scholarly International Relations perspective, but is historically interesting as well. After the end of the Cold War the question emerged whether the institutional security architecture from the era of bipolar power relations would be able to sustain itself, or become irrelevant in conformity with neorealist approaches. Mearsheimer did not shun the 'realist' prediction. For one thing, he predicted Russian resistance against NATO's eastward expansion,

> 'and therefore NATO is not likely to expand eastward in any meaningful way. Regardless, even if those four states [Poland, Hungary, and the Czech and Slovak Republics] joined NATO, the remnant states of the former Soviet Union would still be excluded, and their inclusion would be necessary to transform NATO into an effective collective security system for Europe.'[12]

The ex post incorrectness of this prediction may easily falsify this neo-realism at first glance, but Mearsheimer prudently qualified his statement by leaving open the possibility that an expanded NATO might survive in the long term as a different (i.e., collective security) institution. Indeed, NATO, already for many years, seems to have become entangled in an 'identity' debate, but the present argument focuses rather on its adoption of the additional role of an *ad hoc global security provider* rather than that of a solid pan-European collective security system.

For all its impressive and straightforward arguments, more than a decade later Mearsheimer's 'false promise' thesis, already for empirical reasons, seems not to be able to bear the test of contemporary history. Old institutions like the UN, the International Atomic Energy Agency (IAEA), NATO, and non-proliferation regimes, while certainly undergoing sometimes painful transition processes, cannot yet be written off. They continue to exist and they adapt, and more importantly, sometimes with the help of non-state actors, they demonstrate 'institutional resistance' against states' sidelining manoeuvres. Other ISIs sometimes even seem to grow under oppression, like the Chemical Weapons Convention, or the European Union's slow but evolving European Security and Defence Policy. While this may be enough to reject the baseline argument of international institutions' 'false promises', it requires another argument to measure their actual role and value.

---

[12] Mearsheimer, *supra* n. 9, p. 34 (n. 114).

Best practices?

A remarkable contribution to that effect was launched at the turn of the millennium. In quite a contrasting analysis, the *Human Security Report* of 2005 presented a clear rejectionist view of the 'we can do without institutions' paradigm.[13] It concludes that the world since the breakdown of the Berlin Wall has become a relatively safe place. The number of armed conflicts has decreased markedly (down by some 40%) and one can face a parallel spectacular increase in 'outbursts' of peace or endings of conflicts. The HSR concludes that we owe a great deal of this optimist view to a wave of international activism, in particular to successful NGOs and public institutions. The number of peace operations that defuse conflicts, or which stabilized post-conflict situations, the number of war tribunals and sanctions mechanisms which punished (or possibly deterred) rogue leaders, the number of quiet but effective missions of diplomats and UN emissaries like Max van der Stoel, Jan Egeland or Lakdar Brahimi, rose at least by a factor five since 1992. If only for their degree of unexpectedness, the findings of the HSR may perhaps need more scrutiny, but as of now we can only face the fact that its follow-up *Human Security Briefs* of December 2006 and 2007 signal the consolidation – if not acceleration – of the positive trend since 2002.[14]

Coincidentally or not, parallel to the downward trend in armed conflicts, since the 1960s the number of global multilateral security treaties has risen from some 150 to 400.[15] While it would be premature to speak of a causal relationship, the correlation between institutional consolidation and growth on the one hand, and a less conflictful world on the other, is unmistakable. One might add to this longitudinal correlation another horizontal one, observed by the Stockholm Peace Research Institute (SIPRI), between 1) the regional occurrence of security institutions; and 2) the relative absence of regional armed conflicts.[16] *In concreto*: comparatively more conflicts can be counted in institutionally poor regions like the Middle East, South and North East Asia than in institution-dense regions.

---

[13] HSR , *supra* n. 4.

[14] *The Human Security Brief*, update of the HSR, supplementing the 1946-2002 data to 2005, published on Dec. 20 2006 <http://www.humansecuritycentre.org/images/stories/HSBrief2006/contents/finalversion.pdf>. Recently updated as *Human Security Brief 2007*, id., May 2008 <http://www.humansecuritybrief.info/access.html>.

[15] Michael Zürn, 'From Interdependence to Globalization' (section: What do Interdependence and Globalization Explain? Peace and Cooperation,. In Walter Carlsnaes, Thomas Risse & Beth A.Simmons, eds., *Handbook of International Relations* (London, Sage 2001) pp. 235-254.

[16] Alyson J. K. Bailes, 'Introduction – The World of Security and Peace Research in a 40-year perspective', in *SIPRI Yearbook 2006, Armaments, Disarmament and International Security* (Oxford, Oxford University Press) pp. 1-30, esp.17.

The empirical evidence of institutional contributions, as compiled by the Human Security Project scholars, to global security is supportive of institutionalists at a general level. However, far more research is needed on what specific institutions contribute in what specific way and under what specific conditions. In the security domain, institutions are active at the global, regional, state and sub-state level, they can be of a private and public or mixed nature, and a further distinction can be made according to their single-purpose (i.e., security only) or multipurpose mission.

The institutions-do-matter claim is shared by a leading researcher in the field, John S.Duffield. 'The empirical record indicates that they have had noteworthy effects of different types through a variety of causal mechanisms.' He points at ISIs' modifying effects of state behaviour, evolving autonomy displayed by various ISIs and their capacity to even change states' internal characteristics or at least their policy preferences through their involvement in ISIs. Using a promising matrix typology of inclusive versus exclusive security institutions, as well as operative rule-based *versus* contingent rule-based security institutions, Duffield, however, also does not yet provide the answer to the question of what specific effects can be ascribed to specific institutions. 'There is a need for much more carefully-designed, theory-guided, comparative empirical research on the subject.'[17]

The Duffield typology of International Security Institutions[18]

	inclusive ISIs	*exclusive ISIs*
operative rules	Arms-control agreements, use-of-force arrangements	Arms export control agreements
contingent rules	collective security systems	alliances

---

[17] John S.Duffield, *The Effects of International Security Institutions: a Critical Analysis*. Paper prepared for the AUEB International Conference on 'Assessing Multilateralism in the Security Domain', Delphi, Greece, June 3-5, 2005. Retrieved at: <http://www.ekem.gr/pdf/Duffield.pdf> (April 20th, 2008) esp. pp. 5-9, 21. (Paper stated to be heavily drawn on Duffield, 'International Security Institutions: Rules, Tools, Schools, or Fools?' in R.A.W. Rhodes et al., ed., *The Oxford Handbook of Political Institutions* (Oxford, Oxford University Press 2006) pp. 633-653.

[18] Duffield 2005, *supra* n. 17, at p. 8. The Duffield matrix discerns inclusive international security institutions and exclusive ISIs, the former intended to promote security among participants against threats or aggression from within, the latter to promote the security *of* participants vis-à-vis outside threats or aggression. Collective security, arms control agreements or non-aggression pacts are examples of the former, alliances or arms export controls are examples of the latter. On a second dimension, Duffield discerns ISIs that govern ongoing activities of states (operative-rules institutions) and ISIs that govern hypothetical activities of states (contingent-rules institutions). Examples of the former are arms control agreements and CBMs (confidence-building measures), examples of the latter are collective security systems and alliances, which only become operative in if...then situations.

While hunches, even educated ones, may only serve as hypotheses for further research, one might try and differentiate the institutions-security nexus somewhat further. Operative rule-based ISIs may lose some of their relevance as new power constellations call established routines and mutual control patterns into question. Within that category, inclusive ones may be less resistant than exclusive ones, as the former may be directly affected by the new power distribution whereas the latter address obvious, external targets (e.g., strategic-sanctions regimes against grave human rights perpetrators or hotbeds of conflict) or sometimes have symbolic rather than real value and are therefore easier to sustain.

Contingent rule-based institutions might be expected to be exposed less immediately to new challenges, as their 'if' and 'then' relationship is only of a conditional nature. This might be more true for inclusive rather for than exclusive ones, however, as, e.g., collective security systems address no particular enemy, whereas alliances tend to do just that. The latter might look, therefore, more urgently for new enemies or new missions.

DEINSTITUTIONALIZATION ...

This brings us to the point where the 'ISIs do matter' thesis might be reversed as well. If the reasoning is that international security institutions do well, it would be logical to presume that security deinstitutionalization does not do so well.

Far from being able to present conclusive empirical evidence here, this contribution concludes with a couple of supportive observations on the deinstitutionalization warning. A few examples might serve as a case in point. Arms control agreements seem to have had a relatively hard time during the past decade, suggesting that the first aforementioned hypothesis (including that operative rule-based institutions might erode) might be a fact. The NPT weakening, the CTBT impasse, the ABM termination, the BWC Verification Protocol failure, the CFE suspension are just a few examples catch meet the eye in this regard.

Multilateral arms export regimes, on the contrary, tended to survive, supporting the second hypothesis ('exclusive operative rule-based security institutions live longer'). CoCom, NSG and Zangerrules and the system of UN arms embargos do survive for more than 30-50 years, are still flexible enough to allow for updates and are occasionally even complemented or reinforced by regional regimes (the OSCE embargo or the EU Code of Conduct on Arms Exports).

Collective security systems have shown severe weaknesses in a few salient cases, as the failure to get UN Security Council support for military action on Kosovo (1999) and Iraq (2003) demonstrate. But on the less visible level of minor conflicts, it may suffice to refer to the HSR's findings on the highly successful mediation and other institutional intervention efforts since the 1990s.[19] However, mediation itself, rather than the organizational structure as such, seems to be the successful 'institution' in this respect. The preliminary evidence is that not only organizations but nation states (e.g., Norway, the United States) are successful actors as well in this respect, which warrants 'commented' support for the third hypothesis.

Finally, the emergent preference for *ad hoc* rather than permanent alliances (*Iraqi Freedom, Enduring Freedom*) and manifest NATO masochism (one may briefly refer to the Alliance's repeated 'we can't afford to fail' mantra with respect to the Afghanistan operation here) all incline to support the fourth hypothesis (exclusive contingent rule-based institutions are erosion-sensitive).

Some empirical cases of deinstitutionalization are well in stock and may illustrate the above.

The multilateral treaty system for guaranteeing checks on weapons of mass destruction, especially nuclear weapons, is in deep water. As such, it is a major example of a complex institutional crisis. Since the 1990s, the so-called *horizontal* proliferation of CBRN weapons has accelerated both in perception and in reality.[20] Leaving aside here the story of CBR, the case of nuclear proliferation may be relevated as it is often brought up as the problem case constituting the urgency of the institutional crisis. At the time of the most recent Review Conference on the Non-Proliferation Treaty (2005), IAEA Director ElBaradei supported the warning of the UN High Level Panel calling the state of the *nuclear non-proliferation* regime 'precarious' and signalling 'the risk of a possible cascade of proliferation'.[21] The Conference ended in crisis, the subsequent attempt to address the NPT crisis at the UN World Summit also failed, which led Secretary-General Kofi Annan to call the twin failure 'a terrible signal' and urgently repeating the global risk of a proliferation cascade.[22] In 2007, ElBaradei even

---

19 In-depth research by the Geneva Centre for Human Dialogue has brought to the surface that by 2006 nearly 60% of all armed conflicts 'used' mediation. Even though 50-60% of all mediations fail, one can therefore conclude that still 25-30% of global armed conflict situations benefit through negotiations. The UN is involved in more mediation than any other single mediator, although the combined mediatory involvement of a few leading nation states is much larger. If success is counted as including any progress from a ceasefire to a full settlement, the Geneva Report states that 'regional organizations are significantly better than states, the UN and NGOs.' Centre for Humanitarian Dialogue, *Charting the Roads to Peace – Mediation Data Trends Report 2007* (Geneva 2007).

20 CBRN stands for chemical, biological, radiological and nuclear weapons.

21 <http://www.un.org/secureworld/report.pdf>, p. A/59/565.

22 UN Secretary-General Kofi Annan, *Nuclear Non-Proliferation Treaty Faces Crisis of Compliance, Confidence,* address at the University of Tokyo , May 18, 2006 <http://www.un.org/News/ossg/sg/stories/statments_search_full.asp?statID=29>.

warned of a 'nuclear catastrophe' if the then deadline for action was to be missed.[23]

Of the approximately 60 states that currently have a nuclear industry, at least 40 would be capable of turning to short-term nuclear weapons production if the restrictions were to fade away. This is of course not to say that any loosening of institutional constraints would automatically release the political will to acquire N-status by countries. While some states would still abstain, other states might feel tempted to consider their acquisition. For the past ten years the operational nuclear status of India, Pakistan and Israel is no longer doubted, while North Korea carried out its first testing in October 2006, and is negotiating the conditions for dismantling this position. Less widely-known are the illicit minor activities in this field by at least another handful of states that have come to light. The bilateral negotiations between the United States and India on reaching an exclusive agreement about the nuclear activities of the latter feed the idea that the Non Proliferation Treaty (which India refuses to ratify) is no longer sacred. The most threatening crisis is developing around Iran's nuclear programme, despite its stubborn assertion that it is developing uranium enrichment for energy purposes only. Yet for almost twenty years it has retracted from verification obligations with respect to the IAEA. Although the IAEA has so far not been convinced of the opposite case, namely that Iran is in fact secretly developing its nuclear weapons, an escalation of the current sanction stage towards future military confrontation cannot be excluded. The consequences of such an escalation for the overall security situation in the Middle East and the global energy market – to name but a few outcomes – would be colossal and disastrous. At the moment of writing, another hotbed issue, the regime crisis in Pakistan, demonstrates how precariously close the connection can be between terrorism, radicalism and weapons of mass destruction. The lack of certainty concerning the security of the Pakistani nuclear weapons arsenal, neither in the physical sense nor in political control, generates scary dreams of nuclear weapons falling into the hands of radical Islamic militants.[24] Furthermore, the Pakistan case teaches us that horizontal proliferation has also become a *private* branch of industry, as has been illustrated by the global subdivisions of the Khan network.

Almost forgotten, but still relevant, as ever, is the threat resulting from the advancing *vertical* proliferation. In this regard too complicated to elaborate upon extensively, the established nuclear powers, despite their treaty obligations to

---

[23] Mohammed El Baradei, *International Conference on the Prevention of Nuclear Catastrophe* <http://www.iaea.org/NewsCenter/Statements/2007/ebsp2007n006.html>.

[24] *Increasing Alarm in Washington over Pakistan Nuclear Arsenal*, AFP/Space War, 8 November 2007; *Pakistan Nuclear Security Eyed by US*, Global Security Newswire, 8 November 2007 <www.nti.org>.

reach the point of general nuclear disarmament at any future point in time, are working not so much to expand their nuclear arsenals, as to make them more sophisticated and 'reliable'. The American plans for positioning part of their ballistic missile shield in Europe are answered by Russia with the threat of abandoning old treaties on arms control. This would bring Europe's security directly into play. Some of the measures that Russia has hinted at are the positioning of tactical nuclear missiles at the Eastern border of the EU and the discontinuing of the 1987 INF treaty, which prohibits the placement of medium-range missiles.[25] One does not need to completely embrace the title of the collage 'Approaching Midnight', where various authors exemplify the advancement of the famous doomsday clock to five to twelve, in order to see quite a dangerous world still containing enough megatons to detonate one Hiroshima bomb every second for four days.[26] Another growing problem, only recently institutionally (dis)covered, is the threat of yet another form of proliferation, namely of nuclear material or even weapons technology by and to non-state actors.

The same can be said for global terrorism: more threats, closer to home, and, in a way, both horizontal and vertical proliferation, crossing the public-private frontier by definition. In the name of the Al Qaeda movement, seven major terrorist attacks have been carried out in (by now more than) ten UN member states spread out over four continents. Considering the institutional dimension of this threat: in the eyes of the High Level Panel mentioned above, this group has in a short time grown to a 'universal threat to the membership of the UN and the UN itself,' as well as against 'the rule of law' and against 'human rights'.

... AND THE SECURITY OF THE NETHERLANDS

If the system of ISIs functions (at least) as firewalls which serve to halt the proliferation of major categories of arms, serve to contain conflict and cross-border terrorism, the process of deinstitutionalization can be seen as the dismantlement of the very same firewalls.[27]

Its resulting 'de-securitizing' effects may be found and observed at least at three levels. While the analysis is focused on the impact for a small country like the Netherlands here, where we used to think in terms of relatively well demar-

---

[25] Ko Colijn, 'Kouder', *Vrij Nederland* (17 februari 2007).

[26] 'Nuclear Weapons, Special Report: Approaching Midnight', 63 *Bulletin of Atomic Scientists*, No. 1 (January/February 2007) pp. 33-40.

[27] 'Firewall' is only chosen here to emphasize that ISIs' positive value-minimalistic approach, to the extent that their role is more positive, would be more harmful in the process of deinstitutionalization.

cated territorial security risks during the Cold War, the possible effects could easily be projected for any single country that confronts the new, institution-like world. [28]

At the *state* level, these effects are expressed in the inability of central governments to provide resistance, independently or even engaged in international coalitions, against terrorist activities that brew within national territories and are being exported: in Afghanistan, the Caucasus, East Africa and Asia 'unadministrated' (read: wild) areas as free havens and training facilities for stateless terror movements. This invites (or requires) combating terror and revolts through extensive and risky expeditions (cf., the deployment of commandos to Afghanistan in 2005) by existing or *ad hoc* coalitions (cf., participation in the ISAF missions in Uruzgan since 2006), which no longer shields the relatively minor, prosperous and traditionally militarily low-profile countries like the Netherlands from calls for active engagement, both in soft and hard power operations, the latter bringing about hard-to-explain human and material losses, triggering acts of averse domestic radicalism and the risk of asymmetric revenge acts by foreign terrorists or even military retaliation. All in all, this type of deinstitutionalization may have very unfamiliar security reverberations. Annual surveys show a sobering record of tens of failing states that are often not only a hotbed of civil war, but also an exporter of insecurity.[29]

At the *regime* level, Dutch security interests are damaged by deinstitutionalization, because the strength of treaties and organizations for preventing proliferation has increasingly been doubted for the past years. On the one hand, this is an expression of political scepticism in the United States – that continues to be *the indispensable nation* in any case of global security and weapons control – to multilateralism in general. On the other hand, can this doubt be ascribed to the specific aging symptoms of non-proliferation regimes that seemed to function well during the Cold War, but appear to be losing their swing of disciplining and control?[30] The process of deinstitutionalization at the regime level also applies, *mutatis mutandis*, to alliances such as NATO, whose fixed place and function of deterrence respectively combating military threats is increasingly coming under pressure. The result for a small country like the Netherlands is that its protection clout is no longer unchallenged. For the past years the phenomenon of

[28] The following extract is taken from Ko Colijn, *De Goede Instelling – op zoek naar mondiale veiligheid*' (see author's note).

[29] Cf. 'The Failed States Index 2008', *Foreign Policy* (July/August 2008) pp. 64-73.

[30] Examples include the Non-Proliferation Treaty (unable to effectively prevent *would-be proliferators* from developing nuclear weapons, despite IAEA inspections), the Comprehensive Test Ban Treaty (which appears to fail in getting to the ratifications finish, partly because of US obstruction) and the Biological Weapons Convention (that lacks an effective compliance mechanism).

international *ad hoc* coalitions has appeared as a substitute for permanence in the process of deinstitutionalization. Their performance is inevitably accompanied by politicizing and mounting tensions, as soon as individual (especially smaller) countries are asked to participate in these random coalitions. Whether to take part in *Allied Freedom* (the Kosovo War in 1999), *Enduring Freedom* (several times since 2001), *Iraqi Freedom* (2003), the *Proliferation Security Initiative* (since 2003) and even the prolongation of controversial peace missions (Iraq 2004, Uruzgan 2008) resulted in equally delicate and tense decision moments in Dutch politics, and can easily grow into spots of sublimation for undesirable attention (e.g., internet threats) to foreign terror organizations and of practising external political pressure. One paradox is that as soon as the international community becomes more successful in ending conflicts at the negotiation table, which seems to be the case since the beginning of this century, the need for peacekeeping missions and stabilisation capacity in the involved countries will only increase, because the odds of these conflicts erupting into violence again within five years are relatively high.[31] For those few countries that do possess this capacity, including the Netherlands, they have all the more reason and difficulty not to ignore these sensitive missions.

Third, due to a crisis within the United Nations, the process of deinstitutionalization has even become urgent at the highest *global* level. Concerning content, this translates into strongly disagreeing views about the tolerance of pre-emptive military might and the inability to even come to a broadly accepted definition of terrorism (let alone a working method thereon). At the administrative level the crisis is translated into dragging discussions about the representativeness and competences of the Security Council. As a result, the 'right of war' has moved from a legal *terra cognita* to a politically much more uncertain terrain: the right of armed intervention. These discussions naturally multiply, with all the possibilities of controversies within Dutch society resulting.[32]

FINAL REMARKS

The main question in this chapter has been to what extent the process of deinstitutionalization in the field of global security politics could be considered, on balance, as a threat. The end of the Cold War not only produced new concepts of security (apart from the classical idea of national security and the

[31] *Human Security Brief*, *supra* n. 14, in particular pp. 19-22.

[32] In order to avoid those effects, it is conceivable in foreign policy to opt for risk aversion (read: neutralization), but this can also result in political marginalization and accusations of weakness. Such a policy choice would for that matter not necessarily make the Netherlands less vulnerable for the new security risks, possibly even the contrary.

consequently deriving paradigm of *interstate* security, the 1990s witnessed the emergence of global security and human security as paradigms). The transition to a newer, at least non-bipolar structure, also called into question the 'public administrative' issue of whether the old international security institutions could (be made to) survive as instruments of security policy. The debate shifts between the vision that institutions are irrelevant anyway, and offer only false promises in the tough world of power politics, to the empirical claim that their role has been underestimated during the relative 'decade of peace' following the fall of the Berlin Wall. Inclined to find the last claim to be more convincing than the uncompromising realist 'false promise' thesis, we come to the reverse proposition that deinstitutionalization in the field of security is a risky, if not threatening process. For all the reservations the recent nature of the research may warrant, the conclusion would be markedly different from the false promise thesis: take care of ISIs, institutional conservation in the area of global security would certainly not be a waste of effort.

Global Governance and the Relevance of Social Power

Peter van Ham

Introduction

Soft power, smart power, sticky power, social power, or hard power – obviously power comes in all shapes and sizes, and caters for all tastes. Idealists with rosy views about human nature may propagate the notion of soft power, convinced as they are that persuasion and benchmarking will get the best out of Man, as well as out of states. Sceptics and self-styled 'Realists' who take anarchy for granted will rely on hard, military power as the final judge of who is right, or at least who will get his right.

The debate about power is of all times, and remains central to the study of international politics. The godfathers of the discipline of international relations (hereinafter, IR) like E.H. Carr, Hans Morgenthau, Kenneth Waltz, and Karl W. Deutsch, were all primarily concerned with the working and distribution of power in the international system. Going further back in time, the philosophical roots of IR can be found in the classical works of Thucydides, Machiavelli and Hobbes, whose tracts on war and conflict tried to answer the key questions: what is power and how can, or should it be used?

Power is not just one of the most fundamental concepts in social science, it is also all around us. No one can escape power relationships, we all influence each other and are, in turn, influenced by others. Since the most common definition of power is the sense of someone getting someone else to do something they would otherwise not do, we are confronted with power within the family, as consumers, voters, lovers, and all other social relationships. Why do we buy a certain product, support a certain presidential candidate, or accept a foreign country's political leadership, all boils down to the power of branding, spin doctoring, or loyalty (just to name a few labels). Power is therefore ubiquitous, in the sense that it is in all arenas of social life, as well as complex, since it is often ambiguous who exercises power, and how.[1]

[1] David A. Baldwin, *Paradoxes of Power* (Oxford, Basil Blackwell 1989) p. 1.

J. de Zwaan, E. Bakker and S. van der Meer (eds.), Challenges in a Changing World

Defining the situation

So what is new concerning power? This chapter introduces a particular face of power which I will label 'social power.'[2] Social power, a concept not frequently used in the study of international politics, can be defined as the ability to set standards, create norms, and values that are deemed legitimate, desirable, and, best of all: normal.[3] More commonly used notions such as soft power, but also smart, sticky, and sweet power,[4] can all be accommodated under the generous umbrella definition of social power as the ability to define the situation. In order to set standards and define a situation in international politics, hard power may be used, and has at times proved expedient. Military power has obviously been exercised for millennia to 'define a situation' in international affairs, with mixed results. Even in today's postmodern Europe, one could argue that Kosovo has used terrorism and guerrilla warfare to gain sovereignty, with marked success, as its independence since February 2008 testifies. Military power remains relevant, but requires the legal and/or moral basis of legitimacy to sustain its triumphs. Since social power ultimately depends upon legitimacy and credibility, military force alone is of marginal use. Today's Iraq is a clear illustration of the results of military power without legitimacy. And even Kosovo now has to wait until the international community recognizes its independence, illustrating that neither legitimacy nor credibility can be owned, but are conferred by others.

Social power includes, but goes beyond soft power. Joseph S. Nye's definition of soft power involves the ability to get one's way through attraction, rather than coercion or payments.[5] In order to be successful in international politics, attraction and persuasion are valuable resources. Being popular and admired is important, also for political actors; it makes it easier to sway others, and influence policy decisions. But although soft power is a valuable concept which has widened the debate about the foundations of contemporary power, its scope has become too limited. To compete in today's economic, political, and security pageants, we have to go beyond attraction and persuasion, and study the mechanisms of (global) governance. And we have to do this in quite some detail.

---

[2] For an overview of the sociological literature on power, see John Scott, *Power* (Cambridge, UK, Polity Press 2001). See also Michael Mann, *The Sources of Social Power: A History of Power From the Beginning to A.D. 1760* (Cambridge, Cambridge University Press 1986); and Daniel Philpott, *Revolutions in Sovereignty: How Ideas Shaped Modern International Relations* (Princeton, Princeton University Press 2001).

[3] Mann, *supra* n. 2.

[4] Walter Russell Mead, *Power, Terror, Peace, and War. America's Grand Strategy in a World at Risk* (New York, Vintage 2005); and Michael Mead, 'America's Sticky Power', 83 *Foreign Policy*, No. 141 (March/April 2004).

[5] Joseph S. Nye, Jr., *Soft Power: The Means to Success in World Politics* (New York, Public Affairs 2004).

All major powers aspire to upload their values and norms to the global level; this particularly applies to the United States and the European Union, with China as a relative newcomer, offering its so-called Beijing Consensus as a competing development model to the West's market-based liberalism.[6] Traditionally, Great Powers have used empires, or at least the idea of an empire, to expand their normative reach and ideational range. But since the notion of empire is now frowned upon, conjuring up images of oppression and exploitation, different rationales are offered and different narratives developed. It is no longer *comme il faut* to admit that both the United States and EU are engaged in a *mission civilisatrice*, since this immediately raises the spectre of neo-colonialism, if not full-fledged imperialism. Against this backdrop, the modest aspiration of uploading one's values and norms and influencing the rulebook of global governance sounds innocuous – and it probably is.

Since social power centres around being able to determine what is normal, desirable, and the 'law of the land', legitimacy and credibility are important, if not essential requirements to successfully upload one's norms and values. In contemporary international politics, legitimacy and credibility have become powerful resources and tools to justify and gather support for foreign policy actions. The ability and capability to legitimate foreign policy *in the eyes of others* is the staple of social power. Legitimacy assumes the tacit or explicit agreement on the rules of the game, based on, or rooted in a shared set of norms. Credibility is based on trust that policies will be conducted effectively. The ability to acquire and sustain both legitimacy and credibility requires social capital, which can de defined as the set of norms and values that are shared among members of a group permitting cooperation among them. Every community is based on social capital, based on norms such as honesty and reliability, or freedom and justice.

How, and even whether, social capital can be accumulated in international politics, remains somewhat elusive. But it has become obvious that political legitimacy becomes more strained as the sense of community weakens, and the physical distance between those in authority and the general public grows. As the scale of governance expands, legitimacy becomes increasingly problematic. Since global governance functions without a formal system of authority, the capacity for direct control over actors has been replaced with a capacity to influence processes. Today, global governance centres around the goal of harmonizing the collective preferences of multiple actors. In these efforts to solve problems on a global scale, social power is rapidly growing in importance since it does not apply coercion and makes little use of the hierarchical modes of

[6] Kishore Mahbubani, 'The Case Against the West', 87 *Foreign Affairs*, No. 3 (May/June 2008).

government. Since legitimacy is rare and the normative basis (i.e., social capital) is usually fragile or lacking, social power has become a cherished, while scarce, commodity in international politics.

Contemporary (global) governance embraces governmental institutions (be they states or intergovernmental organizations), but also involves informal, non-governmental mechanisms which all aspire to upload their own norms and values and 'define the situation' on a wide range of policy issues. States now compete with intergovernmental organizations (hereafter IOs), trans-governmental policy networks, as well as non-governmental organizations (hereafter NGOs) and private authorities in a new global governance game. Clearly, the state is usually the *primes inter pares* among them, not least because its territorial embeddedness offers it unique authority as well as democratic legitimacy. But the state's enduring power base is no longer directly linked with its military capacity, since in a governance environment, military force has been duly marginalized and delegitimized. Moreover, since the state can no longer take the loyalty of 'its' citizens for granted, it has to work hard and cleverly to maintain what is left of the traditionally strong emotional bond between country and people. Place branding has become an effective mechanism for states (as well as cities and IOs) to charge citizens' emotional batteries, trying to obtain the attention, affection, and 'brand loyalty' of communities living both inside and outside its borders by using practices developed in the commercial sector.[7]

In order to define the situation, states increasingly look at social power tools. Hard power still lurks in the background, though, reminding us of US President Teddy Roosevelt's famous dictum that smart policymakers 'speak softly and carry a big stick.' This relationship between hard and social power remains largely unresolved, since it is well nigh impossible to clinically dissect their impact on the legitimacy and credibility of political actors and foreign policies. Scholars like Ian Manners maintain that the EU's normative power would be seriously undermined by the development of an European Security and Defence Policy (ESDP) worthy of its acronym.[8] Others, like Robert Kagan, have famously argued that US credibility is sustained by its massive military might, even – or perhaps: particularly – when it is not actually used.[9] Examples can be found proving both scholars right: The EU's model of postnational policymaking has been attractive for Africa, for example, which tries to emulate the EU's

[7] Peter van Ham, 'The Rise of the Brand State: The Postmodern Politics of Image and Reputation', 80 *Foreign Affairs*, No. 5 (September/October 2001).

[8] Ian Manners, 'Normative Power Europe: A Contradiction in Terms?', 40 *Journal of Common Market Studies*, No. 2 (2002).

[9] Robert Kagan, 'Power and Weakness', *Policy Review*, No. 113 (2002).

experience with its African Union. At the same time, America's military preponderance has made it particularly popular in Central Europe, which still credits Ronald Reagan's power-politics with winning the Cold War. Or, as Thomas Friedman claims, '[t]he hidden hand of the market will never work without the hidden fist. McDonald's cannot flourish without McDonnell Douglas, the designer of the F-15. And the hidden fist that keeps the world safe for Silicon valley's technologies is called the U.S. Army, Air Force, Navy and Marine Corps.'[10]

These two cases illustrate that social power is not simply the default option of the weak. Even hard-nosed *Realpolitikers* realize that the intangible qualities of social power are relevant, even to the use of military force. In all conflicts and wars, claims are made to transform brute force into legitimate rule. Whether it is God, communism, international law, or freedom, lofty goals have always been raised to legitimate the use of force, confirming that hard power requires social power to ultimately achieve its goals. On the other hand, one should also recognize that normative power is not always 'nice' power. Social power may certainly have a social ring to it, but is conceptually neutral and says nothing about the moral qualities of the 'situation' it endeavours to define, or the norms and values it attempts to upload to the next governance level. For example, critics claim that Europe's global normsetting is frequently a hidden form of protectionism. Take the EU's call upon all Member States to ban inefficient light-bulbs and to gradually introduce energy-saving CFLs (compact fluorescent light-bulbs). Although a lofty plan from an environmental perspective, this decision also offers splendid new business opportunities for EU-based manufacturers such as Philips and Osram, and keeps the old-fashioned light-bulbs out, which happen to be produced outside the EU, in the developing world.[11] The EU's efforts to upload its social norms can therefore also be seen as a strategy to defend Europe's own social standards against worldwide competition.

Summarizing the ideas of Zaki Laïdi, we may therefore conclude that 'norms' are not necessarily 'nice', but that projecting (or uploading) norms is a major tool and source of social power.[12]

---

[10] Robert W. McChesney, 'Global Media, Neoliberalism, and Imperialism', 52 *Monthly Review*, No. 10 (March 2001) pp. 17-18. See also Jon Alterman, *New Media, New Politics: From Satellite Television to the Internet in the Arab World* (Washington DC, Washington Institute for Near East Policy 1998).

[11] Jeroen van der Kris & Elske Schouten, 'EU Wordt de Regelgever van de Wereld', *NRC Handelsblad* (21 October 2007).

[12] Zaki Laïdi, 'The Normative Empire: The Unintended Consequences of European Power', *Les Essays de Telos* (Paris, Telos 2008).

Making it work

Central to all debates about power in international politics is the so-called 'wielding problem': how can we connect the dots between power tools, instruments, and resources, and concrete policy outcomes. One could argue that social power has a certain Newtonian quality to it, since its effect may be visible, whereas the source of power normally is not. Since social power is most often set in institutions and relationships, it is difficult to actually wield it. Institutions and relationships are socially embedded, moulded as they are by traditions, culture, the media, as well as fads and fashions.

Whereas military power is visible and mediagenic (battleships are moved, and shots fired, often *live* on TV), social power generally lacks visibility and public attention. By their very nature, institutions and relationships are visually unappealing, and often elusive. The simplicity and straightforward quality of military power stand in stark contrast to the complexity and ambiguity of social power. This makes the quality of social power less easy to understand and explain; it also makes it less easy to 'sell' as a preferred tool of statecraft, both to the wider public as well as within bureaucratic organisations. Perhaps the current impasse in the wars in Afghanistan and Iraq offers a window of opportunity for social power to make its case. In Iraq (as well as in Afghanistan) military power has obviously found its limits, whereas the struggle to win the hearts and minds of Muslim communities is an ongoing effort. Obviously, winning the war of ideas requires social power, since it involves a struggle between the West and extremist Islamists to 'define the situation', and to upload conflicting sets of norms. Public diplomacy and place branding have emerged as social power tools to reach these foreign communities, instil legitimacy and credibility, and gain compliance. This is, of course, a tall order – but still feasible, despite all odds.

So, which dots have been connected most clearly, giving us confidence that social power tools indeed form a central part of international politics? As in all social sciences, 100% proof is illusory. Still, some cases prove social power's value beyond any reasonable doubt. The case of culture, especially popular, or 'low' culture, stands out. Since social power involves the capacity to shape and influence motives, attitudes, roles, and interests of actors in international politics (by non-coercive means), culture's qualities hardly come as a surprise. Especially popular culture is uniquely capable of defining what is standard, normal, and legitimate.

These are, of course, rather unspectacular sociological observations. But applying them to the realm of international politics opens up new thinking space about the workings of power in general, and foreign policy in particular. Popular culture has been instrumentalized during the Cold War, when jazz and rock 'n' roll were used to spread the Western values of freedom and consumerism to the communist world and beyond. But arguably more influential has been the complete package of American (and more general Western) popular culture, which has offered the people of Soviet-dominated 'captive nations' tempting vistas of freedom and affluence. Having myself frequently visited Central Europe in the 1980s, I recall the immense attraction these Western lifestyles had on ordinary Poles, Czechoslovaks, and East Germans, feeding the frustration and opposition which ultimately culminated in the 1989 revolutions.

The social power of popular culture permeates Western society, and is most notably visible through patterns of consumption and the impact of the media. Consumers' power of the purse is shaping notions of corporate social responsibility, whereas the rise of the Internet and me-media (blogs and wikis) effectively limits the role and impact of traditional gatekeepers of information. The bearing of these modes of social power becomes most evident if we focus on the resistance and conflicts they provoke, especially with authoritarian governments keen on defending their bubble of identity against the perceived onslaught of a Western-dominated globalization. Obviously, countries like China realize all too well that the free flow of goods and images affects its identity, which in turn shapes the normative codex upon which both domestic and foreign policy are based. China has erected its own Great Firewall to manage the Internet, and is developing its public diplomacy network to counter the social power of its competitors.[13] And so does the EU, which over the last few decades has thrown up its own cultural Maginot line, in a rather desperate attempt to dam off American popular culture – to little avail, of course.[14]

Over the decades, US administrations have persisted in their efforts to use, manage, and manipulate the social power instilled in America's popular pop culture. As a report of the US Advisory Commission on Public Diplomacy suggests, immediately after 9/11: 'Brands, products, popular entertainment, higher education, corporations, and Web sites all may reinforce or undermine U.S. foreign policy objectives.'[15] From cartoons to music, from movies to consumer brands, all modes of social power have been used by the United States (and others) to upload its norms, and define the (global) situation. At times quite successfully.

---

[13] William Thatcher Dowell, 'The Internet, Censorship, and China', 7 *Georgetown Journal of International Affairs*, No. 2 (Summer 2006).

[14] Mel van Elteren, 'GATT and Beyond: World Trade, the Arts and American Popular Culture in Western Europe', 19 *Journal of American Culture*, No. 3 (Fall 1996), and ibid., 'U.S. Cultural Imperialism Today: Only a Chimera?', 23 *SAIS Review*, No. 2 (Summer 2003).

[15] U.S. Advisory Commission on Public Diplomacy, *Building America's Public Diplomacy: 2002 Report* (Washington, DC, 2002).

The most impressive pool of social power comprises the images and narratives that inform the so-called 'Hollywood aesthetic', which has turned itself into the globe's dominant visual language. The normative mode of communication that underlies this aesthetic offers the world a golden mean of images, which explains why it crosses boundaries easily. Hollywood has turned itself into the world's dream factory, producing its hopes and fears, based on shared desires and concerns. Olsen and Blumenberg's notion of the 'Hollywood mythotypos' dissects Hollywood's social power, arguing that its movies are designed to overcome the 'existential dread that our lives might be short, meaningless, and ultimately ephemeral,' and appeal 'to those emotions that block out the absolutism of reality: wonder, awe, purpose, and participation.'[16] This offers popular culture (as well as the mass media) the social power to define the situation, and the capability to set standards and determine normalcy. Taken together, popular culture and media largely shape the general public's views of the world, and its notions of how the world is run, and by whom.

The relevance of these social power resources for international politics should be clear. For example, the fact that US popular culture is based on the dogma of the happy ending, is reflected in (and in turn shaped by) America's 'can do' foreign policy ideology. The US entertainment and media industry supports this image, depicting America as a superhero who 'reluctantly' steps in to rescue passive and usually incompetent communities and peoples. Ranging from Westerns to *Die Hard*-like movies, the notion that Americans should fight evil has become ingrained in the American psyche. This is the myth constructing the United States as a redeemer nation. It is also an image which tickles the egos of US foreign policy makers, and informs their foreign policy decisions. But since these movies, stories, and images are consumed globally, this 'natural' American role has also influenced perceptions and expectations of the rest of the world.

Can Washington wield this pool of social power? Not really, but American policymakers are keenly aware of it, and realize the impact it has on their image and reputation as an actor in international politics. Unlike any other social power tool, America's popular culture shapes the imagination of a global community, and, more importantly, informs expectations of American foreign policy actions. Although trust in American leadership has fallen precipitously, the overall US brand remains strong, despite debacles such as the torture-pictures of Abu Ghraib's and Guantanamo Bay's prisoners, and the atrocities in Haditha, and other Iraqi villages. Imagine if Great Powers like Russia or China would be responsible for disasters of this magnitude – the consequences would be dev-

---

[16] Scott R. Olson, 'The Globalization of Hollywood', 17 *International Journal on World Peace*, No. 4 (December 2000) p. 10. See also Hans Blumenberg, *Work on Myth* (Cambridge, Mass., The MIT Press 1985).

astating, mainly because these states lack the massive pool of goodwill and visual hegemony the Hollywood aesthetic still offers. As long as America presents to the world its *Desperate Housewives* and *The Sopranos*, it seems to get away with policy failures like Iraq.[17]

Combined with the marginal success of America's public diplomacy efforts towards the Muslim world, the conclusion is warranted that social power is a key tool of statecraft, although it is inherently difficult to employ effectively. As far as culture and media dominance is concerned, one can have social power, without being really able to use it. In this sense, social power is structural.[18] America's popular culture offers it legitimacy and credibility, as well as visual and discursive hegemony over the global foreign policy agenda. This has given Washington the ability to dominate the agenda and determine what issues warrant discussion; but it has not shaped ultimate policy decisions and outcomes. Al Jazeera and the surge of new media all add to the erosion of America's social power to frame the global international agenda. These new, and often powerful competitors, make it harder for political elites to control the nature, timing, and content of foreign policy debates. As a result, social power, at least in the realm of culture and media, may still involve the capability to influence and affect, but rarely to determine and control.

Tilting the playing field

This makes social power uncomfortably fluffy for foreign policy analysts, but a great resource for experienced players of the global governance game. Setting rules is the core business in international politics. Both the United States and the European Union are avid norm entrepreneurs, using every possible instrument in their toolbox to encourage others to join their normative spheres of influence. Strong states and IOs may still follow *Realpolitik*'s rulebook of powerplay and coercive diplomacy, but the vast majority of rules, standards, and regulations that cover international society's *acquis communautaire*, are set through non-hierarchical means of policymaking, involving such postmodern processes as best practices, benchmarking, and 'naming and shaming'. In order to play this 'game' well, policy actors have to acquire a particular sensitivity, mindset, and organisational structure to be successful. Here, too, social capital assets like legitimacy and credibility, as well as trust, are indispensable.[19]

---

17 Toby Miller, Nitin Govil, John McMurrian & Richard Maxwell, *Global Hollywood* (Berkeley, Ca., University of California Press 2002).

18 Stefano Guzzini, 'Structural Power: The Limits of Neorealist Power Analysis', 47 *International Organization*, No. 3 (Summer 1993).

19 Tanja A. Börzel, 'Pace-Setting, Foot-Dragging, and Fence-Sitting: Member States Responses to Europeanization', 40 *Journal of Common Market Studies*, No. 2 (2002).

It comes as no surprise that the EU feels comfortable in this new environment of governance and social power. The unique nature of EU policymaking, which comprises elements of intergovernmentalism, supranationalism, and comitology (i.e., the rules of committees and working groups), makes the European integration process a microcosm of global governance, albeit on a regional basis. Over the decades, the European Commission has spun a dense network of advisory, regulatory, and management committees which serve to set the agenda, prepare policy proposals, and implement agreed policies. Obviously, these committees are the preferred entry points for advocacy groups and NGOs, turning the EU's intrinsic hybridity and flexibility into a major *forte* to compete in today's global governance arena.

Interestingly, the soft underbelly of EU policymaking is duly compensated by a rather tough institutional construction supporting Europe to project its norms and values to the global level. *The Economist* even suggested (in 2007) that 'Brussels is becoming the world's regulatory capital.'[20] EU Trade Commissioner Peter Mandelson clarified that it 'is the rules of the single market which gives us the foundation to export our rules and standards around the world – an increasingly important part of my job as a trade commissioner. In short, no single market, no European project and no *Europe puissance*.'[21]

Uploading one's norms is made easier by being a first mover, combined with a certain measure of economic and political power. As Mattli and Büthe suggest, European firms 'possess much better information about international standardization opportunities and proposals and, thanks to this information advantage and more effective interest representation, to be more involved – *earlier and more effectively* – than their American counterparts. [emphasis added].'[22] American firms usually learn about developments of new international standards too late, and therefore often have to pay high switching costs since international standards differ from their current practices. The EU's hybridity, combined with its institutional strictness, have made Brussels into the world champion of global governance, offering a good example of how social power is generated and used. It also suggests that social power facilitates other power resources, adding legitimacy and credibility to policy outcomes that might otherwise be deemed hegemonic. Especially since the EU is considered a postnational actor, a kaleidoscope of interests and norms, its policies acquire credence and authority, which are major elements determining its chances of success.

---

[20] 'Brussels Rules OK', *The Economist* (22 September 2007) p. 42.

[21] 'Openness, Trade and the European Union', Speech by Peter Mandelson, at the Chambre de Commerce et de l'Industrie de Paris (June 30, 2007).

[22] Walter Mattli & Tim Büthe, 'Setting International Standards: Technological Rationality or Primacy of Power?', 56 *World Politics*, No. 1 (October 2003) p. 27.

A similar route has been followed by emerging transgovernmental policy networks, which have become important conduits for social power. These transgovernmental arrangements (or global public policy networks [hereafter GPPNs]) are loose alliances between governments, IOs, firms, NGOs, professional organizations, and cultural and religious groups, joining together to achieve common goals.[23] They embody the new fluid (or liquid) nature of today's governance environment, which privileges arrangements lacking institutional fixity, but rewards flexibility.[24] This also explains the proliferation of Friends groupings, Troikas, Quartets, and Quints, which are merely the top of the iceberg of a major recalibration of the institutional foundation of global governance. The important novelty of these networks is that they are not driven by formal institutions and bureaucracies, and not managed in a modern, top-down hierarchical style. Instead, GPPNs are 'owned' by relevant slices of society, comprising as many stakeholders as is deemed necessary to be effective, efficient, and legitimate.

Especially transnational advocacy coalitions, whose power derives from managing information and mobilizing public support, have shown themselves remarkably adept to influence both formal government channels and GPPNs. Norms established within the UN-sponsored Global Compact and Corporate Social Responsibility (CRS) agreements, for example, are encouraging firms to act as good, responsible corporate citizens. Especially firms selling directly to consumers realize that their credibility and likeability are essential elements of their brand. This implies that NGOs and the wider public of consumers may steer business actors to comply with a wide range of social and environmental goals. Together with the phenomenon of private authority – based on gentlemen's agreements, codes of conduct, ethical guidelines, and partnerships – today's policymaking environment has become a crowded field of actors, all with diverging claims of legitimacy and credibility.[25] The state has become only one of these competing actors, which all try to define the situation, and aim to set rules and standards.

Social power can be used to tilt the playing field, by setting the structural conditions to achieve foreign policy goals and limit the costs in doing so. The EU's institutional structure and its normative authority have proved effective social power tools. This whereas the United States has made use of the social power derived from its hegemonic pop culture, on top of all the other structural

---

[23] David Antony Detomasi, 'The Multinational Corporation and Global Governance: Modelling Global Public Policy Networks', 71 *Journal of Business Ethics*, No. 3 (March 2007).

[24] Zygmunt Bauman, *Liquid Modernity* (Cambridge, Polity Press 2000); and ibid., *Liquid Times: Living in an Age of Uncertainty* (Cambridge, Polity Press 2007).

[25] Rodney Bruce Hall & Thomas J. Biersteker (eds.), *The Emergence of Private Authority in Global Governance* (Cambridge, Cambridge University Press 2003).

qualities inherent in its powerful Brand USA. Especially public diplomacy and place branding are emerging as strategies used by new players – ranging from emerging Great Powers like China, to IOs such as NATO – in order to enhance and capitalize on their social capital. Not always successfully, to be sure, since many of these rather inexperienced actors are feeling their way forward, trying to learn the largely unwritten mores and mechanisms of global governance's rulebook.

One of the bigger challenges for *all* actors involved in public diplomacy and place branding has been to shed the mindset of power-politics, based on control and hierarchy. Instead, the new paradigm of social power has to be embraced, which does not use the megaphone, making claims, but aims to shape an idea or argument in the hope that they will eventually be taken up and reproduced by others, and hence gets a life of its own. Social power is therefore less about authority, telling others what to do, and more about showing others what we consider to be desirable, in the hope that it will be emulated. Without appreciating the nature and workings of social power, contemporary international politics can no longer be understood.

United States and Europe: Two Befriended Giants in a Changing Global Landscape

Willem Post

Introduction

Pre-Cold War international institutions still try to dominate international relations. But because of a variety of transnational problems and challenges we have to adapt to new circumstances. People can change and so can organizations. In transition periods like ours we should learn from decades-old experiences with existing organizations handling crucial security and foreign policy issues. A reformed and stronger NATO-EU alliance comes to the fore.

Transatlantic differences and revival

Transatlantic differences about a possible war in Iraq reached a rhetorical low in early 2003. After the summer of 2002 the centre-left government of Gerhard Schröder had ruled out German involvement in such a war. But Washington persisted and presented its NATO allies with a wish list: support to help defend Turkey and provide Awac-radar aircraft and ships to patrol the Mediterranean. Washington also suggested that NATO could play a role in post-war humanitarian reconstruction operations in Iraq but Germany's foreign minister, Joschka Fischer, declared that Berlin was rather working on a plan aimed at slowing the drift towards war. The German representative on the UN Security Council requested weapons inspectors to present a report by mid-February. 'We want them to continue working,' Fischer declared together with his French counterpart, Dominique de Villepin. 'And if they are to continue working, then they must also report.'

'We knew the Germans had a problem, but we were surprised that the French joined them,' said one Alliance official.[1] In response to a reporter's question

[1] *The Guardian* (24 January 2003).

J. de Zwaan, E. Bakker and S. van der Meer (eds.), Challenges in a Changing World

about the German-French qualm, the United States Secretary of Defense, Donald Rumsfeld, responded: 'You're thinking of Europe as Germany and France. I don't. I think that's old Europe. If you look at the entire NATO today, the centre of gravity is shifting to the east and there are a lot of new members.'

Rumsfeld's 'Old Europe' remark resulted in sharp criticism and a whole range of official reactions. The French government's spokesman advised Rumsfeld to listen to 'old Europe'. 'When one is an old continent, a continent with an old historic, cultural and economic tradition, one can sometimes inherit a certain wisdom, and wisdom can be a good adviser.' The general secretary of the German Social Democratic party, Olaf Scholz, stated that 'Rumsfeld does not understand Europe,' while a spokesman of the conservative Bavarian Christian Social Union even accused Rumsfeld of 'neo-colonialism'. 'The US should understand that the European Union is a partner and not a protectorate.'

Just sixteen months previously, the *nine-eleven* terrorist attacks had been committed after which we saw a remarkable transatlantic revival. NATO allies immediately invoked Article 5 of the 1949 Washington Treaty. It was envisaged by the Treaty's signatories as a mechanism to commit the United States to come to the aid of its European allies. But now the European allies offered Washington their support.

Impressive commemorative events were organized in European countries. Daily life in so many countries was almost totally dominated by the events in the United States. The Italian Prime Minister said on television: 'Against the deaf making sound of hate stands the silence of civilization.' In Berlin, 200,000 people assembled at the Brandenburg Gate . 'No-one knows better than the people here in Berlin what America has done for freedom and democracy in Germany,' the German President said, overcome by emotion. Behind him there was a huge banner with the words: *We mourn*. French radio adjusted its music programmes and John Lennon's *Imagine* became the song of those days.

Long-term relationship

Behind the façade of these sharply fluctuating moods there was a long-term relationship between the United States and Europe that, at first sight, in the end resulted in a growing gap between their interests and a process of ideological alienation.

From the early beginning of the European integration process, American governments focused on coherence between economic and military developments in order to be able to defend the European continent during the Cold War. The concept of a European Defence Community (EDC) was a move on the part of the French to counterbalance the US strategy to re-arm West Germany. The

United States put pressure to provide mutual security assurances between NATO and the EDC (the French Parliament voted against the EDC in 1954.)

Although sceptical about a 'European' EDC, the failure to establish a European army caused serious doubts in Washington about Europe's ability to take on its own defence responsibility:

> 'These doubts are latent, but linger, and might be one of the root causes of more recent scepticism [...] Americans no longer thought of the European institutions as formal defence mechanisms. Four decades later, when the EU began to develop defence mechanisms through the European Security and Defence Policy (ESDP), Americans were still sceptical. While the EDC's demise was not often cited, that failure meant that a generation of American analysts were educated to expect a neat dichotomy: NATO handled defence and the European institutions managed economic integration.'[2]

The EU policy of Democratic and Republican administrations during the Cold War was based on the consensus that NATO under American leadership would take care of 'hard defence' while the EU would focus on 'soft security'.

As a leading superpower it was in the interest of the United States to have a stable world order with a whole range of multilateral institutions like the United Nations, Bretton Woods and NATO. European allies took cover under the American atomic umbrella. Washington supported European integration because this process linked former enemies together. The Marshall Plan, with a total worth of $12.4 billion, was meant to jump-start the engine of integration with the defeated Germany at the heart of it. On to a safe, prosperous and anti-Soviet Europe! The United States offered free Europe a mutual deal in the form of a social and security compact.

Initially, in the first years after the Cold War, there was little reason to have doubts about the close American-European relationship. The end of the Cold War changed the strategic landscape by making possible the reunification of both Germany and Europe. Germany's Chancellor Helmut Kohl took the initiative and negotiated Soviet consent to the one-Germany goal. This *fait accompli* for the other Western allies reassured the United States that Germany would be reunified within the US-led NATO Alliance. The ultimate goal was a 'European Germany' instead of a 'German Europe'. The eastward expansion of NATO secured the hegemony of the United States in post-Cold War Europe by ensuring that the former communist countries of Eastern Europe would not become part of a Russian sphere of influence. At the same time, their membership of NATO, dominated by the United States, was considered preferable by Washing-

---

[2] Esther Brimmer, 'Seeing blue: American visions of the European Union', *Chaillot Paper* (September 2007) p. 9.

ton to their membership of the Western European Union (WEU) in which the United States had no say.[3]

One of the strategic aims of the administrations of George Bush and Bill Clinton was to translate Cold War victory into sustainable hegemony. After the 1991 Gulf War the United States, with the help of Great Britain, conducted a *de facto* low-intensity war consisting of no-fly zones, bombings to degrade the Iraqi military and UN weapons inspections.

> 'Aside from weakening Iraq while keeping its government, this "containment" policy had the added virtue of giving the United States the excuse and opportunity to maintain a permanent presence in the Persian Gulf. Just as the Gulf War itself had been a "resource war" to remind Europe that it still needed America to maintain access to global resources in a post-Cold War world, so the low-intensity war on Iraq served as a continuing reminder to EU nations (and countries such as Japan) that they still needed American protection to maintain stability in the Persian Gulf region and its oil production, on which they depended.'[4]

Especially the US-led NATO war without UN authorization against Yugoslavia in 1998 further demonstrated US military leadership.

In short, it seems crystal clear that the end of the Cold War has increased American power, especially from a traditional military-strategic perspective. US-sponsored globalization and free trade could restore the world economy to high levels that would be more profitable than any EU emphasis on regional markets. On the other hand, the rationale of common positions shared by the free world diminished after the Cold War, as Wallace writes: 'Now the Cold War is over, the Soviet Union gone, and America is the world's only superpower, and the rhetorical justification for this dominant position is more often couched in realist than in liberal terms; with reference to American national interests rather than in liberal shared global values and concerns.'[5]

First nine months of the Bush administration

In retrospect the 'golden' 1990s was the era of the grand illusion. The first eight months of the Bush administration was characterized by an increasingly harsh

---

[3] Michael Lind, *The American Way of Strategy* (New York, Oxford University Press 2006) p. 134.

[4] Thomas McCormick, 'American Hegemony and European Autonomy', in Lloyd C. Gardner & Marilyn B. Young, eds., *The New American Empire. A 21st Century Teach-in on U.S. Foreign Policy* (New York, The New Press 2005) p. 84.

[5] William Wallace, 'Living with the Hegemon European Dillemma', in Eric Herthberg & Kevin W. Moore, eds., *Critical Views of September 11: Analysis from Around the World* (New York, The New Press 2002) p. 101.

climate in the relations between the United States and Europe. Anti-Americanism and anti-Europeanism were on the rise. Francis Fukuyama's prediction that Europe and America would together lead the rest of the world into a peaceful post-historical era of triumphant liberal capitalism was wrong.[6]

On the eve of September 11, 2001 the United States still tried to convey the message that it was at the height of its power. Media commentators labelled the United States as the new Roman Empire. In record time Washington rejected international treaties like the anti-landmine treaty. It was remarkable that US diplomats did not provide many explanations. In wide circles, including befriended nations, the United States was blamed for its arrogance of power.

But Washington stayed the course. Conservative journalist Peggy Noonan quoted President Bush about standing firm when he was criticized by the European leaders during his first visit to the Old Continent: 'I think Ronald Reagan would have been proud of how I conducted myself. I went to Europe as a humble leader of a great nation, and stood my ground. I wasn't going to yield [...] I patiently sat there as all 15 in one form or another told me how wrong I was.'[7]

'Standing tall', that was apparently very important for Bush. Norman Ornstein, the foreign-policy expert of the American Enterprise Institute, could explain that attitude just before nine-eleven:

> 'In the last five hundred years there has never been a situation like now where the leading nation of the world has such a military lead over the number two, with the rest of the world lagging enormously behind. Bush plays out this position of lonely superpower in extremis. Europe has internal problems, the Japanese economy is broke and Russia can not compete with America by any measure.'[8]

In the field of foreign and security policy Washington had created space to manoeuvre as flexibly as it wanted.

Robert Kagan and the changing view of Europe

This was a fertile breeding ground for more tensions between Europe and the United States. Differing European and American views on power, international law and multilateralism lie at the heart of the current controversies. US policy shifts were captured in the National Security Strategy of September 2002 which stated that the United States would pursue 'an American internationalism that reflects the union of our values and our national interests.'[9] Concerning the

---

[6] Francis Fukuyama, *The End of History and the Last Man* (New York, Free Press 1992).

[7] *Wall Street Journal* (25 June 2001).

[8] Willem Post, *Keerpunt, Amerika, voor, op en na 11 september* (Soesterberg, Aspekt 2002) pp. 55-56.

[9] The National Security Strategy of the United States, September 2002, p. 5.

Iraq war and its aftermath the Bush administration repeated its commitment to unilateralism, pre-emptive and preventive war and regime change. The rest of the world was told to accommodate itself or suffer irrelevance or even worse. 'Take it or leave it,' was one of the White House slogans. Washington presented the case for war in Afghanistan, in Iraq and against terror-cells everywhere as a necessary battle of good against 'evildoers'. Europeans who hesitated were rebuked; those who refused to join the coalition of the willing were publicly threatened with retaliation in the form of troop withdrawals and economic boycotts. When European countries such as Germany, France and Belgium discussed plans for the headquarters of an EU military force, a US official belittled the initiative as 'the little bitty summit' of 'the chocolate makers'.[10]

Robert Kagan, a neo-conservative commentator close to the Bush administration, elaborated on these negative views about Europe in a book and a widely cited article. He accused Europe of embracing the morality of the weak by moving into a self-contained world of laws and rules and transnational negotiations. Decadent Europeans were entering an irrational post-historical paradise of peace and relative prosperity where 'the United States remains mired in history, exercising power in the anarchic Hobbesian world where international laws and rules are unreliable and where true security and the defence and promotion of a liberal order still depend on the possession and use of military might.'[11] In short, the United States and Europe were increasingly drifting apart.

Kagan sketched an artificial and unrealistic great divide. He even concluded: 'It is time to stop pretending that Europeans and Americans share a common view of the world, or even that they occupy the same world [...] Americans are from Mars and Europeans are from Venus: They agree on little and understand one another less and less.' Kagan corrected his world view in 2008. The new era after the Cold War was no longer characterized by universal values and with the United States as its lonely, real and truly representative. China and Russia with billions of people and the second and third largest militaries were governed by autocrats able to sustain power for many years because of structural economic growth. The new era 'will be one of growing tensions and sometimes confrontations between the forces of democracy and the forces of autocracy.'[12]

Autocracy made a comeback and threatens the liberal international order (recently typified by Larry Diamond as a 'democratic recession'[13]). Russia's

---

[10] 'US Sneers at "Chocolate Makers"', *News 24* (2 September 2003).

[11] Robert Kagan, 'Power and Weakness', 113 *Policy Review* (June-July 2002). See also the book on the same topic, *Of Paradise and Power: America and Europe in the New World Order* (New York, Knopf 2003).

[12] Robert Kagan, 'The End of the End of History', *The New Republic* (23 April 2008).

[13] Larry Diamond, *The Spirit of Democracy: The Struggle to Build Free Societies Throughout the World* (Times Books, 2008). Also the article 'The Democratic Rollback. The Resurgence of the Predatory State' in *Foreign Affairs* (March/April 2008) was adapted from this book.

model of sovereign democracy and China's open economy under autocratic rule are appealing options for governments in many countries all over the world, especially in Africa and Asia. With less self-confidence than in the 'old days' after September 11, when Kagan supported the one-dimensional world view of the Bush administration, he now urged 'the world democracies to begin thinking how they can protect their interests and advance their principles in a world in which these are, once again, powerfully contested.'

Comeback of international law

Why not a comeback of international law embedded in powerful foreign policy strategies shared by America and European countries? International law can only flourish in a world where we can avoid or overcome the isolation of hostile nations. Strategies of 'offensive détente' and 'peaceful engagement' that were successful toward the end of the Cold War might inspire us once again. Gone are the days of Charles Krauthammer's 'unipolar moment' and Hubert Védrine's 'hyperpower'. The erosion of American power is illustrative of an international order that, in the words of the French political philosopher Pierre Hassner, is no order anymore. 'We live in a time of fundamental heterogeneity and contradiction pertaining both to the nature of political units and the character of tensions, solidarities and opportunities between these units.'[14]

America is still the richest and most resourceful power but its illusions of omnipotence were profoundly shaken by September 11 and the protracted struggle against terrorism in countries like Afghanistan and Iraq. But we have also seen the failure of the European Union to develop into a coherent political actor on the world scene. In that respect the 2005 French and Dutch 'no' votes to the EU constitution and the 2008 Irish 'no' vote against the Lisbon Treaty were big mistakes.

No hegemonic power in history has ever relied exclusively on power. Neither America nor the West can reclaim the authority to act as a hegemon. The rest of the world with rapidly rising economies and military capabilities will simply not accept that. The fundamental question is how we can defend our interests and peaceful principles in a world in which we are increasingly contested.

Hassner is right in stating that '[t]he dimming of America's light cannot herald good tidings for anyone, anywhere, who cherishes the Enlightenment and what it has made of the West over the past several centuries.' When the Cold

---

[14] Pierre Hassner, 'The fate of a Century', *The American Interest* (July-August 2007) pp. 36-48.

War ended international relations experts predicted in their grim assessments that the great powers would clash in a world that lacked a central authority to enforce order. 'NATO's days are not outnumbered, but its years are,' Kenneth Waltz wrote pessimistically in 1993.[15]

There is indeed chaos in the 'greater Middle East region' and issues like nuclear proliferation and energy security threaten mankind and the planet. In a changing and more dangerous world we need to understand that because of shared security and economic interests and basic values of freedom, as formulated by President Franklin Roosevelt, the United States is still Europe's natural partner. All, even critical, European powers still recognize the centrality of the United States to Europe's security and interests in the future. Even those who claim that more independence from the United States would be better, theoretically, cannot reasonably think of real separation. As Justin Vaisse puts it: 'Whether we share the same policy objectives or not, we Europeans find ourselves stakeholders of the same international order as the Americans [...] and others see us as part of "the West," so we cannot pretend we're on our own. All this makes true independence wishful thinking.'[16]

Revived transatlantic alliance

Politicians on both sides of the Atlantic should once and for all consider realist suggestions for a revived transatlantic alliance in our rapidly shrinking global village characterized by an ongoing revolution in the means of both communication and destruction. In transition periods like ours we should learn from decades-old experiences with existing organizations handling security issues, in particular NATO.

In the early 1990s we had NATO 1, from an American perspective created as the military consequence of President Truman's political containment doctrine. With hindsight it is crystal clear that NATO's narrow scope in its very first year was already undermined by the shocking events in China, the Soviet Union's staunch ally. One year later the Korean War began. A country like the Netherlands participated in that war under the auspices of the United Nations and not NATO. NATO, because of treaty limitations, was from the start not allowed to adapt to a changing world, although it proved successful in the 'European' Cold War. In short, NATO was handicapped. The Korean and Vietnam Wars were no

---

[15] Kenneth N. Waltz, 'The Emerging Structure of International Politics', 18 *International Security* (Fall 1993) p. 76.

[16] Justin Vaisse is a French scholar on American foreign policy and transatlantic relations affiliated with the Brookings Institution. Quoted from a discussion with Mona Sutphen, October 2006.

sideshows away from the main European theatre. The United States, in particular, paid a heavy price for this fundamental misunderstanding. The wars were all part of a global struggle against communism.

Nowadays 'NATO 2' is in a much better position to confront security problems on a world scale. NATO was an alliance of sixteen countries that had never conducted a military operation and had no partner relationships. But on 11 August 2003, NATO took over the UN-mandated International Security Assistance Force (ISAF) in Afghanistan. NATO literally entered a new world. In 2008, we have a NATO that has established partnerships with over 20 countries in Europe and Eurasia, seven in North Africa and the Middle East and four in the Persian Gulf. Global partners such as Australia and Japan are working with NATO in Afghanistan. In 2008 more than 64,000 allied military personnel are deployed on three continents.

Almost every military, political and social problem has global implications nowadays. There is a real possibility that this age will become a 'Pacific century', featuring the rise of China as a great power in combination with a Russian resurgence. Almost everywhere sleeping terror cells could suddenly be activated by radical civilians and paramilitary organizations. That means a metamorphosis for NATO in a world with so many different threats. NATO's mandate, structure and personality need to change accordingly.

If, because of internal political circumstances and/or different military skills and traditions, allies prefer nation building in, for example, northern Afghanistan instead of counter-insurgency in the violent south, so be it. At least for the moment. In our times, first and foremost, we need a flexible NATO. There is nothing wrong with a two-tier NATO. The first priority in the near future is (more) commitment from critical European countries which were neglected when Washington almost exclusively focused on its 'global war on terror'. That also means a real dialogue within NATO and a more internationalist approach from a new White House.

Basically, in order to solve international security problems and to prevent future wars in a peaceful way, Ivo Daalder, the foreign policy adviser of the Democratic candidate Barack Obama, and James Goldgeier, have urged NATO in a *Foreign Affairs* article to rapidly transform into a 'global NATO'.[17] Why not expand NATO with staunch, reliable democratic partners in, for instance, Asia and South America? For the moment Daalder's and Goldgeier's ideal is a bridge too far, but they are pointing in the right direction, especially with their 'global partnerships' and the creation of a 'NATO Global Partnership Council'.

---

[17] Ivo Daalder & James Goldgeier, 'Global NATO', *Foreign Affairs* (September/October 2006) pp. 105-113.

League of Democracies

Against the broader context of eroding international institutions their global view is more realistic than the vague new international model which Republican candidate John McCain proposed in a speech and in an article in March 2008.[18] The senator stated that Americans and Europeans share the common goal of building 'an enduring peace based on freedom.' He sees many challenges that we can tackle like terrorism and climate change, but he also explicitly mentioned 'the disturbing turn towards autocracy in Russia.' The key word for him is 'together'. 'We need to renew and revitalise our democratic solidarity. We need to strengthen our transatlantic alliance as the core of a new global compact – a League of Democracies – that can harness the great power of the more than 100 democratic nations to advance our values and defend our shared interests.'

McCain is pointing to the shared interests of the global democracies. But if he is right on this there is no reason why these countries were not already working together in the United Nations. For democracies like India the north-south divide is at least as important as a democratic-non-democratic divide. His proposal lacks a central authority. McCain calls upon the NATO alliance and the European Union to have 'the ability and the will to act in defence of freedom and economic prosperity [...] The US and Europe must lead together to encourage the participation of the rest of the world.' But his League will also function as a counterbalance against Russia and China and fits in a roll-back strategy against 'evil states'. 'It could act where the U.N. fails.'[19] This new actor on the global scene will collapse under its own ambitious and extreme agenda and add to confusion and chaos in international relations. But the League model, especially in a more moderate form, will certainly generate more discussion about reorganizing international relations.

American-European alliance

For the near future, an essentially American-European NATO alliance can function as a bedrock against authoritarian actors and terrorist organizations. NATO's enhanced power is not unlimited because the Alliance cannot overrule the veto power of the UN Security Council. We have to change NATO's 'entrance hall' and take the first measures to enlarge new NATO in a more responsible way. The 'Membership Action Plans' (MAPs) are considered by aspiring non-NATO

---

[18] John McCain, 'America must be a good role model', *Financial Times* (18 March 2008).

[19] Speech by John McCain at the Hoover Institute, 6 May 2008.

countries as virtual and quick guarantees for membership. We need more time to test their democratic qualifications. In the end we can present our allies, our partners, and indeed the rest of the world, with the best reasons why we want newcomers including Ukraine and Georgia, to join our military-political alliance. NATO;s popularity in some countries is still relatively low. An extensive, professional information campaign with reasonable targets must be adapted in MAPs for aspiring countries. Support will increase as was the case with other new members like the Czech Republic and Slovakia.

In our complicated world hard and soft power are not antagonists but are intertwined. Fareed Zakaria wrote in *Foreign Affairs* that 'on every dimension other than military power – industrial, financial, social, cultural – the distribution of power is shifting, moving away from U.S. dominance. That does not mean we are entering an anti-American world. But we are moving into a post-American world, one defined and directed from many places and by many people.'[20] The rest of the world is becoming more powerful but American ideals remain dominant.

In this unstable world, the United States needs Europe and *vice versa*. The United States still has the world's largest economy. It has held a constant share of global GPD: in 1960, 26%; in 1980, 22%; and in 2007, 26%. Most estimates suggest that in 2025 the United States' economy will still be twice the size of China's in terms of nominal GPD. The Euro zone has been growing impressively, roughly at the same pace per capita as the United States. It takes half the world's foreign investment and boasts a strong labour productivity and trade surplus. In the short term the rise of Asia is definitely exaggerated.

The European Union can function well alongside NATO. By acknowledging European concerns, especially in Afghanistan, the United States is in a better position to ask for new resources from EU countries. France has made its new commitment already clear in March 2008 when President Nicolas Sarkozy declared that 'we cannot afford to lose Afghanistan.' In this new Atlantic partnership a renewed and strengthened NATO could undertake a needed 'surge' in Afghanistan. The war in Afghanistan has direct links to '9/11'. These clear ties should give the new US administration in 2009 a sufficient rationale to pressure European allies for assistance. 'One-third of the roughly 20,000-30,000 troops required should come from Europe [...] Even under optimistic conditions, NATO forces will have to stay in Afghanistan for five to ten years.'[21]

The United States and democratic Europe have common security and economic interests. We share the same basic values and must not give in to the

---

[20] Fareed Zakaria, 'The Future of American Power. How America Can Survive the Rise of the Rest', *Foreign Affairs* (May/June, 2008) p. 9.

[21] James P. Rubin, 'Building a New Atlantic Alliance', *Foreign Affairs* (July/August, 2008) pp. 106-107.

temptation of going it alone. We need stronger Atlantic bonds in a more and more chaotic multi-polar world. Given these circumstances and especially also because of a new US President with different foreign policy priorities we now have great possibilities to create an even more stable United States-European partnership.

Russia's Foreign and Security Policy: The Return of the Empire?

Marcel de Haas

Introduction

Since 2000 Russia's defence budget has risen tenfold. Russia has applied its energy weapon against former Soviet republics which followed a pro-Western course. Under President Vladimir Putin's Russia an anti-Western stance unfolded, condemning NATO expansion, unilateral and dominating policies, the deployment of a missile shield and the 'Cold War vestiges' of the current European security architecture. Subsequently, in December 2007, Moscow suspended the Conventional Forces in Europe (CFE) Treaty, which by both sides had always been considered as the cornerstone of post-Cold War European security. This assertive stance has been combined with sabre rattling. The Kremlin has shown its military power by threatening to aim nuclear missiles at Europe, by conducting military exercises with China, by resuming strategic nuclear bomber flights, by conducting naval exercises in the Atlantic Ocean and the Mediterranean, by recommencing the traditional military parade in the Red Square, and by dispatching strategic bombers and warships to Venezuela to carry out joint war games. The assertive posture of the resurgent Russia escalated in August 2008, when Russian armed forces invaded and occupied large parts of Georgia, after its attack on the secessionist region of South Ossetia.

This overview gives the impression that Russia is back as a superpower, capable of projecting power on a global level. Whether this actor in the international arena should be regarded as 'evil' or not – as United States President Reagan referred to the Soviet Union at the time – the question is: has Russia really regained the status of a mighty empire or is the Russian bear still limping?

This chapter provides a brief analysis of Russia's foreign and security policy since Vladimir Putin was sworn in as President of the Russian Federation in 2000. Russia's external policy is manifold and thus too broad to be captured in

J. de Zwaan, E. Bakker and S. van der Meer (eds.), Challenges in a Changing World

a couple of pages. Therefore, the purpose of this contemplation is not to deliver an all-encompassing overview, but to present highlights that give an insight into Russia's foreign and security thinking. These highlights are a mixture of security documents and statements, bilateral and multilateral cooperation and Russian actions in certain regions and against specific states. The analysed period of Russia's foreign and security policy is divided into three parts: the first one explains Putin's external views during his first term in office as Russia's President; the second elaborates on his second term while the third part deals with Russia's external policy under President Dmitry Medvedev. The chapter ends with an assessment of and an outlook on Moscow's external policy and its consequences for relations with the West.

External policy during Putin's first term (2000–2004)

National security policy reflects a coherent and consistent system of political, military, economic and psychological means that a state has at its disposal. National security policy encompasses all activities regarding internal and external security. The grand strategy, or political strategy, is the product of the opinion of the state concerning the optimal guarantee of its security.[1] In Russia's case the National Security Concept forms its grand strategy. Derived from and subjected to this strategy are the Military Doctrine and the Foreign Policy Concept. These three works constitute the major documents of Russia's foreign and security policy. This part compares the 2000 editions of these major three policy documents.[2] In October 2003 the Russian Ministry of Defence published *The priority tasks of the development of the Armed Forces of the Russian Federation*, a document which can best be described and will be referred to as a Defence White Paper.[3] After assessing the security documents in comparison with the

---

[1] *KLu Airpower Doctrine* (The Hague, commander-in-chief Royal Netherlands Air Force 1996) pp. I-4 and I-5; B.R. Posen, *The sources of military doctrine – France, Britain, and Germany between the world wars* (Ithaca/New York, Cornell University Press 1984) p. 13.

[2] See the following sources for the contents of the 2000 editions of the three principal security documents: *National Security Concept (January 2000)*: Russian: 'Kontseptsiya natsional'noy bezopasnosti', *Nezavisimoye Voyennoye Obozreniye*, 1 (14 January 2000) p. 1 <http://www.scrf.gov.ru/documents/1.html>, English: <www.fas.org/nuke/guide/russia/doctrine/gazeta012400.htm>; *Military Doctrine (April 2000)*: Russian: 'Voyennaya doktrina Rossiyskoy Federatsii', *Nezavisimoye Voyennoye Obozreniye*, 15 (28 April 2000) <http://www.scrf.gov.ru/documents/33.html>, English: <http://www.armscontrol.org/act/2000_05/dc3ma00>; *Foreign Policy Concept (June 2000)*: Russian: 'Kontseptsiya vneshney politiki Rossiyskoy Federatsii', *Nezavisimoye Voyennoye Obozreniye*, 25 (14 July 2000) p. 4 <http://www.scrf.gov.ru/documents/25.html>; English: <www.fas.org/nuke/guide/russia/doctrine/econcept.htm>.

[3] Defence White Paper of 2003: *Aktual'nyye zadachi razvitiya Vooruzhënnykh Sil Rossiyskoy Federatsii* [The priority tasks of the development of the Armed Forces of the Russian Federa-

contents of the 2003 Defence White Paper, conclusions will be drawn on the conceptual approach of Putin's foreign and security policy during his first term in office, until his re-election in March 2004. The National Security Concept was produced by the Security Council of the Russian Federation and provides an overall view of the security policy of the Russian Federation, applying all resources available to the state. The Military Doctrine was drafted by the Ministry of Defence and deals with the military means of the state. The Foreign Policy Concept was drawn up by the Ministry of Foreign Affairs, and relates to Moscow's political and diplomatic instruments.

Policy documents as mirrors of security thinking

The 2000 security documents demonstrate the prominence of negative tendencies with reference to Western security policy. In particular, NATO's use of force in the former Yugoslavia (Bosnia and Kosovo) was seen as a clear example of its policy of ignoring Russia, which claimed a decisive role in Europe, as well as of disregarding the United Nations and the standards of international law. Other concerns were NATO's new Strategic Concept of April 1999 and its enlargement with new member states in the East, adjacent to Russia's borders. As concerning external national interests the documents mention strengthening Russia's international position as a great power and cooperation in the military-political area and in the sphere of security through the Collective Security Treaty of the Commonwealth of Independent States (CIS), particularly in combating international terrorism and extremism. Moscow feels threatened by attempts to belittle the role of existing mechanisms for international security, by the economic and power domination of the United States and other Western states, as well as by ignoring Russian interests and influence in resolving international security problems. Particular attention is given to the threatening nature of the reinforcement of military-political blocs and alliances, above all the eastward expansion of NATO, and NATO's practice of using military force outside the bloc's zone of responsibility without sanctioning by the UN Security Council. Russia intends to ensure its security by defending and guaranteeing the legal rights and interests of Russian citizens (compatriots) resident abroad or of the Russian-speaking population, in the CIS as well as in the Baltic states. Furthermore, all forces and facilities available, including nuclear weapons, will be used if necessary to repel armed aggression. And if all other means have been exhausted, the interests of Russia's national security may require a Russian military presence in certain strategically vital regions of the world. The 2000 security

tion], Russian Ministry of Defence, 2 October 2003 <http://supol.narod.ru/archive/official_documents/doctrine/war_doctrine.htm>.

documents demonstrate fine-tuned points of view when it comes to external aspects. For example, they all reject Western security policies and refer to the strengthening of recognized security mechanisms, such as the United Nations, as the appropriate answer.

Russia's Defence White Paper of 2003, formally 'The Priority Tasks of the Development of the Russian Armed Forces', in dealing with the West in general and NATO in particular poses a vision of two minds. The document mentions that the NATO-Russia partnership will be further deepened in spite of major differences. Furthermore, it states that nuclear and large-scale wars with NATO or other US-led coalitions are no longer probable armed conflicts and that Russia expects cooperation with the United States and other industrialised countries to grow in ensuring stability. However, elsewhere in this policy paper this appeasing tone is set aside and replaced by an antagonistic approach, underlining that Russia expects that the anti-Russian entries will be removed from NATO's military planning and political declarations. Even stronger, the document states that if NATO is preserved as a military alliance with an offensive doctrine, cardinal changes will be undertaken in Russia's military planning and the development of the Russian Armed Forces, including its nuclear strategy. At the time of the publication of this document these entries caused considerable concern in circles within NATO. These contrasting entries have made it more difficult to acquire a clear picture of Russia's intentions in the field of security. The 2000 papers mentioned, without any restraint, the dominance of Western states led by the United States in international politics, Western institutions weakening the role of the UN Security Council, as well as NATO's practice of using military force without a UN Security Council sanction. Anti-Western tendencies are still present in this defence white paper, but the overall tone of this policy document is more moderate than the major security documents of 2000.

Objectives of external policy

After the terrorist attacks of 11 September 2001, '9/11', President Putin took a pro-Western course. In the long run Putin desired to strengthen Russia's international position, not excluding military means to achieve this. However, Putin realized quite well, in contrast to many Soviet leaders, that nowadays influence on a global level is more than ever based on economic leverage. Taking this into account, his rapprochement towards the West, and especially towards Europe, did not seem strange. Closer cooperation with the EU served more than one objective of Russian policy. Firstly, economic cooperation with Europe would most likely bring about growth in the Russian economy, which in turn would enhance Russia's international position. Secondly, closer ties with the EU might also weaken the relationship between Europe and the United States, even more so if Russia were supporting, or participating in, the further development of an independent European security policy with its own military power, which possibly could be in contrast with American interests. From a weakening or even a split in the Transatlantic camp Russia could naturally benefit in the international arena, by promoting its foreign policy principle of multipolarity in international politics and Russia's status as a great power.

At the time of the start of the second Gulf War, in March 2003, Putin was well aware of this policy option of splitting the Transatlantic, Western camp. In their plea in the UN Security Council for military intervention against Iraq, the United States and the United Kingdom were diametrically opposed to Germany and France. Putin supported the latter in their rejection of the use of force, just like France, by threatening to use the right of veto, and, after *Operation Iraqi Freedom* was launched, by a strongly worded condemnation of the use of force.[4] Once again the Kremlin's reaction demonstrated the dualistic nature of its policy. On the one hand, Putin used the division in the Western camp to strengthen Russia's status in the international community. At the same time he had apparently instructed Foreign Affairs Minister Igor Ivanov to use more measured words towards the United States, thus serving the opposite part of Russia's dualistic policy: cooperation with the West in order to improve Russia's economy.[5] Putin's policy regarding the war against Iraq was definitely also intended for domestic consumption. His firm stand against the United States raised goodwill among the conservative representatives of the Russian security elite, who had rebuked Putin for his pro-American attitude since '9/11'. Hence, in the case of the second Gulf War, by adhering to the customary dualistic approach, Putin managed to accomplish the national as well as international objectives of Russia's foreign and security policy.

Russia's foreign and security policy during Putin's first term as President was laid down in four major documents, as mentioned above. The major points of view in these documents were an assertive attitude towards the West, a strengthening of Russia's position within the CIS as well as on a global level, and, lastly, an emphasis on military means as an instrument of security policy. The leading security documents originated in a Russian security establishment consisting of generals, politicians, diplomats and scientists. Judging from their criticism of Putin's gestures towards the West, the state of mind of this elite did not change after '9/11'. Putin's positive policy towards the West since '9/11' had only manifested itself in public statements. Thus Putin's rapprochement

---

4 'Putin says Iraq crisis most serious conflict since end of cold war', 4 *Radio Free Europe/ Radio Liberty Security Watch*, No. 13 (1 April 2003).

5 'Foreign minister concerned by US efforts to seize Iraqi assets', 4 *Radio Free Europe/ Radio Liberty Security Watch*, No. 12 (26 March 2003); 'Putin stresses need to avoid conflict with US', 4 *Radio Free Europe/Radio Liberty Security Watch*, No. 14 (9 April 2003).

towards the West did not imply a structural change of Russian foreign and security policy. President Putin had to balance the pressure of his security establishment with reinforcing Russia's economic capacity. Putin's policy was symbolic for the dualistic nature of Moscow's foreign and security policy. On the one hand, international (economic) cooperation was continued and internal conflicts received a higher priority in security thinking. On the other hand, Russia continued to claim a great power status in the international arena.

External policy during Putin's second term (2004–2008)

During Putin's second term as President, due to the rise of global prices for oil and natural gas, energy resources became an essential policy instrument of the Kremlin. The South Caucasus, because of its vital geo-strategic position between Asia and Europe and its vicinity to Russia's unstable area of the North Caucasus, became more important as an element in the Kremlin's objective of strengthening its international position, using the CIS, Russia's sphere of influence, as its major vehicle. For the same purpose Russia reinforced its ties with its eastern neighbours, Central Asian states and China in particular, bilaterally and by way of its leading role in regional organisations.

Energy as an instrument of Russia's power

At the beginning of the 1990s Russia tried to coerce other former Soviet states, such as the Ukraine and the Baltic States, to adhere to its demands by cutting energy supplies.[6] Since the end of the 1990s, due to the rising energy prices and an increasing demand – especially because of China and India – Russia has rediscovered energy as a policy instrument. The most obvious example was provided in December 2005 when Russia stopped energy deliveries to Ukraine to force it to pay a higher gas price.[7] However, the renewed interest in the energy instrument now came as part of a coordinated policy endeavour together with the military instrument. Russia's leadership did not hide this conviction, which was demonstrated in 2003, when Putin called Russia's gas firm Gazprom a powerful political and economic lever of influence over the rest of the world.[8]

---

[6] K.C. Smith, 'Current implications of Russian energy policies', Center for Strategic and International Studies, 12 January 2006; 'Defuse Russia's energy weapon', *International Herald Tribune* (17 January 2006).

[7] 'Russia turns off supplies to Ukraine in payment row, and EU feels the chill', *The Guardian* (2 January 2006) <http://www.guardian.co.uk/russia/article/0,2763,1676556,00.html#article continue>.

[8] 'Russia's Power Play Has High Stakes', *The Wall Street Journal* (2 May 2006); 'Gazprom acts as lever in Putin's power play', *Financial Times* (13 March 2006).

Furthermore, Defence Minister Ivanov stated in 2006 that Russia now needed to think not only about diplomatic, but also about forceful means to safeguard its economic interests. The (renewed) Russian interest in and alertness concerning the importance of energy sources was not limited to its value as an instrument of power. In recent years Russia's political and military leadership has also realised that the protection of its energy resources is of vital interest to national security. Consequently, army general Yuriy Baluyevskiy, Russia's First Deputy Minister of Defence and Chief of the General Staff, added the defence of Russia's mineral resources to the list of tasks for the military at an April 2006 press conference.[9]

Russia's involvement in the South Caucasus

As discussed in the part on Russia's security documents, a primary objective of the Russian Federation is to regain and strengthen its position in the so-called 'near abroad', the CIS, Russia's back garden, of which the South Caucasus is a part. This policy is carried out by diplomatic, military and energy security means. Since the 1990s Russia has supported the unrecognized republics of Abkhazia and South Ossetia in Georgia and maintained peacekeeping troops in these areas, formally under the aegis of the CIS. Russia developed a strained relationship with Georgia, not only for its support of the separatist republics, but also because of Georgia's wish to join NATO and for its membership of the 'anti-Russian' GUAM coalition.[10] These conflicting matters have resulted in a Russian policy of political and economic pressure on Georgia, and, conversely, of occasional confrontational acts by Georgia. Russia's assertive attitude towards Georgia was a demonstration of the transforming geo-strategic relations in the CIS and of Russia's corresponding efforts to strengthen its position in the CIS and in the international arena. Elsewhere in the South Caucasus, Russia maintained good ties with Armenia, the only South Caucasian state that is militarily allied with Russia. Moscow has a military base in Armenia, and Yerevan is a member of the Russian-led military cooperation organisation Collective Security Treaty Organisation. The reason for Armenia's (military) relationship with Russia is pragmatic: in Russia Armenia found an ally against its opponents Turkey and Azerbaijan. Since the latter two are strategically more important to the United States, Armenia turned to Russia as a guarantor of its security, al-

---

[9] P. Gallis, 'NATO and Energy Security', CRS Report for Congress, 21 March 2006, p. 4; K. Giles, *Russian Regional Commands*, Russian Series 06/19 (Swindon, Conflict Studies Research Centre, UK Defence Academy, April 2006) p. 3.

[10] GUAM is a regional organisation comprising of four CIS states: Georgia, Ukraine, Azerbaijan, and Moldova. The group was created in October 1997 as a way of countering the influence of Russia in the area, and it has received backing and encouragement from the United States.

though at the same time it has also maintained military ties with the West, as a member of NATO's Partnership for Peace programme. The oil-rich Azerbaijan maintained good relations with the United States and Turkey, but although it favours the West, it refrained from alienating itself from Russia.

Collective Security Treaty Organisation

The Collective Security Treaty Organisation (CSTO) is a Russian-led military alliance with Armenia, Belarus, Kazakhstan, Uzbekistan, Kyrgyzstan and Tajikistan as the other member states. The origins of the CSTO go back to May 1992, when within the framework of the CIS, a treaty for collective security was signed in Tashkent. The treaty comprises the parties' desire to renounce the use or threat of force. Furthermore, in its Article 1, the treaty forbids parties from joining other military alliances. Just like NATO, the CSTO has a military assistance provision (Article 4), which states that aggression against one party will be considered as an attack on all parties.[11] According to Putin, the main responsibilities of the CSTO are cooperation in defence, the manufacturing of weapons, the training of military personnel, and peacekeeping activities. Other areas of cooperation are a common integrated air defence system and the fight against terrorism and against narcotics, which particularly concerns Central Asia.[12] The CSTO has at its disposal a joint headquarters in Moscow and a collective rapid reaction force. In October 2007, at a CSTO Summit in the Tajik capital Dushanbe, the organisation announced the decision to increase military cooperation.

Russia is of course by far the most dominant member of the CSTO, which makes it a useful instrument for pursuing its policy. At the request of Russia, the member states agreed to buy military arms and equipment from Russia at domestic Russian prices. Furthermore, it was decided at the Dushanbe Summit that its collective rapid reaction force in Central Asia would be supplied with modern *matériel* before the end of 2010. Another Russian initiative adopted at this summit was the foundation of a joint military force for peacekeeping operations. The concept of a joint peacekeeping force encompasses the formation of brigades capable of conducting peacekeeping missions, if necessary also outside the territory of the CSTO.[13] Another Russian success – in countering West-

[11] 'Dogovor o kollektivnoy bezopasnosti', Tashkent, 15 May 1992, *CSTO website*, <http://www.dkb.gov.ru/start/index.htm>.

[12] M. Kaczmarski, 'Russia creates a New System to Replace the C.I.S.', *Power and Interest News Report* (21 December 2005); 'Moscow reinforces military cooperation with CIS allies', 9 *RFE/RL,* No. 120, Part I, 24 (June 2005); 'Korotko: Mirotvortsy ot ODKB', *Nezavisimoye Voyennoye Obozreniye* (26 May 2006).

[13] 'Gendarme of Eurasia', *Kommersant* (8 October 2007) <http://www.kommersant.com/p812422/CIS_CSTO_Russia_Lebedev/>.

ern influence in its neighbourhood – was Uzbekistan. This country demanded that US forces leave its territory, after the United States and the European Union had criticized Uzbekistan for smashing unrest in the city of Andijan. On 23 June 2006, Putin announced that Uzbekistan had become a full-member of the CSTO.[14] Uzbekistan President Karimov's main argument for joining the CSTO was probably his need for Russian protection against a regime change like the ones that had taken place in Georgia (2003), Ukraine (2004), and Kyrgyzstan (2005).[15] Thus, the CSTO meets Moscow's policy goal of increasing its international status, but also of countering pro-Western regime changes in the CIS.

Shanghai Cooperation Organisation

The Shanghai Cooperation Organisation (SCO) is a regional international organisation comprising states in Europe, the Near East, Central Asia and South East Asia.[16] The SCO includes China, Russia, Kazakhstan, Kyrgyzstan, Tajikistan and Uzbekistan as member states and Mongolia, Iran, Pakistan and India as observer states.[17] SCO member states have a total population of nearly 1.5 billion people, which is about a quarter of the world's population, and including the four observers, the SCO encompasses nearly half the world's population. In addition to the member states Russia and China, the observers India and Pakistan bring together in the SCO four states with nuclear weapons. Furthermore, the Chinese and Russian armed forces are amongst the largest armed forces in the world.[18] The SCO provides cooperation in political, military, economic, energy and cultural fields. Important ingredients of economic cooperation are the (conventional) arms trade – with Russia as the supplier – and energy, for which Russia, Kazakhstan, Uzbekistan and Iran are big exporters – while China and India are significant importers. In 2005 and 2007 the SCO conducted large

---

[14] <http://www.jamestown.org/edm/article.php?article_id=2371223> .

[15] 'Sozdayetsa Evrazyjskaya Semerka', *Nezavisimoye Voyennoye Obozreniye* (28 October 2005).

[16] See: M. de Haas, ed., *The Shanghai Cooperation Organisation: Towards a full-grown security alliance?*, Clingendael Security Paper 3 (The Hague, Clingendael Institute, November 2007) <http://www.clingendael.nl/publications/2007/20071100_cscp_security_paper_3.pdf>.

[17] In practice, the observer states participate in many of the activities of the SCO, such as the annual summits, and as observers at military exercises. Their position is specifically mentioned in the regulations of the SCO Energy Club. Therefore, their status is more than simply that of an observer.

[18] For a brief introduction to the Shanghai Cooperation Organisation, see: <http://www.sectsco.org/html/00026.html>. The SCO members and observers account for some 2.7 billion people out of a total world population of 6.4 billion (*Source*: 2005 World Population Data Sheet, <www.prb.org); http://www.nationmaster.com/red/graph/mil_arm_for_per-military-armed-forces-personnel&b_printable=1>.

military exercises, called 'Peace Mission', but with an emphasis clearly other than on peacekeeping, meant as a demonstration of force, to show others (the West) who is in control of the region. Although under the aegis of the SCO, these exercises were dominated by Russia and China, who are the leading actors in the organisation.

For Russia the SCO acts as a means to bring together different policy objectives. Not only China, but India and Iran as well have a special (economic) relationship with Russia. All three states are important actors in Russia's arms export. In addition, China and India are gaining a closer relationship with Russia in the field of joint, bilateral military exercises. The fact that India and Iran joined the SCO as observers by Russian invitation in 2005, underlines that the SCO serves as a platform for Russia's security policy. Another example of the SCO as an instrument of the Kremlin is the fact that it was President Putin who instigated the foundation of an energy club within the SCO.[19] This fits into Russia's policy of using energy as a power tool. It is likely that this development of the SCO, as a tool of Russian foreign and security policy, will continue in the coming years.

Russia's strategic partnership with China

In recent years there has been a comprehensive improvement of bilateral relations between China and Russia. For instance, the long-standing border disputes between both states were settled in agreements in 2005. Furthermore, Russia, in addition to its arms export, will supply China with oil and gas. But even more important, both countries have found each other in a strategic partnership aimed at countering the (Western/US) 'monopoly in world affairs', as was made clear in a joint statement by the Chinese and Russian Presidents in July 2005.[20] Apart from joint political statements, the Russo-Chinese cooperation is most abundant in the areas of war games, arms and energy deliveries.

---

[19] 'Joint Communiqué of 2006 SCO summit' <http://english.scosummit2006.org/en_zxbb/2006-06/15/content_756.htm>; 'Energy outcome of SCO meeting in Dushanbe', 20 September 2006; 'Meeting of the Council of Heads of Government /Prime Ministers of SCO', Dushanbe, 15 September 2006 <http://www.sectsco.org/html/00030.html>; 'Poyavitsya Energoklub ShOS', 3 July 2007 <http://www.scosummit2007.org/news/press/62/>; 'Polozheniye ob energeticheskom klube', 3 July 2007 http://www.scosummit2007.org/files/material/polozhenie_energ_kluba.doc; 'Moratorium on admission to Shanghai Six to hold – F. M. Lavrov', *RIA Novosti* (16 August 2007).

[20] Antoine Blua, 'Joint exercises underscore growing ties between Moscow and Bejing', 5 *RFE/RL Russian Political Weekly*, No. 28 (9 August 2005); 'Putin stresses importance of Sino-Russian economic, military cooperation', 9 *RFE/RL Newsline*, No. 150, Part I (10 August 2005); 'Russian, Chinese presidents discuss expanding political, economic, military cooperation', 9 *RFE/RL Newsline*, No. 125, Part I (1 July 2005).

Military exercises. From 18 to 25 August 2005, for the first time in 40 years, Russian and Chinese armed forces carried out joint exercises, comprising 10,000 military personnel, navy vessels and aircraft.[21] The exercise objectives had little to do with warfare against terrorism, as declared, but were actually nothing other than practising conventional warfare, employing all services except for nuclear forces. The most likely real main objective of the manoeuvres was that in this way China and Russia made clear to the (Western) world that they consider themselves to be in control of the Asian-Pacific region and that others are precluded from interfering in their sphere of influence. At the military exercises Defence Minister Ivanov stated that Russia has an open mind for joint Russian-Chinese peacekeeping operations in the Asia-Pacific region, under the condition that such operations are based upon resolutions by the UN Security Council. Ivanov also mentioned that Russia and China – although no plans had yet been drafted – might conduct joint military exercises on a regular basis.[22]

Arms sales. In 2006, some 45% of Russia's arms export went to China. Since 2000, Russia has delivered weapon systems to China – including fighter aircraft, submarines and destroyers – amounting to an average of $ 2 billion annually. India takes care of some 40% of Russia's arms export and Iran is considered to be an interesting growth market for Russian arms.[23] Hence, China has been the best buyer of Russian military equipment for a number of years. Russia's arms export to China is an important factor in the cooperation between the two countries. However, Russia seems to be well aware that China would like to obtain its most sophisticated military technology, which, in the case of deteriorating relations, might turn against Russia. For that reason Russia is reluctant to provide China with its state of the art products. Moreover, there are indications that China is steadily acquiring enough knowledge to have a solid military industry of its own. Subsequently, in the coming years China will buy less and less arms from Russia, which will diminish the value of this cornerstone of bilateral relations.[24]

---

[21] Igor Plugatarev, 'Kto platit, tot i zakazyvayet ucheniya', *Nezavisimoye Voyennoye Obozreniye*, No. 31 (440) (19 August 2005) p. 3; 'Russia, China may conduct regular exercises – defence minister', *RIA Novosti* (23 August 2005).

[22] 'Joint peacekeeping operations with China possible – defence minister'; 'Russia, China may conduct regular exercises – defence minister', *RIA Novosti* (23 August 2005).

[23] Vitaly Strugovets, 'Potentsial voyennogo eksporta pochti ischerpan', *Nezavisimoye Voyennoye Obozreniye*, No. 24 (433) (1 July 2005) p. 6; Blua, *supra* n. 20; 'Defense minister says Russia, China, India may hold joint military exercises, 9 *RFE/RL Newsline*, No. 195, Part I (17 October 2005); 'Russia to increase military-technical cooperation with China', *RIA Novosti* (31 August 2005); 'Putin steps in to revitalize arms sales to China', *RIA Novosti* (8 September 2005).

[24] 'Alliance with China cost Russia dearly', *RIA Novosti* (22 November 2005).

Energy policy. In August 2005 during a visit to Beijing President Putin stressed bilateral economic ties, especially the work of Russian energy companies in China, bilateral projects that would distribute those supplies to third countries, as well as the delivery of Russian oil and gas to China.[25] Furthermore, in November 2005 Russia and China agreed to double oil exports to China and to consider constructing an oil pipeline from Russia to China and a gas-transmission project from eastern Siberia to China's Far East.[26] However, China focuses on Kazakhstan as well in its need for energy. In due course the Sino-Kazakh pipeline will be enlarged from 1,000 to 3,000 kilometres and will eventually provide China with less than 15% of its crude oil needs.[27] China wants to avoid energy dependency on Russia. Another argument is that by redirecting Kazakh oil pipelines through China instead of through Russia, China's influence over Kazakhstan and Central Asia will increase at the expense of Russia's position. However, although cooperating with China in energy, Kazakhstan has a considerable Russian minority and therefore will be hesitant to follow an anti-Russian political course.

In the coming years Russia is likely to strengthen its ties with China. Not only in the field of security, but also in areas such as military cooperation, energy, (arms) trade and foreign policy, these two states are seeking a closer relationship. Russia has more than once stated that a closer relationship with China is a geopolitical objective in order to strengthen Russia's global position.[28] Nonetheless, this close relationship with China could very well turn out to be for the shorter term. There are a number of conflicting interests. For instance, China is constantly seeking alternatives for its dependence on Russia's energy and arms. Furthermore, in its Far East, Russia is facing increasing illegal immigration from China. Russia has a long border with China, some 4,300 kilometres, and is sparsely populated in its Far East. The numbers may vary but several sources mention a flood of Chinese entering Russia, although this is continuously officially denied.[29] It is not inconceivable that this flood is more than a

---

[25] 'Putin stresses importance of Sino-Russian economic, military cooperation', 9 *RFE/RL Newsline (*10 August 2005).

[26] 'Russia agrees to nearly double oil exports to China', 9 *RFE/RL Newsline*, No. 209, Part I (7 November 2005).

[27] 'Kazakh-China pipeline begins operations', 9 *RFE/RL Newsline*, No. 234, Part I (16 December 2005); 'Circumventing the bear', *Stratfor* (16 December 2005).

[28] 'Presidential envoy: rapprochement with China is Russian geopolitical goal', 9 *RFE/RL Newsline*, No. 133, Part I (18 July 2005).

[29] 'Major players focus on the Great Game', *Stratfor* (6 July 2000); 'Military conflict over natural resources between Russia, US and China by 2012', *Moscow Zavtra* (13 May 2005). This source claims that in 2004 already 4 million Chinese were residing in Russia and with an annual inflow of 600,000 will lead to a number of 10-20 million Chinese in Russia by 2015; 'Russian

coincidence, it might well be a planned policy directed from Beijing, in order to gradually increase its influence over this Russian region. The reasons for such a population policy might be to create an overflow area for Chinese citizens from too densely populated areas in China proper, but also to gain a political and/or economic foothold in this area, which is rich in energy sources. Finally, an indication that Russo-Chinese relations might already be in decline is the fact that China refrained from support to Russia in its August 2008 war against Georgia and its recognition of the independence of the separatist regions. Similarly, China has prevented the SCO from convincingly supporting Russia in this matter.[30]

External policy under Medvedev (2008–)

After his inauguration in May 2008 as Russia's new President, Dmitry Medvedev was supposed to take the lead in foreign and security policy, being the prerogative of the Head-of-State. However, Vladimir Putin, now as Premier, continued to play an important role in these areas of policy. Soon after his installation Medvedev was faced with an armed conflict with Georgia. Among other consequences, this conflict resulted in new foreign policy objectives, in addition to those that Medvedev had recently described in a new document on foreign policy.

The July 2008 Foreign Policy Concept

In July 2008, a new edition of the Foreign Policy Concept was published, President Medvedev's first security document. Major entries in the document are:[31]

On Russia's powerful posture:

> '... A new Russia, basing on a solid foundation of its national interests, has now acquired a full-fledged role in global affairs; Russia wants to achieve strong positions of authority in the world community that best meet the interests of the Russian Federation as one of influential centres in the modern world; Russia exerts a substantial influence upon the development of a new architecture of international

---

politicians see no threat in Chinese power', 9 *RFE/RL Newsline*, No. 189, Part I (6 October 2005). According to this source, citing formal statements, no more than 100,000 Chinese live in Russia's Far East.

[30] 'Russia fails to secure regional backing', *Financial Times* (28 August 2008) <http://www.ft.com/cms/s/0/944f00c2-74d8-11dd-ab30-0000779fd18c.html>; 'Asia sides with West, not Russia, over Georgia', *AP* (28 August 2008) <http://www.msnbc.msn.com/id/26435952/>.

[31] Foreign Policy Concept of the Russian Federation, 12 July 2008 <http://www.kremlin.ru/eng/text/docs/2008/07/204750.shtml>

> relations; Russia will provide comprehensive protection of rights and legitimate interests of Russian citizens and compatriots abroad …'

On the European security architecture:

> '… Russia wishes to create a truly open, democratic system of regional collective security and cooperation ensuring the unity of the Euro-Atlantic region, from Vancouver to Vladivostok, in such a way as not to allow its new fragmentation and reproduction of bloc-based approaches which still persist in the European architecture that took shape during the Cold War period; Russia maintains its negative attitude towards the expansion of NATO, notably to the plans of admitting Ukraine and Georgia to the membership in the alliance, as well as to bringing the NATO military infrastructure closer to the Russian borders on the whole; Russia opposes unilateral actions in the field of strategic antimissile defence that are destabilizing international situation …'

On attention for the East:

> '… Russia will make itself more fully engaged with its traditional partners, the Troika (Russia, India and China); the development of friendly relations with China and India forms an important track of Russia's foreign policy in Asia; Russia will build up the Russian–Chinese strategic partnership in all fields on the basis of common fundamental approaches to key issues of world politics as a basic constituent part of regional and global stability; Russia promotes the CSTO as a key instrument to maintain stability and ensure security in the CIS; Russia seeks further strengthening of the SCO, promoting its initiative for setting up a network of partner ties among all the integration associations in the Asia–Pacific Region …'

In this security paper the Kremlin makes it repeatedly clear that Russia is back as an important power, that it wishes to be treated as such, and that it will influence the international agenda. The August 2008 Russo-Georgian conflict comes to the fore as an example of the latter. After announcing the idea of a new European security architecture during his visit to Berlin in June 2008, Medvedev revisits that concept in this document. However, the document does not make clear what the contents should be of such a transformed European security arrangement, other than that current arrangements, such as the CFE Treaty – which Russia suspended in December 2007 – and NATO, are obsolete and remainders of the Cold War. And as a consequence of the Georgian war Poland was more eager to reach an agreement with the United States on the stationing of the missile defence shield, which is rejected in this foreign policy paper. The emphasis in this document on strengthening ties with India and China and with CSTO and SCO, in combination with its resistance to the current European security structure, gives the impression that Russia is moving from west to east in making security arrangements.

The Georgia conflict and Russia's relations with the West

On 7 August 2008 Georgian armed forces attacked the separatist region of South Ossetia. The following day Russia brought in reinforcements from North Ossetia into South Ossetia which responded with fire, while its air force started attacks on targets in Georgia proper. On 11 August Russian troops from South Ossetia and Abkhazia invaded Georgia proper. On 12 August Georgia and Russia agreed on a cease-fire, drafted by the French President Sarkozy, fulfilling the EU Presidency, and his Russian counterpart Medvedev. In spite of the armistice, Russia continued military operations in Georgia proper until 22 August. As of that day Russia withdrew its military forces from Georgia proper without those remaining in the buffer zones south of Abkhazia and South Ossetia. On 26 August Russia recognized the independence of Abkhazia and South Ossetia. Russia intended to keep 7,600 troops in South Ossetia and Abkhazia with permanent military bases, at the request of the authorities of the regions.[32] During and after the conflict the EU has repeatedly condemned Russia. On 1 September 2008 at an Extraordinary European Council held in Brussels, the EU spoke out against the disproportionate reaction of Russia, and condemned Russia's unilateral decision to recognise the independence of Abkhazia and South Ossetia. The EU decided that until Russia's troops would have withdrawn to the positions held prior to 7 August, meetings on the negotiation of the Partnership Agreement were to be postponed. However, the planned EU-Russia summit, scheduled to take place in Nice on 14 November 2008, was not cancelled or postponed.[33]

The deterioration of the ties between Russia and NATO as a result of the conflict was even worse. The Georgian conflict was partly related to the perspective of NATO membership for Georgia and Ukraine, as announced at the Alliance's summit of April 2008, which was heavily protested by Russia. After the conflict with Georgia, NATO froze most military and political cooperation in the NATO-Russia Council.[34]

---

[32] <http://news.bbc.co.uk/2/hi/europe>; <http://www.rferl.org/section/South+Ossetia+Crisis/454.html; http://en.rian.ru/trend/osset/index1.html>.

[33] Extraordinary European Council, Brussels, 1 September 2008, Presidency Conclusions <http://www.consilium.europa.eu/ueDocs/cms_Data/docs/pressData/en/ec/102545.pdf>.

[34] Meeting of the North Atlantic Council at the level of Foreign Ministers held at NATO Headquarters, Brussels, 19 August 2008 <http://www.nato.int/docu/pr/2008/p08-104e.html>.

Medvedev's five principles of foreign policy

Soon after the Russo-Georgian conflict President Medvedev further elaborated his views on foreign policy by announcing five principles, as mentioned in a television interview on 31 August 2008:

1. The primacy of international law;
2. The world should be multi-polar; not single-pole; no domination, such as by the United States of America;
3. Russia has no intention of isolating itself; it seeks friendly relations, also with the West;
4. Protecting Russians wherever they may be is a priority. Russia responds to any aggressive act against them or Russia;
5. Russia has privileged interests in certain regions.[35]

By invading not only the separatist regions of Abkhazia and South Ossetia, but also Georgia proper, the emphasis on international law is disputed. The principle against (American) unipolar and dominant policies, just as the one on protecting Russians abroad, is a traditional entry in Russian security thinking. In the light of Russia's conflict with Georgia, this reference to the protection of Russian minorities has received a different connotation. One of the grounds to use military force in Georgia's separatist regions was the protection of the Russian minority in South Ossetia. Considering the presence of large Russian minorities on their territory, Estonia and Latvia feel threatened by Russia. The last principle, just as entries in the 2008 Foreign Policy Concept on rebuffing further NATO enlargement, especially with Georgia and Ukraine, underlines that Russia considers the former Soviet area as its sphere of influence from which the West should stay out.

Assessment of and outlook on Russia's foreign and security policy

During the last eight years Russia has re-identified its international position. Together with a centralisation of internal authority President Putin has also restored Moscow's external status. With the collapse of the Soviet Union in mind Putin realized that Russia could only regain its status of a great power or superpower by building a stable and strong economy. Thanks to the enormous rise in

[35] Interview given by Dmitry Medvedev to Television Channels *Channel One*, *Rossia*, *NTV*, 31 August 2008 <http://www.kremlin.ru/eng/text/speeches/2008/08/31/1850_type82916_206003.shtml>.

energy prices the Russian economy has rapidly increased in strength. A solid economy and, consequently, less dependence on Western economies, together with the pro-Western regime changes in Georgia and Ukraine convinced Putin that the time had come to change course in external policy. Moscow's security documents had always contained strong anti-Western tendencies. In Putin's second term in office these entries were now put into practice by adopting an assertive stance against the West and demanding an indispensable position in the international arena. This self-confident policy incorporated alienating from post-Cold War security structures, such as the CFE Treaty and NATO, and attracting closer ties with eastern organisations, such as CSTO and SCO, and countries like Iran and Venezuela. In support of this firm policy of a resurgent Russian state, political action and rhetoric was accompanied by demonstrations of military power, growing into the use of force against Georgia.

Is this the return of an empire? Russia is once more a superpower when the following preconditions are met: the Achilles heel of its insecure and violent North Caucasus region should be stabilised; the decline in population size has to be turned around; the economy should be diversified from its dependence on energy resources; Russia should be a real member of the G-8, based upon its economic rating; and a radical modernisation of the armed forces, resulting in military power which is capable of modern warfare and global power projection, should be accomplished. So far, these preconditions are still far away. Furthermore, new 'challenges', such as the consequences of the Russian invasion of Georgia for its relationship with Western (EU, NATO, USA), but also with Eastern (CSTO, SCO, China) actors, are even more diverting Russia from its return as an empire.

How should the West proceed with this forceful Russia, after the Russo-Georgian conflict? First, the West should get its own act together. Since the conflict is partly due to division within NATO and the EU, these organisations should reach a united stance on issues such as Western interests in the Caucasus; whether independent former Soviet states have the right to determine their future, or that Russia's claim of a dominating role in the region is legitimate; and what the role of energy security should be – alternatives or continued dependence of Russia? Next, how should the West respond to Russia's assertive policy? A dual Western policy towards Russia might be the right approach. On the one hand, a tough stance, by pointing out to Russia what is acceptable, and by taking the initiative instead of reacting to Moscow's endeavours. On the other hand, a policy of encouraging cooperation with Russia. The international isolation of Russia radicalises its external policy. Therefore, sanctions should be avoided. Furthermore, cooperation forums in NATO and EU with Russia should be reinstalled as soon as possible. Moscow should be offered cooperation, by focussing on mutual beneficial and practical projects. And perhaps most important, as lessons learned from the 1990s: treat Russia as an equal partner. Differences between Russia and the West will continue, thus workable conditions have to be established, since both parties will remain important players in the international arena.

China's Post-Olympic Rise and its Place in the Global Concert of Nations

Willem van Kemenade

Introduction

The spectacular rise of China as an economic superpower and in the end a political and military giant as well, is the epic challenge of the early 21st century China's own geo-strategic thinkers have vowed that its rise, unlike the destructive rise of 20th century newcomers Germany and Japan, will be peaceful, but Beijing does not control the agenda of an increasingly complex and unpredictable world. One unanticipated world-shattering event is the current global financial crisis, following the collapse of the American financial system. China unwittingly played a major role in the genesis of the Bush administration's irresponsible financial policies by investing hundreds of billions of its dollar reserves in US Treasury notes and bonds. China's main preoccupation for a few more decades will be the economic development of its vast hinterland and the expansion of its internal market, rather than ever expanding exports, the piling up of trade surplusses and investing these in the United States. This may in due course lead to a shift in the nature of the US-China relationship from overwhelming economic-financial interdependence to a new type of *balance of power*.

In global politics, China's dominant theme is the search for a 'multipolar world' that should replace the unipolar world, dominated by the sole superpower, the United States, but China's relations with the two most important other poles, Russia and the European Union, are not developing very smoothly. Russia has been China's principal arms supplier since the early 1990s, but is no longer willing to provide China with the advanced arms it wants, out of concern that China may turn into an adversary at some point in the future. The 'Strategic Partnership' that the European Union and China agreed to in 2003 is also stagnating, because Brussels is unwilling to lift the arms embargo on China and negotiations on a new long-term foundation for the partnership are at a stalemate over the failure to find a common language on human rights and the Tai-

J. de Zwaan, E. Bakker and S. van der Meer (eds.), Challenges in a Changing World

wan issue. To a significant extent, these problems are rooted in the EU's lack of an effective foreign policy apparatus.

Olympic heights

China has descended from its Olympic heights and is refocusing again on the 'basics' of its rise. It may take a few years to fully grasp the impact that the Beijing 2008 Olympics have had and will have on China's status in the world, the nation's psyche and the further development of its authoritarian political system.

In terms of herculean management, the construction of state of the art hardware and infrastructure, the exertion of national will and energy and the unprecedented avalanche of gold and other medals for the host, the games were a spectacular success and have filled the Chinese people with considerable pride about their country's impressive progress. But that is not the full story. The other side of the coin was that during the prelude and all the way through to the aftermath, an atmosphere of paranoia, repression and preventive overkill has prevailed: draconian censorship of the internet and harassment of journalists; arrests and internal deportations of Tibetans and Uygurs; arrests of dissidents and even of two nearly eighty-year old grandmothers who took seriously their right to demonstrate – in assigned zones – against the government's bulldozing of their houses for Olympic redevelopment.

International image further tarnished

After the selection of Beijing as the venue for the 2008 Olympiad, optimists expressed hope that the seven-year prelude to the Games would be a huge incentive for China to improve its international image in areas such as human rights and its disturbing relations with the rogue regimes of the world (Burma, Zimbabwe, Sudan, Uzbekistan, etc.). The rationale was that the Beijing Olympics would be the apotheosis of China's renaissance as a great power, not only as the third, soon second largest economy in the world (after the United States and Japan) but also as a benign power and a moral force that teaches by example.

China has failed the benevolence and morality test, but only in Europe and North America where it is increasingly reviled as a negative force for its repressive policies in Tibet and Xinjiang, its intrusive restrictions of civil rights, press and internet freedom, lack of market access, violation of intellectual property rights, dumping, recurrent food safety scandals, etc. However, for most Asians, Africans and Latin Americans, China is at the pinnacle of its power and prestige and will only rise further, whereas the United States during the George W. Bush presidency has lost the respect and goodwill of much of the world. Bush has learned somehow from his failures, though. After a turbulent start in relations with China in 2001, Bush has become the most accommodating American president towards China (and India!) in recent history. Bush had been led astray on Iraq and the wider Middle East by his sinister neo-con entourage but on China he did not listen to them, thanks to his father and former Secretary of State Colin Powell. In India Bush is highly respected and credited as having done for that country what the late President Richard Nixon did for China: laying the foundation for its opening and integration in the global order and its subsequent rise as a great power.

Bush was not petulant about the Olympic Games, unlike French President Nicolas Sarkozy and German Chancellor Angela Merkel. Merkel did not go to Beijing at all in retaliation for Beijing's high-handed criticism of her official meeting with the Dalai Lama last year in the Federal Chancery. Sarkozy threatened not to go but when Chinese citizens retaliated with a tentative boycott of French hypermarket Carrefour, the French President immediately caved in. Sarkozy pledged to meet with the Dalai Lama upon his return from the Olympics, but when His Holiness arrived in Paris, Sarkozy dodged him and his spokesperson explained that the Buddhist High Priest did not ask to see the President. This is what you get if you customarily speak loudly without carrying a big stick!

The financial crisis

China can revel in the memory of the glorious Olympics for a while, but what lies ahead for the country in the mid-long and longer term? Over the last two decades China and the United States have become interlinked like Siamese twins with China being the giant industrial manufacturing centre for the American consumer, piling up hundreds of billions of dollars in trade surpluses each year and lending these to the United States to finance its wars and indulge in ever-expanding overconsumption and bottomless deficit financing. Harvard economic historian Niall Ferguson baptized this phenomenon *Chimerica*, one transpacific country, 13% of the world's land surface and a quarter of the population. For a time, this symbiotic relationship seemed almost perfect: The eastern half, China, did the low-cost industrial manufacturing and the government-imposed saving; the western half, America, did the limitless spending.[1] Comparing net national savings as a proportion of gross national income, US savings declined from

[1] Niall Ferguson, 'Not two countries, but one: Chimerica', *Sunday Telegraph* (4 March 2007).

more than 5% in the Clinton era to virtually zero by 2005, while Chinese savings surged from less than 30% to nearly 45% in the same time frame. This divergence in savings allowed a tremendous explosion of debt in the United States, because the Asian 'savings glut' made it much cheaper for American households to borrow money. Meanwhile, cheap Chinese labour and low-priced exports to the United States helped hold down inflation. As this tremendous expansion in borrowing (and lending) was taking place, some economists tried to rationalize what was going on. Some American economists argued that this was 'Bretton Woods II', a system of international exchange-rate management akin to the one that linked Western Europe to the United States after 'the Second World War. Others called it a 'stable disequilibrium' that could be relied upon to continue for some time.

Chinese commentators (with an American passport) did not take to this so kindly. Henry C.K. Liu, the Hong Kong-born chairman of a private investment group in New York, eloquently wrote in a long series of articles, 15 to 25 internet pages each in the *Asia Times* (Hong Kong), that the global economy has been operating as a global *Holy Dollar Empire* with the Federal Reserve as the *Holy Dollar Emperor*. Similar to the Holy Roman Empire (in Mediaeval Europe), which disintegrated from the rise of Lutheran nationalism, this Holy Dollar Empire will eventually disintegrate from the progressive centrifugal forces of a new populist economic nationalism. This new nationalism is not to be confused with regressive trade protectionism. The formation of the new Group of Five (G5 – China, Brazil, India, Mexico and South Africa) is a sign of this new trend of progressive economic nationalism. The 2008 US presidential election may herald in a new populism in US history to reform the structure of US *debtor capitalism*.[2]

China decided in the 1980s to emulate the East Asian model of high economic growth through exports, which had produced miracles, first in Japan and then in Taiwan, South Korea, Hong Kong and Singapore. This meant China would have to play by the rules of the *American Global Dollar Empire*. The United States soon became China's biggest export market and tens of thousands of American enterprises, big, medium and small, moved their operations to China which became the 'workshop of the world'. Labour costs were kept to a minimum so as to encourage ever-expanding foreign investment and container loads of consumer goods were paid for in fluctuating dollars which in recent years steadily decreased in value. The dollars could not be used in China because of strict foreign exchange controls, and exporting enterprises had to turn over their

[2] Henry C.K. Liu, 'China's dollar millstone; Breaking free from dollar hegemony, Part 1', *Asia Times (Hong Kong)* (30 July 2008) <http://www.atimes.com>.

dollar revenues from exports, more than one billion a day in total, to the People's Bank of China (Central Bank).

This has now contributed to China close to $2 trillion in foreign currency reserves, which were subsequently invested in US securities by the State Administration of Foreign Exchange (SAFE), which served as one of the two Sovereign Wealth Funds. Thus far, SAFE has pumped about 70% of its dollar investments into the United States, mostly in Treasury notes.- apart exchange rate fluctuations – the safest bid and some into the stock market. Some were shifted into Euros. China tried to make more profitable investments in the United States, with mixed results. The giant computer firm *Lenovo* succeeded in buying the PC arm of IBM in 2005, but China National Offshore Oil Corporation's (CNOOC) efforts to buy the Californian oil company *Unocal* were vetoed by Congress for political reasons. Occasional measured hints by Chinese officials or academics that the country was losing heavily – depending on the fluctuating interest rate – on its dollar investments and would unload huge chunks of them, caused panic in global financial centres on several occasions, mostly when Premier Wen Jiabao lamented in November 2007: 'We are worried about how to preserve the value of China's dollar holdings.' What held the Chinese back from signalling a loss of faith in the dollar and the American financial system too openly, was that it would lead to a surge in the Chinese currency, the renminbi (RMB) or yuan, which could do colossal damage to Chinese exports, not to speak of the damage to China's one trillion or so dollar holdings in the United States.

Former US Secretary of the Treasury (and the former Harvard President) Lawrence Summers described the financial relationship between the United States and China at the AFL/CIO Trade Summit in 2006 as a *Balance of Financial Terror*… 'a situation where we rely on the costs to others of not financing our current account deficit as assurance that financing will continue…' 'Any miscalculation,' Summers said, 'would lead to *Mutually Assured Economic Destruction* (MAED).'[3]

China subsidizes the American consumer

Writer James Fallows calculated in the *Atlantic Monthly* that every (rich) American gets about $4,000 a year in loans from China, which the Chinese government denies its own (poor) people. What is the rationale of the Chinese government in subsidizing the American high-living standards. 'The obvious

---

[3] Charles Horner, What will China do with all that Money?', *Washington Post* (16 January 2007).

reason for doing this is to keep Chinese-made products cheap, so Chinese factories will stay busy [...] The government doesn't want to let the market set the value of the RMB, because it thinks that would disrupt the constant, stable growth and the course it has carefully and expensively set for the factory-export economy.'[4]

After a long campaign of pressure and threats from the United States, China, on 21 July 21 2005, revalued its currency by 2.1 % and repegged it from the dollar to a trade-weighted currency basket of dollar, euro, yen and won. The yuan was permitted to fluctuate 0.3% daily, which in theory allowed it to creep up. However, central bank intervention made a dramatic appreciation unlikely. The United States had demanded at least 10% but welcomed this as a 'good first step'. China categorically stated that there would not be any more adjustments. By mid-2008, the dollar had fallen to 7 yuan from 8.28 yuan in 2005, a drop of more than 15%.

According to Ha Jiming, the chief economist of China International Capital Corp, one of China's largest financial services conglomerates, it is estimated that China holds up to $400 billion in securities in the now nationalized American mortgage reinsurance giants Fannie Mae and Freddy Mac.[5] In an attack on John McCain, Barack Obama said that China now holds $1 trillion of America's national debt. Mocking McCain's militaristic, jingoistic tendencies, Obama said: 'There has never been a country on earth that saw its economy decline and yet maintained its military superiority.'[6]

As America went into recession in 2008 with the subprime crisis and the Wall Street meltdown, Niall Ferguson wrote that the days when the dollar was the sole international reserve currency are coming to an end. 'The last time the dollar weakened significantly, there was no alternative. There is an alternative now. It is perfectly plausible to imagine a world economy in which the euro is at least equivalent to, if not superior to, the dollar.'[7] For several years Chinese economists have been urging that China should move part of its holdings into stronger currencies and it did happen, but discreetly so as to not upset the 'Balance of Financial Terror' with the United States. China dreaded that if it stopped feeding dollars into US treasuries, it would trigger a dollar crisis and China's own reserves would sink together with the greenback.

However, the retreat is coming from the United States. American consumers are broke and will cut down drastically on buying Chinese products. What magni-

---

[4] James Fallows, 'The $ 1.4 trillion question', *Atlantic Monthly* (January/February 2008).

[5] See Liu, *supra* n. 2.

[6] David Pilling, 'America's chance to kick its Asian addiction', *Financial Times* (1 October 2008).

[7] Niall Ferguson, 'The End of Chimerica' (22 August 2008); a slightly different version: 'Rough Week, but America's Era goes on', *Washington Post* (21 September 2008).

tude this will take and how long it will last is still unclear. The abrupt scaling down of the abnormal, unsustainable commercial-financial US-China relationship intersects with ideas for global economic adjustment that the United States and the European Union have already been discussing with the Chinese government for some years. US Treasury Secretary Henry Paulson opened a high-level 'Strategic Economic Dialogue' with the Chinese government in December 2006 as a regular biannual channel of institutionalized engagement so as to persuade the Chinese to radically overhaul their economic system of overly-heavy reliance on exports, high savings, low consumption – 35% in 2007 against 70% in the United States and 60% in India. China must further develop its financial sector and offer its people higher yield investment options than low-interest bank deposits. Appreciation of the Chinese currency and greater flexibility is high on Paulson's agenda since it could limit the impact of rising world oil and commodity prices on prices in China and at the same time allow Chinese monetary policy to be a more effective tool for ensuring stable growth.[8]

The goals of Paulson's 'dialogue' dovetail fully with EU policy objectives and proposals by global economists that the 'rise of China' should be handled *in a globally coordinated way.* European Commission President Jose Manuel Barroso, accompanied by nine commissioners, inaugurated the EU's own 'high level economic and trade dialogue mechanism'.[9] China should shift away from export-led growth to domestic inland markets and consumption-led growth. The EU and the United States should focus not on sectoral protectionism, but on *coordinated global macroeconomic adjustment* encouraging China to boost domestic demand, modernise its inefficient financial system, reduce the need for savings, reduce the purchasing of hundreds of billions of US treasury bonds and allow the renminbi to appreciate.

The Chinese have a habit of listening stoically to American lectures on how they should reform their systems and answer with a ritualistic call for the United States to reform its own economy, reduce its excessive demand for Chinese goods and loans, thereby sustaining gigantic American trade and budget deficits. China is expected to respond in only a piecemeal fashion to outside *ad hoc*, very specific demands. The transformation from an export-driven economy to a domestic consumption-driven one may take decades. The opening up of the vast interior regions, 1,500 to 2,000 km or more from the coast is socially disruptive and painful, with a permanent *Great Trek* of rural people in search of jobs in new industries. Resource scarcity, social unrest, food and job safety and

---

[8] Henry M. Paulson, Jr., 'A Strategic Economic Engagement, Strengthening US-Chinese Ties', *Foreign Affairs* (September/October 2008).

[9] Charles Grant with Katinka Barysch, *Can Europe and China shape a new world order?* (London, Centre for European Reform, May 2008).

health care are all major challenges and keeping control and maintaining stability are the prime concerns of the regime. That is why the United States and the European Union should not pin too much hope on political liberalization and democratization in the near future.

China's Peaceful Rise

China has been engaging in dynamic *omnilateral* diplomacy since the early 1990s, for regional security in Asia and for energy security globally.

If there is a single, recent programmatic document of note for China's foreign policy, it should be Zheng Bijian's speeches and writings (1997-2005) published under the title *China's Peaceful Rise*.[10] Zheng Bijian is the senior foreign affairs adviser to the Chinese President Hu Jintao and is even in retirement (he is 75) an influential voice in the most prominent think-tanks and committees in China. The essence of Zheng's ideas is that China has become a good global citizen, that it accepts the world order as established under Western domination, that it will not challenge the *status quo*, that its rise will in no way resemble the turbulent, bellicose rise of the new 20th century big players Germany and Japan and that its primary preoccupation for decades to come will be economic development. Below is a key paragraph from one of Zheng's major speeches:

> I reiterate that in speaking of a peaceful rise, I am referring to peaceful development, which is one of the defining characteristics of China's socialism. China has made history in two aspects: First, as an emerging major country, China has transcended the old path of industrialization characterized by rivalry for resources and bloody wars, and has chosen to rise peacefully through sustainable development. This is unprecedented. Second, China has transcended the Cold War mentality that rejects peaceful development and cooperation on the grounds of differences in social systems and ideologies. China is rising peacefully and independently, building a socialism with Chinese characteristics through brave reforms and opening up – in other words, by integrating into the world economy rather than self-imposed isolation. This, again, is unprecedented …

Zheng's ideas are basically a further elaboration of Deng Xiaoping's historical words *Tao guang – Yang hui* ['Hide one's capacities and bide one's time'], uttered in the late 1970s. China will be a relatively weak, emerging great power for another 20 years or so. Its grand strategy is not an 'assertive' one like an

---

[10] Zheng Bijian, *China's Peaceful Rise, Speeches 1997-2004* (Washington DC, Brookings Institution 2005).

established superpower practises, but a 'calculative' one of pragmatism, non-ideology, restraint and the search for asymmetric gains.[11]

TOWARDS A MULTIPOLAR WORLD

One recurrent theme in China's diplomatic strategy is the search for a multipolar world that should replace the 'unipolar world, dominated by the sole superpower, the United States.' China has never specified how many poles it envisages, but Russia and the EU are definitely the most prominent ones. China and Russia have once again been in a (non-military) alliance since 2001, in which China is now the big brother with an economy two and half to more than three times bigger (depending on whether one relies on the exchange rate or Purchasing Power Parity (PPP) figures). The recent crisis in Georgia has interestingly highlighted the limits of the Sino-Russian alliance. At the summit of the *Shanghai Cooperation Organization* in the Tajik capital Dushanbe, China and the four Central Asian member states did not condemn Georgia (as Russia had hoped) and none of them backed Russia's decision to recognize breakaway South Ossetia and Abkhazia. The Russian media reported before the summit that Russia's efforts to insert wording condemning Georgia were thwarted by China. Mindful of its own problems with Tibet and the Uygurs in the western territory of Xinjiang, the Chinese government is usually wary of supporting separatists in other countries.[12] Well before the Dushanbe summit, Chinese President Hu Jintao had urged Russia to resolve the problem through dialogue and appropriate negotiation.[13] Hong Kong commentator Ma Ting-sheng said that employing military means and war to resolve ethnic problems is no longer the trend in the 21st century.

Again, it dramatically illustrates the difference in style between Russia and China. The Russians, like the Americans, cannot kick the reflexes of their assertive, militaristic superpower psychology and the Chinese stick to their calculative strategy of patient negotiations. For 15 years they negotiated with the British and prepared the constitutional framework for the near seamless return of Hong Kong to Chinese sovereignty in 1997. For the future reintegration of Taiwan they are nearly completing the diplomatic preparations and it will happen sooner or later, preferably and probably peacefully, but there is no guarantee. Compare this to the Russian *modus operandi* and decide who is the more reasonable to deal with.

---

[11] Michael D. Swaine & Ashley Tellis, *Interpreting China's Grand Strategy: Past, Present, and Future*, Rand/Project Air Force, 2000, pp. 97-98, 113.

[12] Peter Leonard, 'China faces boost from Georgia War', *Moscow Times* (1 September 2008).

[13] Phoenix Television, Hong Kong, 8 August 2008.

There is another potentially more serious rift in Sino-Russian relations: the arms-supply relationship, vital to China, is in crisis. Russia's arms industry is suffering a near collapse in exports – a 62% decline in 2007 – to China as the Russian top-brass agonizes over which technology can safely be sold to China, as well as Beijing's desire to receive licences to do the work itself. What Russia is willing to sell, the Chinese no longer want and need.[14] Russians feel genuinely concerned that, in the medium to longer term, Russian and Chinese interests may collide once again and that the Chinese may eventually turn against them. To the great chagrin of the Chinese top-brass, Russia is willing to transfer more advanced military hardware to India than to China, e.g., fifth generation fighter aircraft such as the Su-30 MKI and the MiG 35. How the renewed Sino-Russian Pact of 2001 will develop is difficult to say. It is interesting to note what Zbigniew Brzezinski said about this: 'In the longer run, I happen to think that Russia really has no choice but to become gradually more associated with the Euro-Atlantic community. Because if it isn't, then it's going to find itself essentially facing China all by itself.'[15]

That sounds very plausible, but with the steady deterioration of US-Russia relations over NATO expansion, Kosovo, Ukraine and Georgia, it is expected that Russia will improve relations with Europe, particularly Germany rather than with the United States. Most Europeans, including President George W. Bush's best European friend, Chancellor Angela Merkel, consider the American cornering of Russia dangerous. The European Union now has a broader and deeper relationship with China than with Russia, but it is still an unfinished work in progress. The EU is unable and unwilling to lift its arms embargo against China, dating from the bloody 1989 suppression of the student rebellion, because of a lack of consensus among the 27 as well as American opposition. We now have a situation where China remains subject to a long-standing arms embargo by the EU and the United States and a selective embargo by Russia, while the latter two have no restrictions on their military supplies to India.

The Bush administration has, after seven and three-quarter years of inaction, just before its demise, announced that it will provoke China with a $6.5 billion arms deal with Taiwan. It comes at a time when the relationship between China and Taiwan under the new President Ma Ying-jeou is at its most relaxed since 1949. Is it just to please the arms industry and possibly to benefit Senator John

---

[14] Stockholm International Peace Research Institute, *Background Paper on SIPRI arms transfer data* (31 March 2008) <www.sipri.org/contents/armstrad/SIPRI_Backgrounder.pdf/download>. For Russian views, see: 'Russian Arms Exports to China in Collapse – AFP' (WSJ), quoting the Russian independent newspaper *Nezavisimaya Gazeta* (29 January 2008); David Lague, 'Russia and China rethink arms deals', *International Herald Tribune* (2 March 2008).

[15] 'Charlie Rose interviews Zbigniew Brzezinski, Henry Kissinger and Brent Scowcroft', *International Herald Tribune* (18 June 2007).

McCain in the coming presidential election? Chinese academics in the United States are musing on the internet that a much stronger China should no longer take this and should dump $200 billion of its dollar holdings and cause a major currency crisis. After the approval of the long-delayed US-India nuclear deal by Congress last week, American arms dealers are now eyeing long-term multi-billion dollar arms deals with India. The Indian Prime Minister Manmohan Singh was in Paris late September 2008 to sign an agreement on nuclear power cooperation and to discuss possible sales of French fighter aircraft to India. All this will benefit international arms industries but will not necessarily serve security and stability in Asia. It is unlikely that China will take all this hands down.

The EU-China (Non-)Strategic Partnership

Another imponderable is the relationship between China and the European Union. In an effort to curb American unilateralism the two agreed to enter into a Strategic Partnership after the Bush-Blair invasion of Iraq in 2003. After five years, the partnership is still in search of a meaningful content, due to the continuation of the arms embargo. There are many sectoral cooperation agreements, the most important ones concerning energy, the environment and sustainable development, but what is lacking is a solid, well-structured foundation. Since early 2007, negotiations are on the way on a *Partnership and Cooperation Agreement* (PCA), also called the *New Framework,* which will encompass the full scope of bilateral relations, including enhanced co-operation in political matters, such as the arms embargo, human rights and the Taiwan issue. These negotiations will update and expand the obsolete foundation of the Europe-China relationship, the 1985 EEC-China Trade and Economic Cooperation Agreement.

However, the PCA may not be completed unless the EU concedes to lift the arms embargo. In December 2006, the European Council made the lifting conditional upon Chinese acceptance of a strong human rights clause, specific improvements in human rights, such as the release of the remaining Tiananmen (1989) detainees, the abolition of administrative detention without charge, rehabilitation through labour and ratification of the United Nations Covenant on Civil and Political Rights. China must also offer more transparency over its defence budget and account for its close relations with rogue regimes around the world.

It is quite likely that the EU-China partnership will stagnate for an indefinite period of time. A senior EU official guessed five years or longer is quite possible.[16] China is too old, too monolithic and too strong to yield to outsiders on

---

[16] Interview, 7 October 2008.

its core values. These are neo-Confucian, authoritarian harmony and rejection of adversarial, divisive multi-party democracy. As the Israeli scholar Azar Gat wrote a year ago: 'By shifting from communism to capitalism, China has switched to a far more efficient brand of authoritarianism. As China rapidly narrows the economic gap with the developed world, the possibility looms that it will become a true authoritarian superpower.'[17] This need not necessarily be permanent. As national development spreads and the integration of the non-Chinese borderlands Tibet and Xinjiang succeeds, China may eventually evolve towards a more liberal order.

Umwertung aller Werte

The era of Western domination of the world which started in the 16th century and reached its peak in the 19th and 20th centuries is coming to a close. We are living in a neo-Nietzschean transition of *Umwertung aller Werte* ('Re-evaluation of all Values'), with the difference being that during Niezsche's time, the *Leitmotiv*, the main theme, was that 'God is dead'. Now the *Leitmotiv* is: 'The myth of Western superiority is dead.' For decades after political decolonization, numerous Asians continued to think that modernization meant Westernization, but one of Asia's leading intellectuals, Singapore's flamboyant scholar-diplomat Kishore Mahbubani writes in his latest book that Asia's true 'Renaissance' is unthinkable without 'De-Westernization.'[18] The Chinese led the charge for 'De-Westernization' in the 1990s, when the highly public confrontation with the Clinton administration over human rights reached its climax in 1993. Prior to the world conference on human rights in Vienna in June 1993, they convened a preliminary conference with other Asian countries in Bangkok, that basically 'de-universalized' the Western glossary of terms in the human rights field and declared that Asia would set its own standards in the human rights field, the so-called *Asian Values*. The United States mainly focuses on political and civil rights and uses the megaphone; the European Union has more consideration for the priority that China accords to economic, social and cultural rights, and prefers quiet diplomacy, but nevertheless the Sino-European negotiations over a new PCA are bogged down, among other things over the human rights issue.

China is no Soviet Union, which was an autarkic, expansionist military empire with a *cordon sanitaire* of conquered territories and satellites, and without interest in integration in any of the global systems, be they economic, trade or

---

[17] Azar Gat, 'The Return of Authoritarian Great Powers', *Foreign Affairs* (August/September 2007).

[18] Kishore Mahbubani, *The New Asian Hemisphere, The Irresistable Shift of Global Power to the East* (New York, Public Affairs 2008) Chapter 4.

financial. Since the start of its reform-communism in 1978, China has come to accept the Western-dominated world order, has been integrating in the world trading and financial systems and has reached advanced degrees of economic-financial interdependence with many countries including the United States. China plays a constructive role in many problem areas in global politics, e.g., UN peacekeeping, and the North-Korean and Iranian nuclear issues. It even disapproves of the Russian use of force against a former Soviet Republic and refuses to accept the unilateral Russian recognition of the independence of the Georgian enclaves of Abkhazia and South Ossetia. China has also proved to be sensitive to Western criticism of its policies in Sudan and Burma and has contributed to some extent to improvements there. The scope for productive cooperation between China and the European Union under any bilateral or multilateral umbrella is infinite. It would be most regrettable if the European Union fails to reach agreement with China over a Partnership and Cooperation Agreement as this would not be in the long-term interest of either side.

EUROPE AND CHINA IN INTERNATIONAL CONFLICT MANAGEMENT: RIVALS AND PARTNERS*

Frans-Paul van der Putten & Emma van der Meulen

INTRODUCTION

Since the end of the Cold War, the United States and Europe have been the leading actors in global conflict management. China is currently emerging as the third major player in global security governance. Much attention is given to the strategic relationships of the United States with Europe and China. However, in order to understand how the global security landscape is changing, the relationship between Europe and China should also be taken into account. Both Europe and China are permanently represented in the United Nations Security Council and have substantial economic and diplomatic influence in parts of the world far beyond their own regions.[1] This chapter focuses on the roles played by China and Europe in managing regional security crises in Africa and the Middle East.[2]

To understand what Chinese-European interaction on regional security crises could look like, it is useful to consider briefly a current example of Chinese-American relations in a part of the world where Europe is not an active security actor, i.e., East Asia. In 2003 Beijing initiated a mediation effort to address tensions between North Korea and the United States relating to Pyongyang's nuclear weapons programme. This effort became institutionalized in the 'Six-

* This essay is based on Emma van der Meulen & Frans-Paul van der Putten, 'European and Chinese Approaches to International Conflict Management in Africa and the Middle East: The cases of Sudan and Iran' (unpublished manuscript).

[1] On current developments in the relationship between the UN Security Council and the EU, see: Daniele Marchesi, 'The EU Common Foreign and Security Policy in the UN Security Council: Between Representation and Coordination', *Regional Integration & Global Governance Papers 3* (Bruges, College of Europe 2008).

[2] For a recent publication on the overall response of the EU (and the United States) to China's influence in Africa, see: Asteris Huliaras & Konstantinos Magliveras, 'In Search of a Policy: EU and US reactions to the growing Chinese presence in Africa', *European Foreign Affairs Review*, No. 13 (2008) pp. 399-420.

J. de Zwaan, E. Bakker and S. van der Meer (eds.), Challenges in a Changing World

Party Talks' (involving also South Korea, Japan, and Russia). While the Americans became more appreciative of China's role in this crisis, especially after the nuclear test conducted by North Korea in 2006, the Chinese responded positively to US efforts to restrain Taiwan's pro-independence movement. Gradually a picture is emerging in which Beijing and Washington jointly manage potential conflicts in East Asia through their bilateral ties within the region, and through cooperation in the UN Security Council and the Six-Party Talks.[3] At the same time, the North Korean crisis has enabled China to increase its influence in regional security. In terms of regional influence, this emergence of China results in a relative decline in the position of the United States. It remains to be seen how cooperation between China and the United States develops, not only with regard to East Asia but also regarding sources of regional instability in other parts of the world. Nonetheless, the North Korean issue seems to represent a model for great power cooperation on regional security crises that might also apply to great power interaction in other parts of the world.[4]

This chapter discusses how the relationship between China and Europe in conflict (or crisis) management is evolving by taking two recent crises, involving Sudan and Iran, as examples. Two questions in particular are of interest. First, does the growing influence of China lead to a weakening of Europe's role? Second, what is the potential for cooperation between Europe and China in conflict management?

Europe, China and conflict management

One reason why little has been written about Europe as a security counterpart of China is that Europe does not exist as a unified security actor. For the purpose of this chapter, Europe is regarded as an international security actor whose interests and behaviour are shaped in four major centres of decision making: Brussels, Paris, London, and Berlin.[5] Geographically, Europe is taken here to refer to the European Union, while it is taken into account that Europe's three major countries dominate decision making in Brussels and also have – to some degree – a capability to operate individually on the world stage.

More than in any other region, in Africa and the Middle East great powers can play a leading role in managing local security crises. The Middle East has

---

[3] This applies mostly to the situation on the Korean peninsula. Regarding the Taiwan issue, further Sino-US cooperation still faces serious obstacles.

[4] On the North Korean case as a model for Sino-US cooperation, see: Bonnie S. Glaser & Wang Liang, 'North Korea: The Beginning of a China-U.S. Partnership?', 31 *The Washington Quarterly*, No. 3 (Summer 2008) pp. 165-180.

[5] This four-part approach to Europe is also used by the Chinese government in its diplomacy towards Europe: Avery Goldstein, *Rising to the Challenge: China's Grand Strategy and International Security* (Stanford, Stanford University Press 2005) pp. 160-161.

no regional security mechanism, and in Africa's case the African Union has limited resources and external powers are highly influential. The leading great powers are the permanent members of the UN Security Council. They can play their role in conflict management through the Council, but also bilaterally or via other diplomatic platforms. The two crises most often cited as examples of China's growing role in African and Middle Eastern security relate to Sudan and Iran. The violence in Sudan's Darfur region is primarily a domestic crisis. For Europe, however, the failure of the Sudanese government to protect its citizens from large-scale suffering gives the international community a responsibility and a mandate to intervene. International pressure forced China, as a permanent Security Council member and closely tied to Khartoum, to take a stand. The case of Iran revolves around Tehran's uranium enrichment programme, and threats by the United States and Israel to intervene militarily if Iran continues to move towards nuclear weapons capability. Europe, China, and Russia have taken up a role of mediation between Tehran and Washington in order to prevent a military conflict.

Issues at stake

The issues at stake for the Chinese and the Europeans are located at three levels. *First*, there are local interests and local influence. In a given country or region, both Europe and China have certain local economic and diplomatic interests and wish to protect these. *Second*, there is the question of how a given crisis affects the positions of both Europe and China vis-à-vis the Unites States. At the basic level, it is in China's interest to have good relations with both Europe and the United States while in certain instances benefitting from differences between the positions of the Europeans and the Americans. The same is true for Europe regarding its relations with Beijing and Washington. The rise of China could cause Europe to lose its position as the preferred security partner of the United States. Shifts in this triangular relationship affect power relations not only at the local but also at the global level.

Third, there is the general debate on how to deal with the concept of state sovereignty, in relation to both human rights and non-proliferation. This debate is of crucial importance for the future of global governance in terms of international conflict management. The differences between China and the West are the greatest in regard to human rights. Europe, along with the United States, is in favour of a system in which international security organizations such as the UN Security Council intervene in domestic affairs not only if international stability is in immediate danger, but also if a national government cannot or does not protect the human security of its citizens. However, China favours a global security system that leaves a great deal of room for states to manage their internal affairs without external interference. The Chinese leaders believe that human rights norms can be manipulated by great powers to legitimize interventions in other countries.[6] In China, protecting territorial integrity is crucial to the survival of the Communist Party.[7] Local crises in Taiwan, Tibet, or Xinjiang always carry the risk of inviting outside interference, which would enhance the danger of increased autonomy in such regions. So while there is a high degree of confidence in the West that there is no danger of an undesired intervention by foreign powers in Western countries, China does not have this confidence.[8] China's position in the debate on nuclear non-proliferation is based on a similar reasoning, as China believes that, in principle, countries have the right to develop nuclear capabilities for peaceful use. Many Chinese experts also believe that the proliferation of nuclear weapons is inevitable and helps countries to balance against the United States.[9]

Active participation in the debate on the norms and standards relevant to international interventions is a primary line of defence from the perspective of China's leadership. This does not mean that China always favours state sovereignty over human rights or non-proliferation, or that Beijing never actively supports certain interventions. As pointed out by Allen Carlson, in 1999 China criticized the Western intervention in Kosovo, but it supported international intervention in East Timor.[10] The Africa specialist Ian Taylor argues that in the

[6] Allen Carlson, *Unifying China, Integrating with the World: Securing Sovereignty in the Reform Era* (Stanford, Stanford University Press 2005) pp. 174-175.

[7] Russell Ong, *China's Security Interests in the 21st Century* (London, Routledge 2007) p. 15.

[8] For European perspectives on what China's role in global governance should be, see: Charles Grant, with Katinka Barysch, *Can Europe and China Shape a New World Order?* (London, Centre for European Reform 2008) pp.89-92; Marcin Zaborowski, 'EU-China Security Relations', *ISS Analysis Paper* (Paris, 2008) p. 2; François Godement, 'The EU and China: A necessary partnership', in Giovanni Grevi & Álvaro de Vasconcelos, 'Partnerships for Effective Multilateralism: EU relations with Brazil, China, India and Russia.', *ISS Chaillot Paper 109* (Paris, May 2008). On China's perspective see Samuel S. Kim, 'Chinese Foreign Policy Faces Globalization Challenges', in: Alastair Ian Johnston & Robert S. Ross, eds., *New Directions in the Study of China's Foreign Policy* (Stanford, Stanford University Press 2006).

[9] François Godement, 'Is China a Reliable Partner in Non-Proliferation?', *China Analysis*, No. 19 (European Council on Foreign Relations, August 2008).

[10] Carlson, *supra* n. 6, p. 176; also: Allen Carlson, 'Protecting Sovereignty, Accepting Intervention: The dilemma of Chinese foreign relations in the 1990s', *China Policy Series 18* (National Committee on United States-China Relations, September 2002) <http://www.ncuscr.org/files/3.%20Protecting%20Sovereignty,%20Accepting%20Intervention%20(18).pdf> (accessed 25 July 2008); ibid., 'Helping to Keep the Peace (Albeit Reluctantly): China's recent stance on sovereignty and multilateral intervention, 77 *Pacific Affairs*, No. 1 (2004) pp. 9-27; and ibid., 'More Than Just Saying No: China's Evolving Approach to Sovereignty and Intervention since Tiananmen', in Johnston & Ross, *supra* n 8. The changing Chinese perspective on state sover-

longer run, the interests of the West and China in the sphere of human rights in Africa are very similar, implying that Beijing's foreign human rights policy will move closer to Western norms.[11] However, according to Stephanie Kleine-Ahlbrandt and Andrew Small, in the foreseeable future China's policy towards pariah states will show only minor, experimental changes.[12]

For the moment, the focus on specific cases remains crucial in order to understand how the relationship between Europe and China in conflict management is developing. Not abstract theory but actual crises in international relations, whether these relate to human rights, armed conflict, natural disasters, or economic instability, shape the debate on sovereignty and intervention.

Darfur

The crisis in Darfur is rooted in a split within the ruling Congress Party between Omar al-Bashir and Hassan al-Turabi that occurred in the late 1990s. Most party members from Darfur supported al-Turabi, whom al-Bashir ousted in 1999. Hence al-Bashir, fearful of losing influence in Darfur, appointed loyalists in the Popular Defence Forces (PDF), the local police force that later became known as the Janjaweed.[13] The politicization of the PDF increased tensions that escalated into violence in February 2003 when the Sudan Liberation Movement/Army (SLM/A) and the Justice and Equality Movement (JEM), the main Darfuri resistance movements, carried out a series of attacks on military installations. The Government of Sudan responded with a counterinsurgency campaign the extreme brutality of which drew the attention of the international community. Since 2003, over 200,000 people have been killed and two million have been displaced, according to estimates by the United Nations.[14]

---

eignty is also noted by Zhang Yongjin, 'Understanding Chinese Views of the Emerging Global Order', in Wang Gungwu & Zheng Yongnian, eds., *China and the New International Order* (Abingdon, Routledge 2008) pp. 160-161; Shan Wenhua: 'Redefining the Chinese Concept of Sovereignty', in Gungwu & Yongnian, ibid.

[11] Ian Taylor, 'Sino-African Relations and the Problem of Human Rights', 107 *African Affairs*, No. 426 (2008) pp. 63-87.

[12] Stephanie Kleine-Ahlbrandt & Andrew Small, 'China's New Dictatorship Diplomacy', *Foreign Affairs* (January-February 2008).

[13] A. de Waal, 'Briefing: Darfur, Sudan: Prospects for Peace', 104 *African Affairs*, No. 414 (2005) pp. 127-128. See for more information on the origins of the crisis: H. Slim, 'Dithering over Darfur? A preliminary review of the international response', 80 *International Affairs*, No. 5 (2004) pp. 811-828; and A. de Waal, 'Who are the Darfurians? Arab and African identities, violence and external engagement', 104 *African Affairs*, No. 415 (2005) pp. 181-205.

[14] <http://www.un.org/Depts/dpko/missions/unamid/background.html > (accessed 7 July 2008).

China's local interests in Sudan are related to energy security, in addition to which trade and good diplomatic relations are also important. China has invested over $15 billion in Sudan since 1996, much of it in oil-related projects.[15] Because of these large investments, China has an interest in the continuation of good bilateral relations with the Government of Sudan. Oil from Sudan makes up around 6% of China's total oil imports. Most oil-producing regions are located in South Sudan. When the Comprehensive Peace Agreement (CPA) between the central government and the rebel movement in South Sudan (SPLM/A) was signed in 2005, it also became a real possibility that the South would become independent of the North after a referendum to be held in 2011. Consequently the Chinese government invited Salva Kiir Mayardit, vice president and representative of the SPLM/A in the government of national unity, to come to China soon after the CPA was signed.[16] Chinese involvement in oil fields in Darfur is limited to a 95% stake in Block 6 in South Darfur, which produces relatively few barrels per day. However, China recently announced that it would expand its oil operations in Darfur. A political solution to the conflict in Darfur is the best way for China to protect its interests in the country. China has an interest in a stable Sudan to safeguard its large investments. In addition to its local interests in Sudan, China also has a major stake in the implications of the Darfur crisis for global governance. The way in which the UN addresses this particular crisis sets a precedent for future instances. Beijing is determined to defend the principle of state sovereignty, but at the same time it also wants to avoid undermining the legitimacy of the UN Security Council in global governance, or to come into a direct conflict with the United States or Europe.

When the Darfur crisis erupted, Beijing did not pursue an active role. In the Security Council, China threatened to use its veto on resolutions that included economic sanctions against Sudan, but has never put this threat into practice. Instead, China regularly abstained from voting.[17] Key issues for China were the absence of economic sanctions and the consent of the Government of Sudan before any action was taken.[18] China changed its position on international intervention in Darfur in 2006, when it became clear to Beijing that neither Presi-

[15] Chris Alden, *China in Africa* (London, Zed Books 2007) p. 61.

[16] 'Sudanese first vice president to visit China', *People's Daily Online* (12 July 2005).

[17] Key resolutions relating to Darfur are: SC Res. 1556 (arms embargo; China abstained), 1564 (threats of 'additional measures'; abstained), 1574 (expansion of AMIS; approved), 1590 (expansion of UNMIS in Darfur; abstained), 1591 (establishing a sanctions committee; abstained), 1593 (ICC; abstained), 1672 (sanctions on war criminals; abstained), 1679 (transition AMIS into UNAMID; approved), 1706 (deployment of UNAMID, no consent by Khartoum; abstained), 1755 (facilitation of humanitarian operations in Darfur; approved), and 1769 (deployment of UNAMID with the consent of Khartoum; approved).

[18] Daniel Large, 'Oil and Darfur. The evolution of relations between China and Sudan', *Small Arms Survey, Human Security Baseline Assessment*, No. 7 (2008) pp. 7-8.

dent al-Bashir nor the African Union (through its AMIS peacekeeping mission) were able to bring stability to Darfur. The fact that China now saw the need for an international solution became apparent through the firm diplomatic language of high-ranking Chinese officials, such as this statement by the Chinese Premier Wen Jiabao: 'China is very much concerned about the stability in Darfur [...] and of course we support the international society's decision to send in peacekeepers.'[19] Wang Guangya, China's representative in the Security Council, also played an important and constructive mediating role behind the scenes during the negotiations on the 'Annan Plan', the road-map for the deployment of the UN-AU peacekeeping force, in Addis Ababa in November 2006.[20]

The appointment of Liu Guijin as special representative in May 2007 further strengthened China's role as a mediator between the Western call for intervention and the Sudanese resistance to it. China helped to draft a resolution to which the Government of Sudan could give its consent, mainly by ensuring that the peacekeeping troops did not come from Western countries and that the final resolution did not contain any economic sanctions. Liu Guijin also took part in this active diplomacy by visiting Sudan regularly as well as holding meetings with the Arab League and the African Union on the subject.[21] With Khartoum's consent to the deployment of the UN Darfur Mission (UNAMID), China approved resolution 1769 in the Security Council. China also voted in favour of resolution 1776, adopted by the Security Council on 25 September 2007, that authorised the deployment of EUFOR in Eastern Chad, near the border with Darfur in Sudan. China has given some humanitarian assistance to Darfur, but the amount is relatively limited in comparison to other donors. China also contributed $3.5 million to the African Union Mission in Sudan in June 2006,[22] and 435 troops to the UN Mission in South Sudan (UNMIS). In February 2008, China also sent in 140 troops to contribute to UNAMID.[23]

On the European side, France has the most extensive interests in the region. It is especially concerned with the implications that the conflict in Darfur has on the stability of the region. Darfur directly borders France's old colonies Chad and the Central African Republic (CAR), with which Paris maintains close mili-

---

19 Press Statement during a state visit to the Unitd Kingdom: <http://www.number10.gov.uk/output/page10056.asp> (accessed 9 July 2008).

20 Large, *supra* n. 18, p. 9. China's diplomatic activity had already started to change before a group of prominent Americans started the 'Genocide Olympics' campaign in mid-2007, criticising China for its involvement in Sudan. However, China may also have been sensitive to international pressure and criticism as this was damaging to its reputation as a responsible international player which might damage its position on the African continent in particular.

21 Ibid., p. 6.

22 Ibid.; UN News Service

23 'Sudan welcomes Chinese peacekeepers', *The Boston Globe/AP* (1 February 2008).

tary and economic ties. The United Kingdom has few local interests but nonetheless regards the Darfur issue as an important foreign policy priority. This seems related primarily to the more general aim of promoting Western values in combination with the high-profile status of the Darfur conflict in the international media. Germany's interests in Sudan are also limited and are mainly economic. Stability in Sudan would benefit the EU, as it would allow the normalisation of economic relations and – due to the relative closeness of Sudan to Europe – would contribute to Europe's own stability.[24]

France, the United Kingdom and Germany have used largely similar means to address the conflict in Darfur, although France has taken the most active role in addressing the crisis. The big three operate bilaterally as well as through the EU and the UN. Military commitments elsewhere can explain the reluctance of Germans and British to become militarily involved in the Darfur crisis. All three have expressed their support for the African Union Mission in Darfur. In the end, however, Europe has produced much rhetoric but little commitment to actually ending the Darfur crisis. This is in line with its limited local interests and its focus on the more abstract dimension of human rights promotion and its global governance agenda.

When China pressured the government in Khartoum to accept foreign intervention by the UN in 2007, it risked losing some of its local standing. However, China still remains the main diplomatic ally and economic partner of Sudan and the strong pressure from the West continues to make Chinese support indispensable for Khartoum. In spite of Europe committing aid and support for peacekeeping missions and putting pressure on the Sudanese government, its influence at the local level remains insignificant in relation to China's. In terms of the positions of Europe and China relative to the United States, both sides have shown their worth to American foreign policy. On the one hand, Europe has manifested itself as a strong proponent of the same values that underlie US policy. On the other hand, China proves to be a key party when it comes to influencing the government in Khartoum.

In the sphere of global governance, both Europe and China have had to compromise. Beijing managed to defend the principle that external parties can only intervene with the consent of the Sudanese government. However, behind the screens China has had to put pressure on the Sudanese to go along with outside intervention. Europe has seen its sanctions against Sudan counterbalanced by China, and has had to accept a lesser degree of intervention than what would have been possible without China's involvement. Relatively minor areas aside, China and Europe do not act as partners in managing the Darfur crisis, due to

---

[24] European Commission's Delegation to the Sudan, Bilateral Relations, <http://www.delsdn.ec.europa.eu/en/eu_and_sudan/bilateral_relations.htm> (accessed 7 July 2008).

the fact that their main interests are opposed. This is true with regard to the principles of state sovereignty *versus* interventionism, but also with regard to the *status quo*. China benefits from its ties with the current regime, while Europe would benefit more from a regime change. A basis for joint conflict management does exist, since both sides have an interest in stability. The problem is that in this area China's stakes are much higher than Europe's. In other words, China is more genuinely interested in solving the crisis itself, while for Europe the crisis is primarily an opportunity to push its foreign policy agenda.

Iran

The National Council of Resistance of Iran, an Iranian opposition organisation in exile, revealed in August 2002 that Tehran was secretly developing uranium enrichment facilities. The International Atomic Energy Agency (IAEA) started investigations and Iran reported its nuclear facilities officially to the IAEA in February 2003. Iran claimed that the programme had been set up to provide an alternative source of energy for domestic use and that the development of weapons of mass destruction ran counter to Islamic ideology.[25] Contradictory claims and further revelations of nuclear-related activity increased the suspicion of the international community about Iran's intentions. In an attempt to build trust and ensure Iran's future cooperation with the IAEA, Germany, France and the United Kingdom, as the 'EU-3', started a process of 'conditional engagement', whereby the continuation of trade was made dependent on Iran's improved behaviour. Despite its initial successes, such as the signing of an Additional Protocol committing Iran to fuller cooperation with the IAEA and the suspension of uranium enrichment activities for two years, the EU-3 could not prevent that Iran continued uranium enrichment at Natanz on 10 January 2006.

The crisis deepened as the possibility of a military conflict between Iran and the United States, or between Iran and Israel, seemed increasingly likely. The official positions of both the United States and Israel is that a nuclear Iran is not acceptable and that all options to prevent this are open. In addition to the EU-3, also Russia and China – as permanent members of the UN Security Council and because of their ties with Tehran – joined in the efforts to defuse the crisis. Together with the United States they constitute the 'Six Powers' who jointly negotiate with Iran on its nuclear programme. On 31 January 2006, the Six Powers agreed to report Iran to the Security Council. Since then, four resolutions have been adopted requiring Iran to fully cooperate with the IAEA and to suspend all uranium enrichment. Economic sanctions and an arms embargo have

[25] Wyn Q. Bowen & Joanna Kidd, 'The Iranian Nuclear Challenge', 80 *International Affairs*, No. 2 (2004) p. 258.

been imposed to enforce Iran's cooperation. Up until now, Iran has not complied.

China's main local interests in Iran relate to energy resources. Iran has the world's third largest reserves of oil, as well as the world's second largest gas reserves. Iran is currently China's third largest supplier of crude oil.[26] China also has economic interests in Iran beyond energy. Bilateral trade is extensive and growing, totalling $30 billion by the end of 2008, according to Assistant Foreign Minister Zhai Jun.[27] China surpassed the major countries of the European Union, notably Germany, as Iran's largest trade partner in 2006. China is also involved in weapons trade with Iran and played a large role in building up the Iranian army after the revolution in 1979. As with the Darfur crisis, the Iranian nuclear crisis affects China not only in terms of local interests but also at the level of global governance. Here again, Beijing tries to uphold the principle of state sovereignty as much as possible. At the same time, China wants to avoid being regarded as an irresponsible global power that does not care about nuclear non-proliferation.[28] Beijing's reputation in this regard is highly relevant to its standing, and therefore influence, in international organisations. Moreover, China – for whom relations with the United States are also critically important – wants to avoid having to choose between Tehran and Washington in case of a further escalation of tensions between Iran and the United States.

China sought to prevent such escalating tensions from the start of the crisis, without, however, taking a leading role in international mediation. Initially the Chinese government announced its opposition to referring Iran to the UN Security Council, while stressing that Iran should operate in the framework of the IAEA.[29] When Iran openly continued its uranium enrichment in January, China agreed to refer Iran to the Security Council while remaining reluctant about imposing sanctions on Iran. Nonetheless, China voted in favour of each of the four Security Council resolutions aimed at forcing Iran to suspend its enrichment programme. China has emphasised that these sanctions were not intended to punish Iran, but to urge it to return to the negotiating table.[30] For China, Iran

[26] Energy Information Administration, Country Analysis Brief: China, last updated August 2006, available online at <http://www.eia.doe.gov/emeu/cabs/China/Full.html> (accessed 4 August 2008).

[27] 'Iran-China trade to reach dlrs 30b in 2008', *Iranian Republic News Agency* (14 July 2008).

[28] Dingli Shen, 'Iran's Nuclear Ambitions Test China's Wisdom', 29 *Washington Quarterly*, No.2 (2006) p. 56.

[29] Press Release on <http://www.ie.china-embassy.org/eng/NewsPress/t169550.htm>, 'Foreign Minister Li Zhaoxing Pays a Formal Visit to Iran, 7 November 2004' (accessed 14 July 2008).

[30] 'Statements of Wang Guangya after the adoption of resolutions 1747 and 1803, Press Releases on 23-03-2007 and 03-03-2008', available online at <http://www.un.org/Docs/sc/unsc_press.asp> (12 July 2008).

has a right to develop nuclear energy as long as this is done within the IAEA framework. Meanwhile, diplomatic ties between Tehran and Beijing have remained intact, and the crisis has not deterred China from increasing its economic relations with Iran, in spite of American pressure to do the opposite.

In contrast to China's reluctant role, Europe has been highly active in international diplomacy since the start of the Iranian nuclear crisis. France has substantial economic interests in Iran. France's exports to Iran are diverse and encompass the automobile industry, hydrocarbon technology, transport and financial services, while imports are mainly crude oil.[31] Iranian oil accounts for 3% of French oil imports.[32] Iran was France's sixth oil supplier in 2006 and France's third biggest market in the Middle East.[33] French economic interests are being damaged by the sanctions. The value of exports to Iran declined by 20.3% in the period 2006-2007, totalling $1.5 billion in 2007.[34] France has important regional interests in Lebanon, a country in which Iran is an influential actor through its ties with Syria and Hezbollah. Trade between Iran and the United Kingdom was valued at £400 million in 2007 (in 2006: £431m).[35] Iran is Britain's sixth biggest trading partner from the Middle East and Northern Africa region. Britain's involvement in the Iraq war increased its interests in the stability and security of the Middle East.[36] Iran's foreign policy tends to work against British interest. The United Kingdom blamed Iran for giving support to various groups that work to undermine the Middle East peace process and for supplying Shi'a militias in Iraq with arms.[37] The third major European actor, Germany, is Iran's largest trade partner within the EU. The German-Iranian trade volume totalled $7.1 billion in 2007. German exports to Iran declined by 7% in 2006 and 13.5% in 2007.[38] The total volume of trade declined by 8.7% in 2007. The German economy is being damaged by the economic sanctions imposed on Iran and it is therefore in Germany's interests to solve the Iranian

---

[31] French Ministry of Foreign Affairs, 'Economic and Political Relations with Iran', see: <http://www.diplomatie.gouv.fr/en/country-files_156/iran_301/index.html> (accessed 6 August 2008).

[32] Statistics from French Ministry of Foreign Affairs, updated on 10 January 2006 (before international sanctions were enacted).

[33] Energy Information Administration, *Country Analysis Briefs: France*, updated April 2007 <http://www.eia.doe.gov/emeu/cabs/France/Full.html> (accessed 18 July 2008).

[34] 'France and UK reduce trade ties with Iran', *Financial Times* (17 July 2008).

[35] <https://www.uktradeinvest.gov.uk/ukti/appmanager/ukti/countries?_nfls=false&_nfpb=true&_pageLabel=CountryType1&navigationPageId=/iran> (accessed 22 July 2008).

[36] Mark Gasiorowski, 'The New Aggressiveness in Iran's Foreign Policy', XIV *Middle East Policy*, No. 2 (Summer 2007).

[37] <http://www.fco.gov.uk/en/about-the-fco/country-profiles/middle-east-north-africa/iran/?profile=intRelations&pg=4> (accessed 22 July 2008).

[38] German Federal Foreign Office, *Economic Relations with the Islamic Republic of Iran* (18 July 2008).

nuclear crisis swiftly. German companies are fearful that if economic sanctions force them to withdraw, Chinese and Russian companies will take over their position.[39] The interests of the EU as a whole in Iran are largely similar to those of the Member States in this study. The main interests of the EU in Iran are energy resources, trade and investment, while the EU also has an interest in cooperating with Iran in regional security issues because of its interests in the stability of the region.

Under President Chirac France assumed a balancing role in the Middle East after the Lebanon war of 2006, mediating between American and Arab, including Iranian, interests.[40] However, under President Sarkozy France's rhetoric and actions towards Iran have been less compromising and more directly in line with the US's stance. British Prime Minister Tony Blair adopted strong rhetoric, stating it was certain that Iran sponsored terrorism. British soldiers have been taken hostage by Iran's Revolutionary Guards twice, in 2004 and in 2007. Although both crises were solved diplomatically, Iran sent a strong signal of its power in the Persian Gulf.[41] London's policy towards Iran is largely similar to American policy, as the United Kingdom is the main ally of the United States in the region. The United Kingdom is the most active European power lobbying for additional European sanctions. Germany has assumed an active diplomatic role in trying to solve the Iranian nuclear crisis, mainly within an EU or UN context. The fact that it is losing its business interests to China is an extra stimulus for Germany to work towards a diplomatic solution. When the UN took over the case from the EU, Germany's active role remained unchanged. The P5+1 construction, the five permanent members of the UN Security Council plus Germany constituting the Six Powers to deal with the Iranian issue, elevated Germany's status as an important international actor.

Although the EU is seen as having taken the lead in solving the Iranian nuclear crisis in the EU-3 context, this was an initiative of the 'Big Three', France, Germany and the United Kingdom, which was only two years later fully supported by the European Council. The three countries' foreign ministers visited Iran for discussions on the nuclear issue for the first time in October 2003. The talks led to the Tehran Agreed Statement in which the EU-3 recognised Iran's right to peaceful nuclear energy under the Non-Proliferation Treaty and promised cooperation on economic and security issues when the nuclear issue was fully resolved. Iran signed the Additional Protocol of the IAEA and suspended

---

39 Kathy Gockel, *Energy, economic interests complicate Iran dealings* (The Stanley Foundation 2007), accessed online at: <http://www.stanleyfoundation.org/resources> (18 July 2008).

40 Patrice de Beer, 'France and Lebanon: the diplomacy of tragedy' (2006) <http://www.opendemocracy.net> (accessed 23 July 2008).

41 'What the end of the hostage crisis means for the world', *The Independent* (7 April 2007).

uranium enrichment on a voluntary basis from 10 November 2003 onwards.[42] This was perceived as a major breakthrough in the crisis. European diplomacy had prevented the crisis from further escalation and had built a bridge between the American and Iranian positions.[43]

During the following months, Iran was perceived as further obstructing IAEA's access to nuclear facilities. As a result, the European and American positions converged, as both were now willing to refer Iran to the UN Security Council in case of further non-compliance and the provision of contradictory information.[44] The EU-3 presented Iran with a new incentive to continue working with the IAEA on 21 October 2004. This proposal included more economic benefits and cooperation and the delivery of light water reactors, in exchange for the suspension of uranium enrichment and full cooperation with the IAEA. This became the Paris Agreement, signed in Paris on 14 November 2004. The key issue in the follow-up negotiations remained uranium enrichment. Iran was not legally bound to suspend enrichment and did so voluntarily to increase the confidence of the international community. China supported Iran in this position on the ground that enrichment was an internal affair of Iran. The EU maintained that suspension was a prerequisite for further negotiations and a resumption would lead to referral to the UNSC.

In 2005 the newly elected President Ahmadinejad took a hard line and started converting uranium. The EU's diplomacy subsequently failed to convince Iran to cooperate in exchange for economic benefits. Iran was now brought before the UN Security Council, where the EU continued to play the leading role in ensuring a united international stance by adopting a 'twin-track' strategy.[45] This strategy consisted of mediating between the position of the United States, on the one hand, and China and Russia, on the other. EU diplomacy achieved results in both tracks, as the United States expressed its willingness to negotiate with Iran for the first time, subject to the condition that uranium enrichment was suspended first. The other track consisted of getting support from China and Russia, and the United States, for a 'package proposal', a set of economic and political incentives to convince Iran to cooperate with the IAEA. The resulting 'package proposal' was offered to Iran in June 2006. Iran did not accept the offer, leading to a UN Security Council resolution in July 2006 demanding that Iran suspended all enrichment activities. Resolutions that imposed sanctions followed in December 2006, March 2007, and March 2008. On 14 June

[42] Eileen Denza, 'Non Proliferation of Nuclear Weapons: The European Union and Iran', *European Foreign Affairs Review* , No.10 (2005) p. 305.

[43] Tom Sauer, 'Coercive Diplomacy by the EU: the Iranian nuclear weapons crisis', 28 *Third World Quarterly*, No. 3 (2007) p. 618.

[44] Denza, *supra* n. 42, p. 307.

[45] Report of the FCO, *Global Security: Iran* (20 February 2008) p. 18.

2008, a renewed and more extensive 'package proposal' was offered to the Iranian authorities. The European strategy for dealing with Iran has so far succeeded in uniting the positions of China and Russia, on the one hand, and the United States on the other. This has increased its international prestige, but has failed to produce real results. A failure to produce a breakthrough may damage the credibility of the EU as an international actor in the long term.[46]

Europe uses mediation and sanctions to deal with the Iranian crisis. Whereas the EU and Germany tend to favour mediation, the United Kingdom and – under Sarkozy – France put more emphasis on sanctions. In comparison, China puts a greater emphasis on mediation. Still, China has also supported a number of Security Council resolutions. The differences between the European and the Chinese approaches to Iran are most visible in terms of economic relations. While many European firms have severed their ties with Iran, Chinese-Iranian economic relations continue to expand. Thus, with regard to influence at the local level, China has clearly benefited while Europe has suffered. If we look at the global level, relevant factors are changes vis-à-vis the United States and the debate on global governance. As the European position gradually moved closer to that of the United States, Europe's value as a diplomatic ally grew. At the same time the fact that Beijing has much influence in Iran means that China, too, is an important potential partner of the United States. In fact, Europe lost part of its influence when it cut its economic ties with Iran. In terms of global governance, the Iranian crisis caused both Europe and China to compromise. In order to obtain support in the Security Council, Western proposals for resolutions had to take into account the Chinese and Russian positions. Beijing, in order to avoid an escalation of tensions between Iran and the United States, had to vote in favour of four Security Council resolutions on the Iranian nuclear programme.

To an important degree, and although Europe has been far more active, China and Europe have acted as partners in dealing with this crisis. Both sides share a preference for diplomacy, consensus-building and dialogue within existing frameworks. The Iranian nuclear crisis has provided an opportunity for Europe to present itself as an international actor with a preference for diplomatic solutions and multilateralism. By cooperating with Europe in the Iranian nuclear crisis, China has added to the credibility of Europe's efforts. In press conferences on the Iranian nuclear issue, China has called on Iran to continue dialogue with Europe. European policy preferences and initiatives have therefore strengthened the role of China, by allowing China to be integrated into the main international structure that has worked on the crisis. This position also enabled China

[46] Sauer, *supra* n. 43, p. 631.

to ward off criticism of protecting Iran too much, while ensuring that sanctions imposed did not hamper trade with Iran.

However, there is growing pressure from Europe to apply sanctions. Germany has tried to avoid unilateral European sanctions, but the United Kingdom and France under President Sarkozy have been pushing for more sanctions. China is reluctant to accept sanctions that would be detrimental to its energy interests. It delayed the referral of Iran to the Security Council, because it wanted to wait for tangible evidence that Iran was in breach of the IAEA statute. China thus insisted on the correct application of existing structures, while Europe showed a preference for operating pre-emptively as it saw the Iranian threat as more imminent. As the European countries limit their economic relations with Iran, Chinese and European local interests become less similar. While China continues to have good relations with the Iranian government, Europe would benefit more from a regime change – or at least a sharp policy change. At the same time, differences in the approach to global governance become more marked. Europe tends to support tougher sanctions that are more in line with US policy. With local interests becoming less similar, the differences between China's and Europe's approach to global governance become more visible. This makes it more difficult for Europe and China to act as partners.

Sino-European rivalry

The experience of Europe in dealing with the Darfur and Iranian crises suggests that China has an important impact on Europe's role in international security. This is most visible in regard to European influence at the local level. In both Iran and Sudan, local influence seems to a large degree to be mutually exclusive. While China has strong diplomatic and economic ties with both countries, Europe's ties are weak. The decision of the European countries to scale down their economic involvement allowed China to strengthen its relationship with Sudan and Iran. A core element in the European approach actually consists of trying to isolate the Iranian and Sudanese governments, while China's strategy is to uphold and protect its good relations with the same regimes. The European strategy of downgrading or severing ties to put pressure on certain countries is seriously weakened by the fact that China provides an alternative source of economic and political support. In this sense, the rise of China has a negative impact on Europe's position in international relations.

To some extent, Europe benefits from its close security relationship with the United States. American leadership in international security can provide those who are allied to the United States with added prestige and influence. Europe clearly remains an important partner of the United States in dealing with global hot spots, as the European and American approaches tend to be similar. The growing international influence of (undemocratic) China enhances Washington's need for 'like-minded' (democratic) security allies such as Europe, Japan, and Australia. But at the same time, the strong local influence of China and its eagerness to avoid military conflicts in countries where it has large interests make Beijing a key partner for Washington when it comes to finding fundamental solutions to crises. China's rise does not end the close relationship between Europe and the United States, but it does result in Europe not being the only major partner for the United States in dealing with crises in the Middle East and Africa.

In terms of setting norms for global governance, the emergence of China also has a limiting effect on Europe's role. In the early 1990s, with the Soviet Union having collapsed and China keeping a low profile in international relations, the West was in an ideal position to set the agenda and define the norms of global governance. When it comes to international conflict management, Europe and America prefer an outcome that contributes to the spreading of democracy and open markets. While focusing on human rights violations and support for international terrorism as the key problems, Western governments promote (pro-Western) democracy as the best long-term solution. The emergence of China and other non-Western nations as great powers forces the West to compromise. The United Nations and other international organisations can preserve their central role in global governance only if influential powers such as China are included in the system. China, as a non-Western and non-democratic state, does not benefit from a global governance system that is aimed at spreading pro-Western democracy. Its sense of insecurity with regard to separatism within China is an added reason why Beijing is reluctant to allow international organisations to interfere in countries' domestic politics. This is a setback, especially for Europe, because it relies more on soft power, norms setting, and multilateralism than the United States.

The Chinese government also needs to compromise in order to keep the international system going and to retain European support for multilateralism. China faces not just the United States but also Europe in many issues. China can never be sure that countries like Iran and Sudan will not one day improve their relations with Europe to the detriment of China. However, in the regional security crises in Iran and Sudan, the current development is that Europe's role is receding while China's position is becoming more prominent.

POTENTIAL FOR COOPERATION

Rivalry between Europe and China over influence in international conflict management exists, but this does not necessarily mean that the two cannot act as partners. There is rivalry between China and the United States, but also a growing partnership in dealing with the North Korean issue. A Sino-European partnership can work in two ways. First, the two sides can be complementary. While one side puts pressure on the local government, the other side acts as a mediator. This is what happened in Sudan. The situation may be perceived as a partnership if European pressure is genuinely aimed at creating a solution to the crisis, and if Chinese mediation involves instances of serious pressure on Khartoum. The second form of partnership is China and Europe both acting as mediators. This is what happened in the Iranian case. Both parties have been trying to prevent a military conflict by getting Iran to change its nuclear policy.

The triangular relationship between the United States, China, and Europe plays a central role in global security governance, certainly in Africa and the Middle East. Cooperation between Europe and China is a major precondition for progress in this field. The Sudan and Iran crises show that there are restrictions to the Sino-European partnership. Since Europe has fewer local interests than China, there appears to be less inclination to aim at conflict resolution or prevention. Instead, Europe tends to push for more ideological objectives, such as promoting democracy and human rights. These objectives do not necessarily constitute the best or the quickest way out of a crisis. This is most clearly visible in Sudan, but increasingly also in the Iranian crisis. China, on the other hand, is reluctant to become too involved in conflict management. Beijing wants to avoid having to choose between good relations locally or good relations with the West. China may also feel that its local interests are not directly threatened by a security crisis. Chinese reluctance to approve sanctions generally creates tension between Beijing and the European capitals over which course to take. However, in spite of the rivalry and limitations to cooperation, the two examples of Sudan and Iran suggest that there is no reason why Europe and China cannot cooperate – within certain limits – in conflict management in Africa and the Middle East.

Recuperating the European Union's Foreign Policy Machinery: Beyond Institutional Fixes

Louise van Schaik

Introduction

The European Union's foreign policy is rapidly developing, and is heavily criticised at the same time. Internationally, the EU would not be able to bear the fruits of its economic power. Its position would be undermined by a lack of military capabilities and Member States being unable to unite over important foreign policy questions. The various formats it uses for external representation, reflecting various degrees of Community competence and independent national powers of EU Member States, causes confusion among outsiders. Complex decision-making structures and a diffuse allocation of responsibilities are moreover at the root of turf wars between (staff working for) EU Member States, the Commission, the Council Presidency and the High Representative of the EU's Common Foreign and Security Policy (CFSP). The entry into force of the Lisbon Treaty would allegedly improve the situation, but its survival has now become uncertain after the Irish people rejected it in a popular vote.

This chapter will first of all discuss the various formats in which power is carefully distributed between the EU and the national level. Then it will go on to discuss the prevailing images or characteristics of EU foreign policy existing in the academic literature. In a subsequent section the institutional changes proposed in the Lisbon Treaty will be discussed. We will see that the provisions of the Lisbon Treaty are no *panacea* to cure the shortcomings resulting from the many disguises of how the EU operates and represents itself internationally. The benefits will depend to a large extent on the implementation of the provisions. The concluding sections will therefore consider what could and should be saved from Lisbon in case it would not survive, what options are available for implementing them and what other options still exist to strengthen EU foreign policy-making.

J. de Zwaan, E. Bakker and S. van der Meer (eds.), Challenges in a Changing World

The struggle over competences in EU external relations

A key question in the field of EU external or foreign policy is how competences are divided between the EU and the level of the Member States. It influences the decision-making processes which apply and the key actors involved in external representation. It moreover indicates to what extent the EU is able to operate as a unitary and coherent actor on the international stage. The most important distinction is whether a policy falls within the Common Foreign and Security Policy (CFSP) or within the range of issues covered by the European Community Treaty.[1]

Within the CFSP the EU Member States are the dominant actors. Decision-making is more intergovernmental, with only a marginal role for the European Commission and the European Parliament. The external representation of the common positions and strategies, when decided upon by consensus in the (European) Council, is taken care of by the Council Presidency, assisted by the High Representative for the CFSP, and sometimes the incoming Presidency (the so-called troika construction).

With regard to *external policy issues falling within the remit of the Community pillar*, policy-making practices depend on whether there is an exclusive competence, a shared competence or only a complementary competence for the European Community to act. As a rule of thumb, the principle of implied powers, that was established by the European Court of Justice, prescribes that in areas where the European Community (EC) has the authority to legislate, the European Commission has the authority to represent the EC externally.[2] This is understandable when one considers that international agreements often contain policy obligations affecting Community policies. The Community system would be undermined when EU Member States could shift issues from the European to the international arena without the EC being involved. This would also undermine the position of the Commission which has the power of initiative for new Community policies and is usually in the best position to assess international commitments, since it oversees the implementation of EU policies.

For areas of exclusive competence, such as trade, it is clear that Member States are no longer in the position to conduct an independent policy. Since the establishment of a common external border tariff in the 1960s, the Commission

---

1 This chapter will not discuss explicitly the external dimension of the EU's Political and Justice Cooperation on Criminal Matters, since this is generally similar to the CFSP.

2 Cf. P. Eeckhout, *External Relations of the European Union – Legal and Constitutional Foundations* (Oxford University Press 2004); F. Hoffmeister, 'Outsider or Frontrunner? Recent Developments under International and European Law on the Status of the European Union in International Organizations and Treaty Bodies', 44 *Common Market Law Review* (2007) pp. 41-68.

is in charge of representing the EC externally in trade matters. Its autonomy is curtailed somewhat by a negotiating mandate decided upon by the Council. Further supervision is exercised by a committee with Member States' representatives, which is called after the EC Treaty article in which it is established, Article 133.

For many other EU policies legislative authority is shared. Either there are both EC policies and national policies, which is the case with regard to, e.g., the environment, transport and development cooperation policies, or EC powers are only minor and complementary, implying only that a few EC policies exist, which is the case with regard to, e.g., health, education and culture. This means that in these areas the EU Member States also have authority to act on their own behalf in international affairs. The EU will normally still strive to operate with a coordinated position decided upon in the EU Council (e.g., the Environment or Transport Council), but the Member States can decide to grant authority for external representation to the Council Presidency. The Presidency will usually operate in close cooperation with the Commission and the incoming Presidency.

When EC competence exists, even if it is shared or complementary, operating with a joint position is obligatory, but Member States often argue that no such competence exists or that the thrust of the matter is in the Member States' competence. In a large number of cases brought before the European Court of Justice, the Commission has contested a decision by the Member States to deny competence in an issue, sometimes with success.[3] The Court has ruled that EC competence exists at the moment when legislative powers are transferred to the EC, but it has also recognised the independent powers of the Member States where no clear competence exists.

Beyond legal competence: the persistence of national sovereignty

For the Member States, the competence question is sensitive since the authority over external representation clearly illustrates that sovereignty has been transferred to the EU level and touches upon the fundamental characteristics of statehood. They, moreover, do not always trust the European Commission or EU Presidency to operate in their interest and to stick to its mandate.

EC competence can sometimes also be hindered because international structures are traditionally geared towards states being the prime actors. States control decision-making in international organisations, and membership is a reflection of the sovereign equality of Member States.[4] Operating with a joint

---

[3] Cf. Ibid., Eeckhout; Hoffmeister.

[4] Cf. K.V. Laatikainen & K. E. Smith, eds., *The European Union at the United Nations – Intersecting Multilateralisms* (Palgrave Macmillan 2007) p. 3.

EU representation can at times be incompatible or difficult within the context of international organisations. As a result, even in cases where EC competence exists, negotiating partners may not accept that the Commission participates in the negotiations or acts on behalf of the EU Member States, for instance because the EC is not, or cannot become, a member of the international organisation (e.g., in the World Health Organization (WHO), International Civil Aviation Organization (ICAO), International Maritime Organization (IMO)). In other cases some EU Member States may lose a prominent position if external representation is taken over by the European Union. Prominent examples are the IMF and World Bank, where individual EU Member States, notably Belgium and the Netherlands, preside over constituencies composed of both EU and non-EU states granting them a permanent seat on the board of governors.[5] Another example is the IMO where negotiating partners oppose a uniform EU representation, since they fear that it would become too dominant. Demanding reform with a view to establishing a joint EU representation can in such circumstances come at a political cost or a loss of influence for individual EU Member States.

Even when the exercise of EC competence is constrained, it is usually still considered that operating with a joint position and speaking with a single voice add to the powers of the individual EU Member States, also the bigger ones. Even the United Kingdom, France and Germany are at best middle-range powers in a multipolar world order that is rapidly emerging due to the increased powers of the upcoming economies. A joint EU representation would prevent third states, such as Russia, the United States and China, from exploiting their negotiating power vis-à-vis individual Member States. Operating as a bloc could prevent deals that may incur benefits for an individual Member State, but not for the EU as such. A common EU policy could, moreover, rightfully be considered a prerequisite in order to effectively address important cross-border policy questions, such as climate change and terrorism. There is also a clear added value in operating a common policy towards countries in the vicinity of the EU with a view to strengthening their stability and economic prosperity.

This tends also to be the case for matters falling within the remit of the *Common Foreign and Security Policy (including the European Security and Defence Policy)*, but here it is more understandable that EU Member States are still very sensitive when it comes to transferring competence. Consider, for instance, a decision to send national soldiers on a mission where it is difficult to

[5] Cf. L. Bini-Smaghi, 'A Single EU Seat in the IMF?', 42 *Journal of Common Market Studies*, No. 2 (2004) pp. 229-248; B. Coeuré & J. Pisany-Ferry (2007), 'The Governance of the European Union's international economic relations: how many voices?', in A. Sapir, ed., *Fragmented Power: Europe and the Global Economy* (Brussels, Bruegel 2007).

see a legitimate basis for decision-making at the EU level. Exactly because the CFSP covers issues related to war and peace, its decisions are more sensitive for the EU Member States in comparison to the issues where EC legislation is in place. In particular the United Kingdom is wary of deepening EU cooperation on these issues. Together with France, it is in a special position given its permanent membership of the UN Security Council, the supreme body for discussing international conflicts. The two are supposed to inform and take into account the view of the Union as a whole, but since the CFSP falls outside the remit of the European Court of Justice this obligation is not enforceable in legal terms.

A practice of mixed involvement and representation

Although structures of authority and decision-making are very different, in practice international policy issues are frequently related to both Community and CFSP policies. The use of economic sanctions is the most mentioned example, but there are many other issues. As a consequence, contractual relations with third countries (e.g., the partnership and association agreements) usually cover a range of policy areas including economic issues and typical foreign policy issues such as human rights. For this reason the European Security Strategy,[6] the EU's most important foreign policy statement, has called for a holistic approach to EU external relations. The structures beneath this holistic approach are, however, still divided and often there are also still national foreign policies at work. Indeed, most Member States have historic and cultural ties to, or economic interests in, certain countries or regions of the world. In such cases national foreign policies may complement and even strengthen EU foreign policy.

To alleviate conflicts over competences usually various 'EU representatives' are involved, such as the relevant Commissioners, the rotating Presidency, the High Representative and Foreign Ministers of the countries most involved. This, however, has led to confusion over who is in charge and to duplications and bureaucratic turf wars among support structures – it has been a key reason why politicians and EU foreign policy experts advocated institutional reform.

Below, proposals on institutional reform will be discussed. Before looking at them, some more general images of EU external relations will be analysed, both with regard to the complex structures regarding a joint approach and external representation, and with regard to its policy orientation and visibility in world affairs.

[6] 'A Secure Europe in a Better World' (12 December 2003).

Images of EU external relations

In terms of economic power the European Union is a major player in the world. With almost 500 million inhabitants, which is more than the population of the United States and Russia combined, it is the largest international trade block and generates about one fourth of the global wealth. The euro is the world's second currency and jointly the European Community and EU Member States are responsible for around 55% of total development aid, making the EU the biggest donor in the world. In the area of trade the EU has already long practised a joint policy and it is also acting with a common position and a single voice in a wide range of other policy areas. With regard to sensitive foreign policy questions the EU Member States cooperate within the framework of the CFSP. Within the related European Security and Defence Policy (ESDP), the EU is even developing a modest defence capability and is involved in small-scale military operations.

Despite this impressive overview, scholars and media observers are generally critical about the EU's capacities to act effectively in global matters. They have focused on what kind of power the EU is, how its foreign policy-making machinery is organised and how it is viewed in terms of leadership and visibility.

What kind of power?

Perhaps the most important image of the European Union's external relations is the *expectations- capabilities gap* as identified by Christopher Hill.[7] The EU would be outstanding in creating high expectations, for instance in its Council conclusions. It would, however, not have the means and instruments to act upon its statements, particularly not when it comes to what is generally considered to be the instrument of last resort, military intervention. Despite remarkable progress made in the ESDP, and the recent establishment of a European Defence Agency to work more closely on purchasing military equipment, the EU's military might is still modest in comparison to NATO, or to global players with a comparable number of inhabitants and welfare. The EU's CFSP budget is relatively small and there is hardly any staff to consider strategic foreign policy questions. ESDP missions are subject to a separate financing mechanism and depend on the *ad hoc* willingness of the EU Member States to deliver well-trained soldiers and military equipment. Therefore the image of having a limited (military) capacity still seems valid.

---

[7] Cf. C. Hill, 'The capability-expectations gap, or conceptualizing Europe's international role', 31 *Journal of Common Market Studies*, No. 3 (1993).

This brings us to a second and related image, *civilian power Europe*, already propagated in the early 1970s by Duchene.[8] Although the EU would be a political dwarf and even a military worm, it still is an economic giant. It would at times be able to use its economic powers to grant political concessions, thereby contradicting a traditional view on power being related first and foremost to military might.[9] Smith calls this the *flag follows the trade*.[10] On the flip side, the image of *fortress Europe* emerged. The EU would be an area of prosperity, but difficult to penetrate for outsiders, both with regard to export products as with regard to labour opportunities (migration). The EU would moreover dump its own subsidized agricultural products on world markets, thereby ruining agricultural sectors in developing countries. As a result, attention to how development policy and other EU policies interrelate, notably trade and agricultural policies, has increased. This focus on *policy coherence* or consistency concentrates both on the substance of policies and on how policy-making processes could be better integrated.[11]

According to Manners, the EU has increasingly been able to influence world politics by its emphasis on normative issues, such as human rights and environmental policies.[12] It would have been transformed into a *normative power*, able to influence what is considered to be 'normal' in world politics. Its ability to do so would derive from it being a normatively constructed polity itself, and from its ability to draw upon its economic powers (the concept thereby builds upon the civilian power concept). Prominent examples include the EU's efforts to establish the International Criminal Court and to keep the Kyoto Protocol alive despite strong US opposition.[13] Where Manners first and foremost referred to the EU's ability to frame discussions, scholars more recently emphasise the EU's ability to literally set global standards with regard to many economic goods and services being produced. It would be a *regulatory power*.[14] Another recent

---

[8] F. Duchêne, 'Europe's Role in World Peace', in R. Mayne, ed., *Europe Tomorrow. Sixteen Europeans Look Ahead* (London, Collins 1972) pp. 32-47.

[9] J. Orbie, ed., *Europe's Global Role: External Policies of the European Union* (Aldershot, Ashgate 2008).

[10] M. Smith, 'Does the flag follow the trade? "Politicisation" and the emergence of a European foreign policy', in J. Peterson & H. Sjursen, eds., *A Common Foreign Policy for Europe? Competing visions of the CFSP* (London/New York, Routledge 1998).

[11] CEPS, *Policy Coherence for Development in the EU Council: Strategies for the way forward* (Brussels, Centre for European Policy Studies 2006).

[12] I. Manners, 'Normative Power Europe: A Contradiction in Terms?', in: 40 *Journal of Common Market Studies*, No. 2 (2002) pp. 235-258.

[13] M.L.P. Groenleer & L.G. van Schaik, 'United We Stand?, The European Union's International Actorness in the Case of the International Criminal Court and the Kyoto Protocol', 45 *Journal of Common Market Studies*, No. 5 (2007) pp. 969-998.

[14] E.g., A. Sapir, 'Europe and the global economy', in Sapir, ed., *supra* n. 5.

development, coined by Keukeleire, is that the EU also increasingly influences structures of international politics. By combining its economic (including aid), normative and military powers it would increasingly manage to operate as a *structural power*,[15] leaving lasting effects on global developments.

A unified position and external representation?

One of the main criticisms with regard to how the EU organises its external relations is its *lack of a single voice*. Kissinger's question about which phone number to dial to speak to Europe clearly illustrates what is at stake. Authority over EU external relations is unclear and diffuse as has been described above when discussing the competence struggle between the national and European level. The creation of the position of High Representative of the CFSP to assist the rotating Presidency represented only a partial answer. A related issue is the EU's inability to unite over tough questions of foreign policy, such as the war in Iraq, or more recently the independence of Kosovo. Also the ever-lasting EU coordination meetings contribute to the image of Europe being indecisive. Its internal discussions on which position to take and how to develop its foreign policy directions involve a lot of navel gazing, with limited attention for the rest of the world. A process of the 'Brusselsisation' of EU foreign policy-making would have occurred, where senior diplomats of EU Member States spend the majority of their time in meetings of Council bodies and less time in their own capitals or in meetings with third countries. The shift towards 'Brusselsisation' was accelerated by the increased foreign- policy making capacity within the Council.[16] The High Representative's Policy Unit can be considered an indigenous foreign-policy making capacity, although it is modest in terms of size.

The strengthening of the Council Secretariat as the EU's foreign policy centre has highlighted the tensions with the EU's most important administrative body, the European Commission. Whereas this organisation is in charge of implementing aid, trade and other external policies, EU external relations often also include political dialogue. At this stage the EU Presidency and High Representative of the CFSP step in. It is often said that due to good personal contacts, notably the choice to appoint Javier Solana as the first High Representative, *coherence problems* between the Commission-led external relations and Council-led CFSP positions have been diminished. Perhaps this should not come as a surprise given that Solana's position was new and resources available for exter-

---

[15] Stephan Keukeleire, 'The European Union as a Diplomatic Actor: Internal, Traditional and Structural diplomacy', in W. Rees & M. Smith, eds., *International Relations of the European Union* (London, SAGE Publications 2008 [forthcoming]).

[16] The HR CFSP position was created by the Amsterdam Treaty (1998).

nal relations were still first and foremost located at the Commission. At the working level the situation proved more cumbersome and resulted in duplications of activities, contradictory statements and confusion over authority.[17] This has added to the image of the EU not being an effective global player.

Europe, leading the world?

At the same time, the Union's external relations have become more important as a means to increase the visibility of the EU and to justify its added value towards an increasingly Eurosceptic population. The EU would be able to provide shelter against the negative effects of globalisation. Its size would ensure that influence can be exerted in areas where particularly the smaller Member States would otherwise not be able to play a significant role. Its *international leadership* and focus on seeking multilateral solutions to address international policy problems fit within the logic of its own construction. Other parts of the world have noticed the benefits of European integration, but they have also been critical, arguing that the EU would be too mild-mannered and on the sidelines in global politics, behaving like a 'giant Switzerland'.[18] This appears to be another flipside to the civilian power ideal. Establishing a well-functioning trade relationship, even if linked to conditionality with regard to human rights, will not be sufficient to guarantee the emergence of peace and prosperity in (all) other parts of the world. For some of the world's most complicated and difficult conflicts, it will be inevitable that the EU will become actively engaged in order to find long-lasting and stable solutions. For such situations to be credible, it may require more than just being able to deploy small-scale military operations.

The provisions of the Lisbon Treaty

The previous section illustrated that criticism of the EU's international performance centres around a lack of (military) capabilities, a unified and coherent external representation and a visible leadership role matching its economic powers. The new provisions of the Lisbon Treaty mainly address the latter two. They address concerns with regard to the system of a rotating Presidency in representing the EU in the world, coherence problems between the Commission and Council and foreign-policy making capacities.

---

[17] Cf. A. Missiroli, 'Introduction: A tale of two pillars – and an arch', in: *The EU Foreign Service: how to build a more effective common policy*, European Policy Centre, Working Paper No. 28, 2007.

[18] Cf. G. Rachman, 'Irrelevance, Europe's logical choice', *Financial Times* (20 May 2008); K. Mahbubani, 'Europe is a geopolitical dwarf', *Financial Times* (22 May 2008).

First of all, the Lisbon Treaty would abolish the term European Community, which is considered to be confusing by outsiders, and replace it by the European Union. The EU would obtain legal personality and Community competence is to be renamed as Union competence. The EU would be able to accede to international organisations and treaties, as the EC does today. The renaming of EU resembles intentional desires to merge the CFSP into the Community structure, but this proved to be a bridge too far. Two declarations have been attached to the EU treaty to underline that the CFSP would continue to be subject to specific intergovernmental procedures and rules.

Secondly, a set of general provisions on the Union's external action was decided upon. Article 21 of the Lisbon Treaty stipulates that action on the international scene 'shall be guided by the principles which have inspired its own creation, development and enlargement, and which it seeks to advance in the wider world: democracy, rule of law, the universality and indivisibility of human rights and fundamental freedoms, respect for human dignity, the principles of equality and solidarity, and respect for the principles of the United Nations Charter and international law.' The statement is particularly relevant for external relations where a Community competence exists, such as trade, development cooperation and climate change policies. The CFSP also has to adhere to it, but it would be difficult to oblige the Member States to stick to the Treaty objectives, since CFSP activities would continue to fall outside the remit of the European Court of Justice.

Thirdly and probably most importantly, the Lisbon Treaty would establish an 'EU foreign policy coordinator'. Officially the post is entitled *High Representative of the Union for Foreign Affairs and Security Policy*. Although this title is similar to the current position of High Representative CFSP Solana, the scope and mandate of the new function have considerably expanded. It merges the current High Representative position and the position of the Commissioner for External Relations, supplemented by the chairmanship of the Foreign Affairs Council, and the vice-Presidency of the Commission, which has led to a common use of the acronym *HR/VP*.[19] His or her tasks would include conducting the CFSP and ensuring the consistency of the Union's external action.[20] Another task is to supervise a new, still to be established European External Action Service (EEAS) composed of national diplomats and Commission and Council staff dealing with external and foreign policy. Although the Lisbon Treaty provides for the establishment of the EEAS, its scope, organisation and functioning would still need to be decided upon. It was subject to intense debate within the Commission, the Council Secretariat and the capitals of the EU Mem-

---

19 Missiroli, *supra* n. 17.

20 Art. 18, Treaty on European Union (Lisbon Treaty).

ber States before the Irish no vote jeopardised the entry into force of the Lisbon Treaty. A sensitive question is whether the Member States would allow the EEAS to become a genuine diplomatic service. Another sensitive question is which parts of the Commission's services dealing with external relations (e.g., DG Development, DG Trade) would be transferred to the new organisation. Since the EEAS would be working both for the intergovernmental and hitherto Council-led, CFSP, and for the hitherto Commission-led areas of external relations, a key question appeared to be where the EEAS would be hosted, or whether a hybrid organisation should be decided upon (e.g., an agency).

The establishment of the EEAS would clearly affect the practice of EU diplomatic representations in third countries. Currently more than 40,000 officials work in the foreign ministries of the Member States and the approximately 1,500 diplomatic missions abroad. Each Member State maintains between 40 and 160 diplomatic missions, while the Commission has a network of over 120 delegations around the world. In comparison, the United States has about one-third of the human resources that the EU devotes to diplomacy and one-fifth of its diplomatic missions.[21] With the entry into force of the Lisbon Treaty, the EC delegations would become EU delegations reporting to the HR/VP. This means they would need to increase and improve their political reporting capabilities. One of the problems is that the Commission has never recruited staff for traditional diplomatic tasks and has never put adequate resources into training. Most of the current staff lack the specific know-how and expertise of modern diplomacy and international crisis management, as their culture is still predominantly one of (development cooperation) project management and trade. An important question is whether the EU delegations would be able to take over some of the activities of the embassies of the Member States or whether they would remain complementary to them.

The creation of the more centralised foreign policy position HR/VP and EEAS raised concerns about too much power being placed in the hands of one person, and foreign policy objectives prevailing over economic, environmental and development cooperation objectives. However, others emphasised the continued existence of multiple players in EU external relations, while arguing in favour of strong coordinating powers for the HR/VP. Notably competition with yet another newly created position, the permanent European Council President, has been feared.[22] Competition with fellow Commissioners and the Commission President would likely occur as well. Finally, also the role of the rotating Presi-

---

[21] Missiroli, *supra* n. 17.

[22] According to Art. 15 of the Lisbon Treaty the European Council President will 'at his level and in that capacity, ensure the external representation of the Union on issues concerning its common foreign and security policy, without prejudice to the powers of the HR/VP.'

dency in EU's external relations could continue to exist, although probably less prominently. The rotating Presidency would continue to chair the general affairs Council and the 'regular' Ministerial formations (environment, agriculture, etc.) and Coreper (Council of Representatives).

Issues have been raised with regard to whom the HR/VP would be accountable to. According to the Lisbon Treaty he or she would be appointed by the European Council, acting by a qualified majority, with the agreement of the President of the Commission (and may end the appointment by the same procedure). The HR/VP would, however, also have an accountability relationship with the European Parliament since he or she would be one of the members of the College of Commissioners. The Treaty stipulates that Commission procedures apply when the HR/VP is exercising responsibilities within the Commission, so it seems the European Parliament would be able to hold him or her accountable for issues where an EC competence exists. However, when there would be a hearing in the Parliament, it would politically be difficult to claim that the person appointed by the European Council is not fit for the job.

Finally, the Treaty of Lisbon would bring more powers to the European Parliament in external relations. Although the CFSP would continue to fall outside its reach, except for some power over its budget, the EP would obtain the powers to reject nearly all international agreements to which the EU subscribes.[23] This means it could threaten not to ratify an agreement when certain of its demands would not be taken into account. Whether the European Parliament would start to make use of its expanded powers remains the question, since in political terms it may prove difficult to reject high-profile international treaties that are the result of long and intense negotiations.

Too high hopes of institutional reform?

Taken together, the Lisbon Treaty would have implied considerable changes for EU foreign policy making. After the Irish no vote and critical voices by, among others, the Presidents of Poland and the Czech Republic, it has become politically incorrect to further discuss the implementation of the Lisbon Treaty. At the same time, some have remarked that world events will not stop and wait for the EU institutions to catch up. Recent tensions with Russia, following the conflict in South Ossetia, have underlined the need for a stronger external representation. EU foreign policy making would be in desperate need of reform. Less openly it has been mentioned that the HR/VP position and EEAS could still be put in place, if EU Member States would allow it.

---

[23] See Art. 218 (6a), TFU.

The more important and politically difficult issue is that the HR/VP and EEAS would only be likely to contribute to making EU's external relations more coherent and effective when they would obtain a broad remit and sufficient resources. One could easily image these institutions being able to push a powerful EU foreign policy, when within them development cooperation resources would be combined with trade powers and foreign policy instruments. But would Member States and the Commission President allow such a bundling of power to occur? It would require several Commissioners to be subordinated to the HR/VP. Member States would have to accept a permanent spokesperson in a range of international activities, which are now the remit of the rotating Presidency. The HR/VP would, moreover, be likely to press them to agree more quickly and decisively on sensitive foreign policy questions. The EU's trade and aid relations would become more political. From a legal perspective it could be argued that authority, responsibility and accountability would need to be clearly attributed, which may be tricky when the Treaty in force would still formally grant these powers to the rotating Presidency. Perhaps most importantly, whether the EU would be coherent and effective would still depend on EU Member States being able to reach consensus on important foreign policy questions. A mandate by the Council would still be needed for most policy directions.

Final remarks

Strengthening EU unity in external representation does not seem to depend mainly on institutional rules, but on a willingness by EU Member States to give up more easily specific foreign policy preferences in the spirit of compromise. In addition, it is clear that the institutional changes proposed in the Lisbon Treaty mainly address the concerns regarding a unified and coherent external representation, and those regarding the EU's ability to be more visible in international politics. It does not address the sensitive question of scaling up (military) capabilities. With the establishment of a European Defence Agency, and the growing number of EU missions, some progress has been made. However, for most Member States, NATO is and will remain the most important organisation for military cooperation.

Finally, it seems relevant to look at what other improvements could be considered when Lisbon will not survive and when also the HR/VP and EEAS proposals would be dead and buried. In such a situation an important question is how the system of the rotating Presidency could be made more effective. The burden of external representation is currently extremely heavy. It could be considered to offer more support by the Council Secretariat and/or Commission to the rotating Presidency. Member States could also decide to work more often with a lead negotiator covering international issues on behalf of the EU over a longer term (under the formal responsibility of the Presidency). Other issues could be to restructure the organisation of the Commission (DG external relations, DG development, DG trade, etc.) and the Council Secretariat. More training could be offered to Commission officials and diplomats from EU Member States on EU foreign policy objectives and methods, and how 'Europe' is viewed in the world.

Although a number of the negative images of EU foreign policy would undoubtedly continue to exist, it would still be important to consider such small steps. In a world order that is increasingly becoming multipolar and in which other countries look to the EU to demonstrate normative leadership, it cannot afford to stay on the sidelines.

CLOSING THE GAP: PERSPECTIVES ON HOW TO TACKLE THE EU'S LEGITIMACY CRISIS

Mendeltje van Keulen

'There are no riots, no extremists in power, no abrogation of civil liberties, no postponement of elections. Still, I think there is a crisis in Europe. It is a crisis in minds rather than on the streets—and disorder in the mind, in our ideas and loyalties, can be even more dangerous than its more visible counterparts. Europe is suffering a crisis of legitimacy.'

Larry Siedentop[1]

INTRODUCTION

The question of how to remedy the legitimacy deficit of the European Union's politics and policies seems more urgent than ever in the EU's history. Until the 1990s, the EU institutions and the member states were primarily focused on effectively delivering policy output. The Maastricht ratification crises in 1992 initiated a period of structural concern with regard to the EU's democratic underpinnings, with incidental shock waves following the subsequent negative referendum outcomes (most notably those in France and the Netherlands in June 2005 and in Ireland in June 2008). The cumbersome ratification of much wanted treaty revisions constitutes, however, the tip of an iceberg of public discontent with EU policy-making that is perceived as being elitist, disembedded or 'post-democratic'.[2] The depth of the latest institutional impasse on the Treaty of Lisbon suggests that the challenge of legitimizing the EU is here to stay for the coming years.

This chapter reflects upon a number of cited remedies to enhance the legitimacy of the European Union. As reviewing cures imply a basic consensus over

[1] Larry Siedentop (Kebble College, Oxford) is the author of the highly acclaimed and best-selling essay 'Democracy in Europe' (2000). More recent contributions by Larry Siedentop on the EU's democratic deficit include: 'A crisis of legitimacy', *Prospect Magazine*, special issue: 'A Europe of illusions' (July 2005); and 'No to this EU proves self-respect', *NRC Handelsblad* (12 July 2008).

[2] C. Crouch, *Post-democracy* (Cambridge, Polity Press 2004).

J. de Zwaan, E. Bakker and S. van der Meer (eds.), Challenges in a Changing World

the diagnosis, the issue of legitimacy is first unravelled and its dimensions identified. Subsequently, attention turns towards solutions that have been proposed. Three broad methods of re-legitimating the EU are discussed: first, improving the EU's output and performance; second, communication strategies aimed at developing the European public sphere; and, third, remedies under the heading 'politicisation' and strengthening the political domain of European Union affairs. The discussion in the final section focuses on the merits and potential pitfalls of these remedies and the particular role national politicians can play in enhancing the EU's legitimacy by their actions within the national political arena.

DEFINING THE PROBLEM

Unravelling legitimacy

Overseeing the heated scholarly and policy debates on the EU's alleged democratic deficit, to say that the EU and its member states suffer from problems in this respect is like stating the obvious. But although legitimacy is commonly assumed as a crucial requirement for any stable polity, including that of the EU, the concept is notoriously ambiguous. First, legitimacy cannot be measured or enforced and it is by definition rather implicit: it becomes problematic once it is disputed. Second, the problem is multifaceted: indicators for malaise range from voter disaffection, political extremism and the demise of traditional party membership, via non-compliance with EU rules and declining public support for EU policies, towards complaints about the simplicity of national EU debates by technocratic elites.[3] Third, both the definition of the problem and the assessment of solutions cannot be separated from differing perspectives regarding the nature of the EU. On the one hand, there are those who regard the EU as a particular form of special-purpose organisation, which can and should rely on providing common goods for the citizens of its member states. On the other side, an image of the EU prevails as nascent polity with particular legitimisation strategies. As the debate continues, 'whether describing a threatening superstate or a welcome replacement for the national state, Europhiles and Europhobes alike portray a fictional future disguised as a fact'.[4] Both schools judge fundamentally differently about the EU's capacity to provide legitimate policies and politics and the necessity to do so. Any analysis of how to re-legitimize the EU should thus start by unravelling the concept.[5]

[3] M. van Keulen & T. van den Brink, 'Towards Strengthened Legitimacy of Dutch EU Policy', in: 6 *Horizons stratégiques*, No. 5 (2007) pp. 112-116.

[4] A. Menon, *Europe: the state of the Union* (London, Atlantic Books 2007) p. 42.

[5] See for an extensive discussion of the concept of legitimacy: WRR [Dutch Scientific Council for Government Policy], *Rediscovering Europe in the Netherlands* (Amsterdam, Amsterdam University Press 2007).

Legitimacy does not equal acceptance

That the lack of a clear concept definition can give rise to serious controversy becomes clear when efforts to enhance the EU's legitimacy are equated, in public discourse, with attempts to strengthen public support or acceptance of the EU.[6] Inherent in the traditional concept of legitimacy in democratic systems is the recognition that (democratic) politics by necessity involves compromise. Politics is a process of give and take, the outcomes of which may not always reflect individual preferences. This 'diffuse support' implies a stable belief and acceptance of the leaders' right to rule and citizens who may recognise a particular policy as legitimate, even when they do not necessarily support it.[7]

By separating legitimacy from support, it is acknowledged that (European) policies do not necessarily require the assent of all of the citizens, all of the time. The EU cannot and should not always be loved or liked by the respective constituencies of the member states and its decisions may be individually disputed and contested. But if policies, perceived as coming from Brussels, face consistent and widespread opposition among European citizens, there is reason to reconsider the legitimacy of the EU as a polity, however disputed the precise nature of that polity may be.

Lack of legitimacy does not equal a democratic deficit

A second relevant distinction in which the role of perception becomes relevant is that between legitimacy and the *democratic deficit*. Crucial here is the requirement of representation: the extent to which the democratic process guarantees that preferences are reflected in political decision-making. The assumption behind input legitimacy is that the more (often) citizens are involved in decision-making, the higher the possibility that they will accept the outcomes. The corollary of representation is public control or accountability: the degree to which politicians can be properly held accountable by the electorate for their actions at the EU level.

The literature focusing on the democratic side of the legitimacy discussion has been accused of deploying different, sometimes unclear standards in order to measure the degree of democracy.[8] But that the EU also has problems in this

[6] Beetham and Lord warn in this respect against the tendency to over-simplify and 'to reduce the many dimensions of legitimacy to a single one: to legality or procedural regularity alone, to effective performance, or to consent, as the case may be' (as quoted in Chr. Meyer, 'Political Legitimacy and the Invisibility of Politics: Exploring the European Union's Communication Deficit', 37 *Journal of Common Market Studies*, No. 4 (1999) p. 618).

[7] D. Easton, *A framework for political analysis* (Englewood Cliffs, Prentice Hall 1965).

[8] Chr. Lord, 'Assessing Democracy in a Contested Polity', 39 *Journal of Common Market Studies*, No. 4 (2001) pp. 641-661.

vein is clear, if only because many citizens regard the EU as, at best, a 'pseudo-democracy'.[9] On the one hand, the European Parliament has not yet acquired co-decision powers in fields where decision-making is shared or 'pooled' by the member states at the EU level. On the other hand, national parliaments in the member states fall short of making politicians accountable for their EU-level actions. This is not only because of structural impediments in their own structures which prevent them from effectively controlling government representatives, but also because any government representative can be outvoted by a qualified majority in the Council of Ministers. The EU's structure, in short, empowers governments and disempowers parliaments.

Seen from the perspective of representation and accountability, the solution for the EU's 'democratic disease'[10] lies primarily in improving its democratic mechanisms. Many investments have been made in the past decade to remedy this situation by piecemeal institutional and procedural reform – the latest invention being the much hailed 'orange card' procedure, by which a group of national parliaments can raise objections against newly proposed European legislation. More radical options for reform include a further strengthening of a true European government at the EU level, for example by holding an open contest for the post of European Commission President.[11] A third stream of approaches, coined 'post-parliamentary', focus on making the work of the EU's institutions more transparent and to increase public participation by public and civil groups.[12]

The relevance of output and identification

These types of solutions are sharply contested; however, from 'the other side' as described above. This is the perspective from where the EU is primarily regarded as a functional regulatory organisation, which is 'necessarily undemocratic'[13] and '...at its best when it is boring.'[14] When talking about ways to enhance the public legitimacy of this type of organisation, the focus is on delivering output, which most international organisations rely on. The legitimacy of

---

[9] Siedentop (2008), *supra* n. 1.

[10] Ph. Riès, *L'Europe: malade de la démocratie* (Paris, Guillard).

[11] See, e.g., S. Hix, *What's wrong with the EU and how to fix it* (London, Polity 2008); and A. van Staden, *The right to govern: the democratic legitimacy of the European Union* (The Hague, Clingendael paper 2003).

[12] Chr. Lord & D. Beetham, 'Legitimizing the EU: is there a post-parliamentary basis for its legitimation?', 39 *Journal of Common Market Studies*, No. 3 (2001) pp. 443-463.

[13] Riès, *supra* n. 10.

[14] A. Moravcsik, 'Brussels Diary: the EU is at its best when it is most boring', *Prospect Magazine*, Issue 115 (October 2005).

NATO, for example, is in this view mainly derived from the security perceptions it offers to its member states, while the World Trade Organization draws its legitimacy from the perceived economic benefits of removing trade barriers on a global scale. The EU's effectiveness in delivering concrete output by solving problems is for these authors the most important source of its legitimacy.

A last dimension of legitimacy has thus far remained uncovered, namely that of identification. The idea of a 'government *of* the people' rests upon the assumption that citizens who feel attached to their community will be more inclined to accept public policy decisions. For the EU, this implies that its policies become more legitimate the more citizens feel a sense of belonging and connection to the European Union as a polity. Thus far, there is a common agreement that identification with the EU has accordingly had the character of a functional process among a small, Euro-centric circle of politicians, senior officials, lobbyists and a small group of higher educated citizens. Although opinion polls show that many citizens recognise that in times of globalisation and internationalisation the EU is the place to address cross-border problems, for many of the EU's citizens allegiance remains primarily attached to their locality, city or region. Whether this empirical finding is consistent with ideal types again depends on the vision one holds about the Union. For some, any feelings of a European identity will always remain a composite of diverse national and European elements. Others regard the lack of a European *demos* as being explanatory for the legitimacy problems experienced in this domain and suggest the development of a European public sphere where citizens and politicians interact and communicate. The idea is that increasing the engagement of intermediary actors within that space, such as political parties and civil society actors, will build bridges between politicians, policy-makers and the citizens, which would strengthen political arrangements and ultimately lead to more identification with this European community.

Interrelated dimensions

These four dimensions of legitimacy (representation and accountability, output and identification) can function independently of each other. European citizens may acknowledge the legitimacy of the democratic process, even where this leads to decisions which they do not (always) like. A minimum degree of identification with the EU as a policy may lead to greater tolerance of policies which do not correspond with individual preferences. Similarly, European citizens may have their doubts about the functioning of the political process at the EU level, yet accept these shortcomings because they feel connected to 'Europe' as an idea. But if the policies of a rather abstract and uncontrollable organisation, towards which people feel no sense of belonging, fall short in the longer term, legitimacy problems become more serious. People may become sceptical about the political system that is held accountable for these (unwanted) outputs, as well as on how their preferences are systematically (mis)represented. This is the situation with which the member states of the EU are currently confronted.

The identification of the composite elements of legitimacy provides a useful starting point for discussing proposals about how to solve the gap. For one thing, it points attention to the fact that most debates on how to increase the EU's legitimacy have focused on the institutional dimension, whereas this is only one part of the puzzle. One account of the elusiveness of the solutions is to be found in the work of Beetham and Lord.[15] The main difficulty for the EU in their view lies in tension between democracy and identity. Democracy requires at least enough of an identity for people to accept that their deliberations and electoral processes take place *within* a particular community. However, there is no guarantee that this sense of identity will be available at the moment a political system democratises its decision-making. *Eurobarometer* surveys consistently indicate that European citizens identify overwhelmingly more strongly with national states than with the EU as a polity. As long as this is so, those approaches to EU legitimacy which focus on strengthening representation, but entail a high probability of national democratic institutions being overridden by European ones, could even have the opposite effect.

Discussing remedies

In the following sections, three main headings in this menu will be discussed from the perspective of the different elements of legitimacy: first, the often cited focus on output and performance to address the EU's delivery deficit; second, strategies deployed to 'communicate Europe'; and, third, remedies focusing on the purposeful politicisation or political highlighting of European issues both at the national and the EU level.

Improving EU output

From a very pragmatic point of view, the most direct way to address the EU´s alleged delivery deficit is by presenting clear policy solutions to the concerns and problems of European citizens in their day-to-day lives. Presenting output legitimacy as the core solution to the current problems was the response of the European Commission and the heads of state to the ratification crises haunting the draft European Constitution in 2005. It also forms the core of a plea, just

[15] Lord & Beetham, *supra* n. 12.

after the Irish rejection of 'Lisbon', to 'go on doing things that matter to Europeans and the world.'[16] But providing more added value by Brussels or making its real achievements more visible to the public could also work positively on the other dimensions of legitimacy. If national politicians, political parties or members of parliament would proudly present EU policies that do, in fact, work – concerted European action against unfair competition or lowering mobile phone costs within the internal market – they would perhaps no longer fear being held accountable by their electorate for what they do or do not do in Brussels. A positive perception of the EU as a successful polity might foster feelings of identification by European citizens. It has been argued that precisely this mechanism has contributed to the weak but nascent identification with the concept of Europe: not so much due to a shared history or 'essence', but to an appraisal of its common policies over the past fifty years.

This perspective of the EU's legitimacy as solely output-driven is problematic, however, in at least two respects. One is that an organisation whose legitimacy is only based upon criteria of delivery or effectiveness is very vulnerable, as experiences with the EU have shown. Once its outcome becomes disputed, the legitimacy is under fire. As the expectations of citizens have for long been mainly instrumental and functional, their declining appreciation of decisions of a more contested nature are reflected in empirical findings, including opinion polls pointing towards declining approval ratings.[17] The EU's mere focus on output has also contributed to the image of an elitist and technocratic playground for politicians and bureaucratic elites. Due to broader macro level developments such as globalisation, unemployment and threats to the traditional welfare state, citizens feel threatened by the loss of existing safety nets and blame the EU for that.

A second and related problem is that at the same time the EU institutions, by the voices of national politicians, aspire to be much more than a functional delivery organisation, merely relying on results. In the course of the 1990s, the growing impact of policies and regulations from Brussels, the creation of the euro and eastward enlargement have created the impression, for European citizens, that power is escaping towards the EU level.[18] From this perspective, the process by which the EU makes policies both at the national and the EU level is characterised by opaque, technocratic and undemocratic politics. These con-

[16] Timothy Garton Ash, 'Instead of bullying the Irish, Europe should be working on plan D - and E', *The Guardian* (19 June 2008).

[17] H. Schmitt & J. Thomassen, *Political Representation and Legitimacy in the European Union* (Oxford, Oxford University Press 1999)

[18] Siedentop (2005), *supra* n. 1.

cerns are set aside as misperceptions by national politicians – but 'if perceptions of citizens contradict the reality, then the latter is wrong.'[19]

The realisation, from the part of both politicians and citizens, that the outputs of EU policy do not always create positive sum games, does not imply that output legitimacy is no longer a valid way to re-legitimize the EU. However, it does imply that a sole focus on results is insufficient, if it is not matched with parallel investments into the alternative sources of legitimacy. To begin with the input side: without sufficient attention for mechanisms of representation and accountability, there is no incentive for politicians to actively contribute towards improving the EU's output, let alone to credit the EU for the results. This is because the EU's political structure facilitates a 'perverse incentive' for national politicians to claim EU successes as their own and blame the EU for results that are less politically appealing. Although this strategy may be electorally appealing in the short term, it is obvious that it feeds into negative misperceptions of the EU by citizens. One way to soften this very persistent reflex is the introduction of procedural safeguards to the policy process: openness, transparency and the adequate representation of citizen groups and societal interests within the policy process. However, due to problems with representation and access of these groups, participatory democracy is a challenge in itself.[20] In the end, if citizens are to value the significance of concrete policy results, adequate accountability mechanisms must be in place to control the actions of politicians. Third, in order to feed into the identity dimension of legitimacy, these results have to be adequately communicated to the citizens. Here we touch upon a second strand of solutions: that of communication on the EU.

Communicating the EU

A well-known reflex of politicians when confronted with public opposition regarding EU issues (negative referenda, falling turnouts for European Parliament elections) is to 'spin' the problem away from the contents and towards an alleged lack of knowledge. This hypothesis was sustained by the results of opinion research into the outcomes of the French, Dutch and Irish referenda, all of which were driven by a reported lack of information from the side of the voters.[21] In

---

[19] As is argued by Ries, *supra* n. 10.

[20] E. van den Berg & T. Brandsen, *The Dutch Third Sector and the European Union: Connecting Citizens to Brussels* (The Hague, WRR publication no. 22, 2007)

[21] In the Irish case, survey and focus groups revealed that 42% of people said they had voted 'no' due to a lack of information or understanding (source: Millward Brown IMS, September 2008). In the Dutch case, the lack of knowledge was an important explanation (see: Kees Aarts & Henk van der Kolk, eds., *Nederlanders en Europa: Het referendum over de Europese grondwet* (Amsterdam, Bert Bakker 2005)).

order to better communicate Europe, a number of strategies are feasible, including government-sponsored information campaigns and partnership with organisations which stimulate debates on European issues; improving attention for European co-operation in civic education as well as attempts to enhance media attention for European affairs.[22]

From the perspective of the above-mentioned legitimacy dimensions, there is much to say for this line of thought. Obviously, all forms of participation and engagement are based upon a certain basic level of knowledge about the available channels and ways for influence. In order for politicians to adequately represent the electorate's views on a particular matter, it is necessary that the voters are informed about the issues at play. Advocating institutional reform to an electorate which does not perceive its own knowledge about the EU as adequate is particularly difficult. A lack of information increases the perceived complexity and lack of transparency of the EU (as demonstrated by the highly effective 'no' campaign in the June 2008 Irish referendum: 'if you don't know, vote no'), which complicates the satisfactory functioning of accountability mechanisms even further. If the scope, the content and the effects of EU policies are not made sufficiently clear to the public, output legitimacy is also jeopardised. And it is clear that any kind of affection towards or positive identification with the EU is based upon a proper understanding about what the EU is and how it affects daily lives.

However, there are at least two problems to this approach. First, a serious complication for all recent efforts to improve EU policy communication is that they often land on seemingly unfertile grounds. Government EU communication strategies are easily perceived as a management strategy, steered from above, without taking into account how essential deep, pre-existing mind-sets are in judging new information. A well-known mechanism in cognitive psychology is that people are biased in picking up information that confirms existing beliefs, whilst ignoring information that may suggest alternative views on a particular matter. This has proven to be a serious impediment for successive 'yes' campaigns in the member states.

Second, the problem with EU communication is that it is essentially about a fragmented system of governance which depoliticises conflict and obfuscates political accountability. Just because the complications to this system are often gratefully used by national politicians to circumvent public scrutiny and externalise public dissatisfaction to the EU, it takes a double effort to re-steer attention towards the virtues of the same system.[23] This is one of the reasons

---

22 See, e.g., the Commission's White Paper on a European Communication Policy (CEC 2006) which complements the 'Plan D' response to the institutional crisis. The Dutch government presented a national action plan for Communicating Europe in December 2007.

23 Meyer, *supra* n. 6.

why all recent referenda have demonstrated the efforts for politicians to display confidence and passion in attempting to persuade their electorate to vote 'yes'.[24]

To add insult to injury, third, information campaigns and media attention concerning the EU is normally incidental and focused upon isolated 'events' such as elections for the European Parliament or national referendums on EU issues,[25] whereas people have a conservative tendency to only gradually adapt existing mind-sets.

This does not mean that information and communication cannot contribute to the legitimacy deficit. Rather paradoxically, the crucial influence that communicative strategies of political elites and parties may have on the way citizens end up identifying with Europe can be demonstrated by the results of similar strategies in the past.[26] In recent years, politicians in a number of member states have adopted a populist 'framing' of pro- or anti-European standpoints, thereby fuelling fears of a European 'superstate'. Moreover, the line between information and propaganda has sometimes deliberately been crossed, as the implicit agenda of the EU's institutions was one of persuasion instead of communicating Europe.[27] In the eyes of many citizens, the EU has become simply a 'soulless' and remote technocratic project and any attempt to contribute to this image will be associated with propaganda. There are lessons to be learned from this experience. First, the effects of communication can be considerable, but, second, if politicians do not take seriously (the effects of) these reception strategies and existing mental blocks (for the creation of which they were mostly responsible), information will not 'land'. Perhaps more importantly, the relative success of the aforementioned 'blaming and shaming' by national politicians, as compared to long-standing efforts by the EU institutions to increase public interest in their operations, demonstrates that communication on the EU should be focused at the local, regional or national level. These offer political spaces to which citizens do feel an allegiance, for which there are channels available and which remains the most likely location, in the absence of Europe-wide mass media and politics.

One particular requirement in this respect is that national differences are to be taken into account. Schmidt differentiates between compound polities, including the EU itself and Germany and Italy, and more simple polities such as

---

[24] 'Charlemagne: Democracy in Europe', *The Economist* (21 June 2008).

[25] H.-J. Trenz, 'Understanding media impact on European integration: enhancing or restricting the scope of legitimacy of the EU', 30 *Journal of European Integration*, No. 2 (2008) pp. 291-309.

[26] See V. Schmidt, 'The EU: Democratic Legitimacy in a Regional State?', 42 *Journal of Common Market Studies*, No. 5 (2004) pp. 975-997.

[27] J. Lodge, 'Transparency and democratic legitimacy', *Journal of Common Market Studies* (1994).

the United Kingdom and France. In the first case, including a fragmented political system such as the Netherlands, politicians have developed this vital communicative skill only on a very insubstantial level. In these member states in particular, the challenge lies in an investment in the quality of structural and consistent communicative discourses on EU policies within the member states. Efforts should focus on communicative discourse which informs the national news media and national citizens in appealing and accessible terms about the *why* and *how* of specific policy choices, let alone involving them in the drafting or assessing of possible alternatives. As will be discussed in the next section, enhancing the possibility of open contestation is perhaps one of the most fruitful solutions to the legitimacy problems of the EU.

Politicisation

The intensity of the scholarly debate on politicisation may suggest that introducing more of it into the EU system is a value *per se*.[28] Instead, it is widely considered as primarily an instrument to prevent that contrasting opinions are persistently covered up or left out of the political debate, so that public unease may grow gradually and unnoticed and suddenly spill out, as happened in the French and Dutch referenda in 2005. Politicisation refers to the conscious revelation and articulation of contrasting opinions or positions on a given issue. This requires that political actors hold different opinions, that these potential conflicts are highlighted rather than covered, and that the process by which an assessment of these values, sealed by a political decision, is made, has real consequences for the content of policies. For the EU, this implies that its EU policies are subject to '... a battle for control of political power and the policy agenda at the European level, between rival groups of leaders with rival policy platforms.', according to Hix. Pleas from a more politicised debate stem from the realisation that the traditional 'permissive consensus' as well as the technocratic ways of policy-making are no longer regarded as consistent with the development by which the EU has entered into the realms of 'high politics', notably in the sensitive fields of foreign, justice and home affairs policies.[29]

A number of solutions have been put forward which could increase the contestability of EU policies. Most radically, these include a reshuffle of the

---

[28] S. Hix & S. Bartolini, *Politics: The Right or the wrong sort of medicine for the EU?* (Paris, Notre Europe paper series, no. 19, 2005).

[29] The distinction between 'low' and 'high' politics was introduced and later modified by Hoffmann (1966). 'Whether an issue falls into one or the other category depends on its momentary salience – on how essential it appears to the government for the survival of the nation or for its own survival, as well as on the specific features of the issue [...] and on the economic conjuncture.'

EU's party structure, the installation of more state-like governmental characteristics in its structure, including a presidential system with the European Commission as an elected 'government' being accountable to the European Parliament, or holding EU-wide referendums for concrete policy choices. In terms of policy contents, the introduction of a more politicised debate could be facilitated by the introduction of former 'taboos' to the European discourse, such as introducing European taxes, which would no doubt heat up the debate. As these solutions are inevitably linked to a particular vision of the future development of the European Union, it is unlikely that such radical redistributions of power would be accepted by the member states in the near future.

Less radical alternatives for introducing a more contested EU debate include piecemeal reforms at the national level, that of politics within the member states. Here, a number of obstacles remain. First, the 'classical' route via political parties and election campaigns has proven problematic, which has been explained by the fact that the discussion of EU issues remains stuck in the one-dimensional sphere of 'in favour or against Europe.' If politicians do take up contrasting positions on EU issues, these are rarely translated into political power struggles at the national level, due to compound problems of a lack of political steering, information exchange and co-ordination between actors.[30] The timing, scope and impact of parliamentary involvement differ considerably across the member states. In most member states, national parliaments could more fully exploit existing competencies to control the executive in their European tasks. Even in the much cited case of Denmark, where an active parliamentary 'European Committee' plays an important role in devising mandates for Danish EU policy, a lack of information and resources prohibits Parliament as a whole from playing a proactive role in shaping national EU policy. This has inspired pleas to politicise not all EU dossiers all the time, but to select or 'target' certain dossiers or decisions for more (explicit) political contestation. This would not necessarily require procedural innovations, such as the 'yellow' or 'orange' card procedure introduced in the Lisbon Treaty, but rather a more conscious and committed use of existing arrangements.[31]

Secondly, and rather paradoxically, it should be noted that the current political emphasis on 'subsidiarity' (which implies that the EU should focus on the policy issues that are truly transnational or require international attention) may turn out to be counterproductive for involving or engaging European citizens. It implies that political 'fireworks' on those issues that really matter to many citi-

[30] C. van der Eijk & M. Franklin, 'Potential for contestation on European matters at national elections in Europe', in Gary Marks & Marco R. Steenbergen, eds., *European Integration and Political Conflict* (Cambridge, Cambridge University Press 2004).

[31] Ph. Kiiver, 'Europe in Parliament: Towards Targeted Politicization', Scientific Council for Government Policy (WRR) online paper no. 23 (2007).

zens (welfare policies, health care, education, housing) remain located at the national level, whereas the remaining issues for which the EU is competent (free movement, trade, agriculture) are normally not electorally decisive.

Thirdly, the particular features of the European decision-making arena pose particular difficulties to making it more political. Negotiation mandates that politicians have realised in a more (explicitly) 'politicised' way may turn out to be inflexible, in the sense that they are so different from the positions of the European partners that it is impossible to realise the political consensus that EU negotiations normally aim at.[32] If the results of a politicised policy process thus cannot be realised, disillusion or frustration may be the – counterproductive – result. This sets a number of requirements for the process. First, efforts to politicise should come with the silent agreement that *all* outcomes from agreed procedures should be respected. In other words: there are no wrong answers by the electorate in popular referenda or elections – as could be the impression from some of the political reactions to the subsequent rejections of the Constitutional and Lisbon Treaty in France, the Netherlands and, most recently, Ireland. There is a serious risk here, which should be duly taken into account. As politicisation sensitises people to value conflicts, they may become less willing to accept a decision that favours other values than their own preferences. Thereby, politicisation could in the end undermine the degree of diffuse support that is necessary for a legitimate political system. The paradoxical situation with the latest rejection of the institutional treaty shows that the effects of politicisation may run counter to efforts to improve governability, effectiveness and efficiency, as the Lisbon Treaty was meant to remedy precisely these alleged shortcomings of the EU's structure.

A second requirement is a sufficient degree of realism, both from the part of national politicians and the electorate, that taking part in European cooperation structures essentially implies 'to win some and lose some' in concrete policy negotiations. This political realism is part of the deal, but may be difficult to openly admit in a climate of electoral competition. In other words: it may be politically appealing in the short term to continue 'blaming and shaming Brussels'; in the long run, however, this tendency undermines all serious political efforts to enhance the EU's legitimacy. Politicisation is therefore ultimately dependent on the sense of responsibility of national politicians to take this challenge seriously.

---

[32] P.W. Meerts & F. Cede, *Negotiating European Union* (Palgrave, EU series, 2004)

Conclusion

This chapter has discussed several perspectives, from which the current crisis of legitimacy that haunts the EU and its member states can be perceived. It has identified a number of indicators of the current malaise, depending on the views of commentators on the current and desired state of the Union in general. In order to analyse solutions, a number of composite elements of EU legitimacy (output, representation, accountability and identification) have been identified, as well as a portfolio of methods to 're-legitimise' the EU. It has been argued that for remedies to work in the long term, these solutions should work positively on more than one element of legitimacy and be deployed consistently over time.

Whichever angle is chosen, however, the main challenge seems to lie with national politicians in the member states, who in daily practice function as the hands and faces of the EU. Perhaps paradoxically, their failure thus far to effectively communicate EU actions, in a way that appeals to citizens, demonstrates the crucial influence that communicative strategies of political elites and parties may have on the way citizens end up identifying with Europe. Institutional solutions focusing on procedural reform, including an overhaul of competencies or a rearrangement of responsibilities, may facilitate the processes of politicisation. But whatever the institutional arrangements selected, the key challenge lies in the contents, words and visions that are offered by national politicians themselves. As national discourse on European issues remains largely focused on procedures and institutions, the 'communicative discourse' is the main challenge for the coming years.

How to Repair the Legitimacy Deficit in the War on Terror: A Special Court for Dealing with International Terrorism?*

Bibi van Ginkel

'Liberty and security can be reconciled; and in our system they are reconciled within the framework of the law.'

Justice Anthony Kennedy, US Supreme Court[1]

Introduction

Seven years after the terrorist attacks that marked the beginning of the so-called 'war on terror', the record shows many new policies, regulations and commitments to co-operate on all levels. While the shock at that time, and the call for an immediate response explain the fact that not all adopted measures excelled in their balanced approach, the time has come to evaluate and to repair the flaws in our system. Many of these flaws relate to the ever-lasting debate on whether security can be guaranteed while respecting liberty rights. Some would argue that respecting liberty to the full extent will jeopardise the discretionary power which the government needs to guarantee security, and that abandoning some of our freedom rights is but a small sacrifice in order to ensure our security.

* The author would like to thank Gijs de Vries for his valuable comments on an earlier draft of this contribution.

[1] Justice Kennedy made this comment after the US Supreme Court's ruling regarding the right to *habeas corpus* of detainees at Guantanamo Bay, Cuba, issued on 12 June 2008 (US Supreme Court, *Boumediene et al.* v. *Bush, President of the United States et al.*, No. 06-1195, 12 June 2008). In that ruling the Supreme Court decided that foreign suspects at Guantanamo Bay have the right to challenge their detention in the US civilian courts. President Bush, however, criticised the judgment, saying that they would 'study this opinion to determine whether or not additional legislation may be appropriate.' See BBC News, 12 June 2008. The American Bar Association, on the other hand, commented that this ruling would help restore the credibility of the United States as a 'model for the rule of law across the globe.' See also, BBC News, 12 June 2008.

Justice Kennedy, however, reminds us that '[t]he laws and constitution are designed to survive, and remain in force, in extraordinary times.'[2] Indeed, the framework of human rights conventions shows that rights to liberty go hand in hand with possibilities of governments to derogate from these rights by law, when necessary in a democratic society to serve a legitimate aim, such as national security. And in absolutely dire moments, a state of emergency can be invoked,[3] which gives the state even more room to manoeuvre without being hindered by human rights limitations.[4]

Apart from the many legal arguments in favour of upholding human rights, one should also keep in mind that terrorism is a threat to the core values of our free democratic society, such as the rule of law, and that these core values should not be lost in our battle against terrorism. Because if that were to be the case, and we sacrifice these values in our response, 'we are handing a victory to the terrorists,'[5] and we lose the moral high ground.

It is with that remark in mind that a survey of the current practices in different states does not strike a positive note. On the contrary, even though the international community is joined in the 'war on terror' and many new (international) instruments have seen the light of day after 9/11, the story that sticks in the mind is a collage of horror pictures from Abu Ghraib, hooded detainees in Guantanamo Bay, CIA rendition flights, witness reports of torture, and government officials legitimating harsh methods of interrogation. This collage is accompanied with sound-bites, such as the remark by the current Dutch Minister of Foreign Affairs, who claimed that it is better to put ten innocent people in jail, than to let one terrorist with a bomb walk free,[6] or US Vice-President Dick Cheney who said that international terrorist suspects 'don't deserve the same guarantees and safeguards that would be used for an American citizen going through the normal judicial process.'[7]

Although images and sound-bites do not necessarily reflect the real situation, in this case many evaluations underline the assessment that in the war on

---

[2] BBC News, 12 June 2008.

[3] See e.g., Art. 4 of the International Covenant on Civil and Political Rights.

[4] Of course, even in these situations, certain core principles, the so-called *Notstandsfest Rechten*, can never be suspended. But most importantly, the possibility of derogation and the option to claim a state of emergency provide a state with a balanced framework within which it can act to provide security when needed. To this category belong, e.g., the right to life, the prohibition of torture and slavery, the right to freedom of thought, and respect for the principle of legality in criminal law. See Arts. 6, 7, 8 (I and II), 11, 15, 16 and 18 of the International Covenant on Civil and Political Rights.

[5] Kofi Annan in a key-note address to the Closing Plenary of the International Summit on Democracy, Terrorism and Security, 10 March 2005.

[6] Maxime Verhagen, Member of Parliament for the Christian Democrat Party, during a Plenary Debate on 11 November 2004, Kamerstukken 29854 (25 November 2004), no. 22, p. 1280.

[7] *International Herald Tribune* (16 November 2001).

terror, we are dealing with a legitimacy deficit. For a large part, this follows from the flagrant violations of the fair trial principles. Various news reports and NGO alerts[8] remind us almost on a daily basis of legal black holes and other judicial wrongs, such as minimal or no procedural guarantees for suspects that occur in different parts of the world, and which seem to survive any criticism as it is taken for granted that they form part and parcel of the global 'war on terror'.

Mindful of the bad image which the United States carries, a debate has emerged between two camps in relation to the future of Guantanamo Bay. Ironically enough, some are now arguing in favour of closing down 'Gitmo', but are meanwhile struggling with fear for the potential human rights abuses against detainees when sent back to their countries of origin.[9] With that dossier still open, new alarming reports are already being broadcast suggesting that the United States is operating 'floating prisons' to house terrorist suspects.[10]

Clearly, there is not yet an end to the perceived dilemma between security and liberty. The negative impact of these policy choices on the overall image of the international coalition against terrorism is not to be neglected. It might in some instances even contribute to the motivation of potential terrorists. The question is thus how to repair the legitimacy deficit in our struggle against terrorism?

An absolute requirement for the answer to this question is the conviction that the response to terrorism should have a long-term character, taking into account all human rights principles and preventing measures from having a negative effect on, for example, radicalisation processes. Even though the panic right after the attacks of 9/11 explains the short-term solutions adopted with less respect for liberty rights, the repairs to these flaws have to be made in order to remain credible as defenders of freedom and the rule of law. Part of the answer to the question of how to repair the legitimacy deficit can thus be found in better guarantees for respecting fair trial principles during the different legal procedures that relate to terrorism. There is certainly much to gain in this respect.

Both national procedures as well as international procedures, such as the UN Security Council's sanction regime on blacklisted individuals,[11] would benefit

---

[8] See the endless list of country reports on the websites of Human Rights Watch and Amnesty International.

[9] BBC News, 21 May 2008.

[10] D. Campbell & R. Norton-Taylor, 'US accused of holding terror suspects on prison ships', *The Guardian* (2 June 2008).

[11] This sanction regime was first adopted with Security Council resolution 1267 (1999) to pressure the Taliban to, *inter alia*, surrender Osama bin Laden, and members of the Al Qaida organisation. The freezing of financial assets had to be implemented against the individuals on the blacklists. Later the regime was revised on many occasions to also include Osama bin Laden

from procedural improvements. However, notwithstanding these possibilities, there will always be concerns with regard to the procedures in terrorist trials in certain states. Whether that sprouts from the politically-biased situation in a certain conflict, or just because the human rights level is not particularly high, the impact on the international community's image in the struggle against terrorism will always be there, since after 9/11 we all joined the global war on terror. These concerns have triggered the call for a special international court for international terrorism as a possible answer to the legitimacy deficit.[12] Such a tribunal could contribute to rectifying this bad image, because it would be impartial and independent and it would respect procedural guarantees.

This chapter will therefore examine this particular option as a possible answer to the legitimacy deficit. First, the phenomenon of the recent emergence of international criminal tribunals will be dealt with. Next, a comparison will be made between the option of leaving the situation as it is, and three possible models of international criminal tribunals to deal with terrorism. The chapter will conclude with an assessment of the best option.

Tribunals

Since the Security Council for the first time adopted a resolution establishing the *ad hoc* International Criminal Tribunal for the Former Yugoslavia in 1993,[13] a proliferation of different forms of international criminal tribunals has taken place. Some have been established by the Security Council to deal with a specific – recent or old – conflict, limited in both time and regional applicability, and are completely manned by international judges.[14] Others are hybrid forms,

---

and members of Al Qaida as well as others associated with them on the sanctions list. A delisting procedure was first adopted on 7 November 2002 in the Guidelines of the Security Council's Sanction Committee established pursuant to Res. 1267 (1999) concerning Al-Qaida and the Taliban and associated individuals and entities, as amended on 10 April 2003 and revised on 21 December 2005. See <http://www.un.org/Docs/sc/committees/1267/1267_guidelines.pdf>.

[12] Recently, the Dutch Parliament adopted a resolution in which the government was encouraged to look into the options for creating a special tribunal. The resolution adopted in the Dutch Parliament in November 2007 (Kamerstukken 31200 V 51, 8 November 2007) stated that human rights should be respected while countering terrorism, and that terrorist suspects also deserve a fair and transparent trial, and Parliament therefore requested the government to promote the effectualisation of universal jurisdiction, and explore as an interim measure the possibility of establishing an international tribunal to prosecute international terrorism.

[13] SC Res. 827 (1993).

[14] Examples are the International Criminal Tribunal for Rwanda (1994) and the *Ad Hoc* Court for East-Timor, established by the United Nations Transitional Administration in East-Timor.

seeking a combination of local judges and international judges.[15] Yet another option is to place the tribunal on neutral territory.[16] Apart from all the specific solutions, the landmark achievement of the international community was the establishment of the International Criminal Court in 2002, which is, contrary to the other tribunals, a permanent court.

A proposal for an international criminal court with jurisdiction to deal with crimes of terrorism is not new in history. As early as 1937 there was an initiative to establish an international criminal court. This initiative coincided with a draft international convention on the combating of terrorism, and this court would henceforth also have jurisdiction with regard to terrorist crimes. However, the problem which prevented the conventions from becoming operational in those days is still the same problem which the international community is dealing with now: there is no internationally accepted definition of terrorism.[17]

Many attempts to draft a universal definition have been made,[18] but so far without any success. Especially within the United Nations, negotiations on a universal definition have now been going on for more than 10 years.[19] However, in order to be able to respond to certain issue-specific acts of terrorism, such as, for example, the taking of hostages or terrorist bombings, the international community did manage to agree on definitions with a limited scope, and henceforth laid down agreements on the criminalisation, prosecution and extradition of such acts.[20] Furthermore, on a regional level, disagreements on the

---

15 Examples are the Special Court for Sierra Leone, established on the basis of an agreement between the UN and the government of Sierra Leone (2002); the Khmer Rouge Tribunal, established on the basis of an agreement between the UN and the government of Cambodia (2003); and the Special Tribunal for Lebanon, based on SC Res. 1644 (2005)

16 An example is the Lockerbie Trial dealing with the perpetrators of the terrorist attack on an aircraft over Lockerbie (Scotland) that took place at Zeist, the Netherlands.

17 See in more elaborate detail on this issue: B.T. van Ginkel, 'Developments within the United Nations: Towards a comprehensive convention on combating terrorism', in: Marianne van Leeuwen, ed., *Confronting Terrorism: European experiences, threat perceptions and policies* (The Hague, Kluwer Law International 2003) pp. 207-225.

18 Ibid.

19 In 1996 India submitted a proposal for a Comprehensive Convention on Combating Terrorism to the Legal Committee of the UN General Assembly, including a definition of terrorism. See A/C.6/51/L.15.

20 Today, 13 sectoral conventions in the field of terrorism have been adopted: the 1963 Tokyo Convention on Offences and Certain Other Acts committed on Board Aircraft, UKTS 126 (1969), Cmnd. 4230, entered into force 4 December 1969; the 1970 Hague Convention for the Suppression of Unlawful Seizure of Aircraft, UKTS 39 (1972), Cmnd. 4965; (1971) ILM 133, entered into force 14 October 1971; the 1971 Montreal Convention for the Suppression of Unlawful Acts Against the Safety of Civil Aviation, UKTS 10 (1971), Cmnd. 5524, entered into force 26 January 1973; and its 1988 Protocol for the Suppression of Unlawful Acts of Violence at Airports Serving International Civil Aviation, 27 ILM 627 (1988); the 1973 UN Convention on the Prevention and Punishment of Crimes Against Internationally Protected Persons, Including

scope of a definition were less fierce, and hence, several regional treaties have been concluded.[21] In the European Union, a Council Framework Decision on Combating Terrorism was even adopted with a definition of terrorism, with the intention that Member States would ensure that terrorism would be qualified as a crime, and an appropriate punishment would be applicable.[22]

The lack of a universal definition of terrorism plays a role in many international initiatives regarding the battle against terrorism, but especially complicates any legal instrument in this regard. The general principle of legality, after all, dictates that any punitive measure should find its basis in a law and can only be imposed when the described criminal act has been proven. When the criminal act is not clearly laid down in a legal norm, the general principles of *nulla crimen sine lege, nulla poena sine lege* (no crime without a law, no punishment without a law) are not met. Thus a definition of the criminal act of terrorism is a

---

Diplomatic Agents, Misc. 19 (1975), Cmnd. 6176, entered into force 20 February 1977; the 1979 UN Convention Against the Taking of Hostages, (1979) 18 ILM 1456, entered into force 4 June 1983; the 1980 IAEA Convention on the Physical Protection of Nuclear Material, Misc. 27 (1980); (1979) 18 ILM 1419, entered into force 8 February 1987; the 1988 IMO International Convention for the Suppression of Unlawful Acts Against the Safety of Maritime Navigation and its 1988 Protocol on the Suppression of Unlawful Acts Against the Safety of Fixed Platforms Located on the Continental Shelf (1988) 3 IJECL 317; the 1991 Convention on the Marking of Plastic Explosives for the Purpose of Detection, on 27 January 1977, entered into force 4 August 1978, UN Doc. S/22393, Annex; the 1997 International Convention for the Suppression of Terrorist Bombings, adopted by the General Assembly of the United Nations on 15 December 1997, UN Doc. A/Res/52/164, entered into force 23 May 2001; the 1999 International Convention for the Suppression of the Financing of Terrorism, adopted by the General Assembly of the United Nations on 9 December 1999, UN Doc. A/Res/54/109, entered into force 10 April 2002; and the 2005 International Convention for the Suppression of Acts of Nuclear Terrorism, adopted by the General Assembly of the United Nations on 13 April 2005, A/RES/59/290, entered into force 7 July 2007.

[21] See e.g., the 1971 OAS Convention to Prevent and Punish Acts of Terrorism Taking the Form of Crimes Against Person and Related Extortion that are of International Significance, 10 ILM 225, 1971, entered into force 16 October 1973; the 1977 European Convention on the Suppression of Terrorism, ETS no. 90; UKTS 93 (1977), entered into force 4 August 1978; the SAARC (South Asian Association for Regional Cooperation) Regional Convention on the Suppression of Terrorism, signed at Kathmandu on 4 November 1987, entered into force 22 August 1988; Treaty on Cooperation among State Members of the Commonwealth of Independent States in Combating Terrorism, on 4 June 1999 (Minsk); Arab Convention on the Suppression of Terrorism, on 22 April 1998 (Cairo); Convention of the Organisation of the Islamic Conference on Combating International Terrorism, on 1 July 1999 (Ouagadougou); OAU Convention on the Prevention and Combating of Terrorism, on 14 July 1999 (Algiers); Council of Europe Convention on the Prevention of Terrorism, adopted on 16 May 2005 (Warsaw), CETS no. 196, entered into force 1 June 2007.

[22] The Council Framework Decision on Combating Terrorism, adopted on 13 June 2002, 2002/475/JHA, in: *Official Journal of the European Communities* (OJEC), 22 June 2002, No. L 164, p. 3.

prerequisite for any criminal code or any scope of subject-matter jurisdiction of an international criminal code.

Apart from this major impediment to the realisation of any option with regard to an international criminal court with subject-matter jurisdiction to deal with the crime of terrorism, there are certainly some more arguments against such an initiative (see the next section: 'Pros and cons of the status quo'). Yet, an international tribunal might offer a solution to the fact that prosecution and extradition can easily be thwarted by threatening the government of unstable or weak states with adverse political consequences or even more violent repercussions.[23] Such could be the case in, for example, Pakistan. Another problem could be that a state is suspected of having some involvement in the attacks, as was the case with Libya after the Lockerbie attack. It could, moreover, be an advantage for less-developed states to provide an international tribunal with jurisdiction to prosecute crimes of terrorism because they, in many cases, lack the financial resources to prosecute terrorism.[24] It is, after all, not unlikely that the case is complex, and the evidence trail runs through different states, bringing along travelling expenses and costs for translation. Furthermore, establishing a criminal court with jurisdiction to deal with international terrorism could create a neutral forum for prosecution, where impartiality is now, in many cases, doubted. In any case, it would offer a solution to the problem that, as a general rule, a country's domestic courts only have jurisdiction to prosecute perpetrators who have committed acts of terrorism against its nationals or on its territory, and sometimes if the perpetrators have its nationality. The last-mentioned factor is, to a great extent, dependent on extradition to be able to prosecute.

The systems between the various nations usually vary, for example, with regard to the severity of punishments and the impartiality of the courts and, henceforth, might create legal uncertainty and create friction between states.[25] And, even though the creation of an international criminal tribunal might not be a major deterrent for terrorists, making them change their mind on a plotted attack out of fear for prosecution by such a tribunal,[26] the states that intend to fight terrorism stand stronger when their fight is legitimate and their trials are fair. Any declared ambition to create a form of international jurisdiction for terrorist crimes therefore springs from this principle.

The international co-operation in the struggle against terrorism, however, is both needed as well as a hindrance in effective responses. However, threat percep-

23 Mira Banchik, 'The International Criminal Court & Terrorism', 3 *Peace Conflict and Development* (2003) p. 9.

24 Ibid, p. 9.

25 Richard J. Goldstone & Janine Simpson, 'Evaluating the Role of the International Criminal Court as a Legal Response to Terrorism', 16 *Harvard Human Rights Journal* (2003) p. 16.

26 Steven C. Roach, 'Courting the Rule of Law? The International Criminal Court and Global Terrorism', 14 *Global Governance* (2008) p. 17.

tions are not the same in every corner of the world. Also, internal political agendas might colour the adherence to the agreed international policy goals, and governments might even seek the opportunity to get international support for dealing with their internal problems under the heading of fighting international terrorism.[27] In order to find common ground for laying down these policy goals, the difficult issues, such as defining terrorism, are commonly avoided. At this moment in time – much to the dismay of the less powerful states – that is not likely to change, since the most powerful states, which in most cases dictate the international agenda, find more benefit in *not* defining terrorism, giving them more freedom in the way they draft their policies without any set boundaries. However, the tide is turning. Lessons learned in the last five years of combating terrorism have pointed out that the international community should enhance the legitimacy of the policies in order to be more effective. Formulating a definition of terrorism is one of the improvements that are needed. This would contribute to the transparency of governance in this field and would henceforth facilitate the establishment of a special international tribunal.

When arguments are made in favour of an international tribunal for terrorism, three options spring out:

- A Special Court for Terrorism;
- An *Ad Hoc* Tribunal pursuant to a Security Council resolution; and
- An extended subject-matter jurisdiction for the International Criminal Court.

Although many more varieties are possible, these three options will be the focus of this chapter. To that end, the arguments in favour and against the three options for creating individual criminal responsibility for committing international terrorism before an international tribunal will be laid out in light of the international field of powers. The question will be, first of all, what requirements need to be fulfilled to make it possible. And, secondly, whether such an international special court would serve the interests of the different states.

The pros and cons of the status quo

Before going into the arguments in favour and against the three options, it is interesting to remind ourselves of the pros and cons of the current situation. For this assessment several aspects are taken into account, such as financial costs,

---

[27] Examples are the Russian Federation with regard to Chechnya, and China with regard to the Uighurs in the province of Xinjiang.

the gathering of evidence, issues with regard to extradition, legitimacy and procedural guarantees, and political desirability and possible consensus. Without claiming to be exhaustive, some of the arguments relating to the pros and cons are laid down in Table I.

***Table I.* Status quo**

Pros	Cons
No extra costs	High costs for smaller states; lack of capacity
Evidence gathering on site easier	Legitimacy deficit; Legal uncertainty; no guarantees for procedural rights
Use national definitions of terrorism	Problems with extradition

Staying as we are surely saves direct costs that otherwise need to be invested in a new tribunal. National legislations can use their own definition of terrorism, their own powers for investigation and detention, and choose their own severity in punishment. Evidence gathering for those acts committed within their boundaries is also much easier compared to when such cases are tried outside that country. On the other hand, international co-operation for investigation and extradition always creates obstacles in the operation. States might refuse to co-operate because of a lack of trust in the other legal system, and because they criticise the level of procedural guarantees. The differences between legal systems create legal uncertainties. Moreover, some states might lack the capacity to hold such high-profile cases. But most importantly, with the *status quo* one runs a risk of illegitimacy and furthering the poor image of the war on terrorism.

With that in mind, the three most common suggestions for an international tribunal for terrorism are assessed. In the next sections, the requirements that will have to be fulfilled for realising the three options will be laid out. Some of the arguments in favour or against the different options can easily be transplanted to the other options.

Special court for international terrorism

Starting with the option of a new special court for dealing with criminal responsibility for acts of international terrorism, one needs to realise that this will probably be the most time-consuming option. First, drafting a convention to establish such a court normally takes years of international negotiations. And second, once an agreement on such a statute has been reached, it again takes time before the required amount of ratifications by the signing partners is attained. On the other hand, in terms of international law-making, this option is probably the most in accordance with the classical principle of state sovereignty, which also entails the rule that it is the state's prerogative to decide to which rules of international law or which treaties it will abide by expressing its consent to be bound.

The most important requirement that needs to be fulfilled before any agreement on a special court for international terrorism can be reached is deciding upon the scope of the subject-matter jurisdiction of this court. Questions that can be raised in this respect entail, first of all, whether the court will only deal with large-scale terrorist attacks, the ones that shock the international community at large, or whether all terrorist attacks that match the definition in the treaty can be dealt with. Should it list various forms of terrorist activities or acts comparable to the acts that are already covered by the existing international conventions? Or should it strive for a general definition? The latter option will certainly send the states back to the drawing board over and over again, since agreement on a general definition of terrorism, despite endless attempts, has so far not been reached. One could of course take a minimalistic approach and only use the formulation of the different elements of a definition on which there is common agreement.[28] However, the question is whether this would accommodate the ambitions of establishing a special court in the first place.

Other questions that need to be dealt with in respect of the scope of the jurisdiction is whether or not the tribunal can only deal with acts of terrorism that bear an international or cross-border element, or whether also local acts of terrorism can be the subject of an investigation by the tribunal's prosecutor. Moreover, states might not be in agreement on whether or not the death penalty should be allowed as a punishment.

And finally, it must be decided whether this tribunal's jurisdiction will be autonomous or complementary to domestic jurisdictions. In the latter case, similar to the arrangements of the International Criminal Court, the international tribunal will only have jurisdiction if a state is unwilling or unable to prosecute. This option would respect the state parties' own judicial systems. However, someone would have to judge whether or not the investigations and prosecutions stand the test of a credible trial with respect to the severity of the crimes committed and the necessary procedural guarantees adhered to. Some authors therefore argue in favour of a primacy rule for any such tribunal over national procedures.[29]

On the other hand, if all these hurdles have been cleared, then it will be possible to create an impartial tribunal with a geographical representation of the

[28] Reuven Young, 'Defining terrorism: the evolution of terrorism as a legal concept in international law and its influence on definitions in domestic legislation', in: 29 *Boston College International and Comparative Law Review,* No. 23, pp. 23-102.

[29] See e.g., Ken Gude, *After Guantanamo, A Special Tribunal for International Terrorist Suspects,* Center for American Progress, April 2006, p. 9.

different legal systems. No political involvement in the procedures, and moreover, absolute transparency and the highest respect for the fair trial principles. Trials brought before this court will contribute to the simplified image of the good against the bad.

A disadvantage, though, of establishing an international tribunal with jurisdiction for crimes of terrorism, instead of leaving it to national courts, are the problems that will occur in relation to gathering evidence[30] and the dependence on the cooperation of other states with regard to extradition. Related to that is the secrecy that always surrounds the use of intelligence information. Moreover, trials are not easily accessible for witnesses and victims.[31]

***Table II.* Special court for terrorism (Special permanent tribunal)**

Pros	Cons
A permanent solution to a long-term problem	Takes a long time to adopt
Respect sovereignty of states	US will not likely become a state party
Geographical representation in the court and prosecution office	How to deal with the death penalty?
Independent, no political involvement, impartial, respecting internationally recognised principles of fair trial.	How to deal with intelligence gathering and sharing?
Transparent procedures	No definition
	Evidence gathering complicated.
	No easy access for victims and witnesses to attend the trials
	Cooperation by states is needed for investigations and extraditions
	High costs

Ad hoc TRIBUNAL

The second option entails an *ad hoc* tribunal for dealing with cases of terrorism established pursuant to a binding resolution of the Security Council. According to Articles 39 and 41 of the UN Charter, the Security Council is empowered to take decisions that entail non-military measures to maintain or restore international peace and security, after a determination of a threat or a breach of the peace has been made. The establishment of the *ad hoc* International Criminal Tribunal for the Former Yugoslavia (ICTY) came into being after such a resolution. The only requirement that needs to be met is the Council's determination

30 Jacob Katz Cogan, 'The Problem of Obtaining Evidence for International Criminal Courts', 22 *Human Rights Quarterly*, No. 2 (May 2000) pp. 404-427.

31 Goldstone & Simpson, *supra* n. 25, p. 15.

of a threat or breach of the peace. Since several resolutions have already been adopted stating that international terrorism, in general, possesses such a threat,[32] this requirement does not pose an impediment. Furthermore, the Council has also determined that several terrorist attacks with a more national character qualify as threats to international peace and security.[33]

With this option, one would avoid the dragging process of negotiations by the interested states. After all, in this option only 9 of the 15 Security Council members will have to cast a concurring vote to adopt a resolution. An important hurdle to overcome, though, is avoiding a veto by one of the permanent members of the Security Council, not to mention the newly evolving practice of striving for unanimity within the Security Council. Given the current positions of the most powerful states with regard to a definition in general and jurisdiction for international tribunals in particular, it is not very likely that a broad jurisdiction for an *ad hoc* tribunal will be attainable, if such an agreement is at all feasible. If at all, an *ad hoc* tribunal would be established whose jurisdiction would most likely be limited to a specific incident.

However, such a tribunal would have the peremptory powers of the Security Council and would not necessarily have to rely on cooperation treaties to obtain evidence and could also avoid complicated extradition procedures.[34]

Another advantage would be the fact that no process of ratification is needed. This means that a great deal of time can be gained and the tribunal can become effective as soon as the logistical aspects, such as nominating judges, and appointing a prosecutor and a register, are taken care of. Moreover, the existing *ad hoc* tribunals can serve as an example for the institutional aspects and the tribunal's statute.

With this model, it could be an option to make any prosecution dependent on a decision to start such an investigation by the Security Council.[35] This would probably assure some states that the powers of the *ad hoc* tribunal can be controlled. However, at the same time this would render the procedure highly political. The United States could, for example, still veto any initiative to deal with Guantanamo suspects when it so chooses. Another option would be to make the prosecutor independent from the Council. In the latter case, though, the question on the autonomous or complementary function of the tribunal will have to be dealt with.

---

[32] See e.g., SC Res. 1377 (2001) in which the Council declares terrorism as one of the most serious threats to international peace and security in the twenty-first century.

[33] Examples are the resolutions issued in relation to the hostage taking in the Moscow theatre, SC Res. 1440 (2002); the bomb attack in Bogota, SC Res. 1465 (2003); and the bomb attack in Istanbul, SC Res. 1516 (2003).

[34] Goldstone & Simpson, *supra* n. 25, p. 20.

[35] See also ibid., pointing to the possibility of political sabotage.

Surely, the Council should agree upon a definition of terrorism to set the limits of the scope of the jurisdiction of the tribunal, but since various previous resolutions already attain formulations that come very close to a definition, this might not be as big a problem as formulating a definition of terrorism in other situations would cause. Problems in relation to the delimitation between terrorism and the legitimate struggle for self-determination can be avoided after all.[36]

***Table III. Ad hoc* Tribunal pursuant to a Security Council Resolution (established on the basis of an SC decision)**

Pros	Cons
SC decision binding on all States. Quick procedure	A permanent problem deserves a permanent solution. *Ad hoc* tribunal sets aside state sovereignty
If decided, US will be bound	Permanent members of SC have to agree on its necessity
Peremptory powers of SC might force states to cooperate with investigations on site and extraditions	New tribunal generates extra costs
Ad hoc tribunal will work in accordance with international procedural guarantees	Political decision might jeopardise the perceived impartiality
Tribunal can be composed of a bench with a geographical representation	No easy access to attend trials for witnesses and victims

Extending the Subject-Matter Jurisdiction of the International Criminal Court

Finally, the last option would be to extend the International Criminal Court's subject-matter jurisdiction to encompass crimes of terrorism. The ICC's jurisdiction now entails genocide, crimes against humanity, and war crimes.[37] Immediately after the attacks of 9/11, several arguments were made to claim that the attacks would qualify as crimes against humanity[38] and, as such, could fall

[36] See in more elaborate detail: Van Ginkel, *supra* n. 17.

[37] Arts. 6, 7 and 8 of the Rome Statute of the International Criminal Court. The Statute was adopted on 17 July 1998 by the United Nations Diplomatic Conference of Plenipotentiaries on the Establishment of an International Criminal Court, 2187 UNTS 3. The Statute entered into force on 1 July 2002.

[38] *Inter alia* Mary Robertson, United Nations High Commissioner for Human Rights, on 17 October 2001, while speaking at the US Institute of Peace in Washington, expressed the opinion that the attacks of September 11 would constitute a crime against humanity. Also former ICTY Judge Antonio Cassese is of the opinion that the international community should revisit the Rome Statute with regard to crimes against humanity. See: Antonio Cassese, 'Terrorism is Also Disrupting Some Crucial Legal Categories of International Law', 12 *European Journal of International Law*, No. 5 (2001) pp 993, 994. See also P. Krisch, the author and Chairman of the Preparatory Commission for the International Criminal Court, who argues that although international terror-

under the subject-matter jurisdiction of the ICC,[39] except for the fact that the Rome Statute would not enter into force until after the attacks[40] and the United States withdrew its signature from the Statute prior to its entry into force.[41] On the other hand, as the negotiations on the Rome Statute unfolded, it became clear that there was no agreement on this issue. The opinion that such crimes should be addressed by the treaty was voiced by Algeria, Armenia, Congo, India, Israel, Kyrgyz Republic, Libya, Macedonia, Russia, Sri Lanka, Tajikistan, and Turkey.[42] However, others, among which the United States, took an opposite view, fearing not only the politicization of the Court, but also pointing to the lack of a definition and the disputed effectiveness of international courts in comparison to national courts.[43]

In order for acts of terrorism to fall within the scope of crimes against humanity, several requirements have to be fulfilled. According to Article 7 of the Rome Statute, any such attack should be inhumane in nature and character, causing great suffering, or serious injury to body or mental or physical health. Moreover, the act should be committed as part of a widespread or systematic attack against members of a civilian population. Furthermore, the perpetrator should have knowledge of the widespread or systematic character of the attack. The widespread or systematic practice of the act entails that it can never be a single act, but it should always be a 'multiple commission of acts [...] pursuant to or in furtherance of a state or organisational polity to commit such an attack.'[44] Thus, the connection between the single act and the widespread act is the central theme.[45] And even though customary international law has evolved to include non-state actors as a category of 'policy makers', it will be difficult to

---

ism does not fall under the jurisdiction of the ICC, it could qualify as a crime against humanity, and thus be subject to international punishment: P. Krisch, *Terrorisme, crimes contre l'humanité et Court Pénale Internationale* (2001). See for another overview of arguments: Vincent-Joel Proulx, 'Rethinking the jurisdiction of the International Criminal Court in the Post-September 11th era: Should acts of terrorism qualify as crimes against humanity?', 19 *American University International Law Review* (2004) pp. 1009-1089.

[39] Art. 7 of the Rome Statute encompasses the Court's jurisdiction for crimes against humanity.

[40] The Rome Statute entered into force on 1 July 2002.

[41] On 6 May 2002 the Bush Administration declared it would no longer cooperate with the ICC. See also, Roach, *supra* n. 26, pp. 13-19. Moreover, not only did the United States withdraw its signature, but it also adopted the American Servicemember's Protection Act (signed by the President on 2 August 2002, H.R. 4775, 107th Cong. (2d Sess. 2002)), which includes the prohibition of cooperation with the ICC. And the United States remains a persistent objector to any international tribunal; see also Raphael F. Perl, *International Terrorism: Threat, Policy, and Response*, CRS Report for Congress, 3 January 2007, p. 20.

[42] See Proulx, *supra* n. 38, p. 1023.

[43] Ibid.

[44] Art. 7 (2) (a) Rome Statute.

[45] Banchik, *supra* n. 23, p. 12.

prove a systematic policy of destruction.[46] Can there be intervals between the attacks? What if the attacks are carried out by different groups? How many attacks are needed before one can speak of a regular pattern? And how many victims are needed before the attack qualifies as a widespread attack?

In 2009, the Review Conference will take place to consider possible amendments to the Rome Statute of the International Criminal Court. During this Review Conference one of the options is to include terrorist crimes as a separate crime under the subject-matter jurisdiction of the ICC Statute, thereby lowering the high threshold that has to be surpassed when prosecuting terrorist crimes under the subject-matter jurisdiction of crimes against humanity. There is, however, still the issue of the definition. It does not seem likely that a definition will be formulated by that time. Meanwhile, the interim solution could be to install subject-matter jurisdiction with regard to those acts of terrorism that have been described in the existing sectoral conventions, with a back-up option of using crimes against humanity for those widespread systematic attacks that do not fit any of the other definitions.

In comparison to the possibilities of an *ad hoc* tribunal, the ICC can only exercise its jurisdiction in limited cases. The ICC's jurisdiction is based on the territoriality and nationality principle, which means that a criminal act either has to be committed on the territory of a State Party to the Rome Statute, or by a person with the nationality of a State Party.[47] Moreover, the ICC can only exercise its jurisdiction when the State Parties are unable or unwilling to investigate or prosecute,[48] and when a case is referred to it by a State Party or the Security Council, or when the Prosecutor takes the initiative.[49]

***Table IV.* Extending jurisdiction of the ICC**

Pros	Cons
Structure is already in place	US is not a member
Neutrality and impartiality. Works in accordance with the international procedural guarantees	Effectiveness is doubted, since it takes a long time for cases to be heard
Complementarity principle: State Parties can choose to prosecute themselves	
Crimes against humanity can be used, but do not cover all kinds of terrorist acts. Review Conference in 2009 with opportunity to extend jurisdiction.	No definition of terrorism
Permanent tribunal	Only applicable if states are party
Smaller states will not have the ability to prosecute themselves	Costs for the international community

46 Ibid.
47 Art. 12 (2) (a) and (b) Rome Statute.
48 Art. 17 Rome Statute.
49 Art. 13 Rome Statute.

An international tribunal: a reality or merely a dream?

Let us imagine that Osama bin Laden would be arrested tomorrow by Pakistani authorities. What would they do? Will they prosecute him for terrorist crimes claiming universal jurisdiction? What kind of trial will he get? Will fair trial principles be respected during the process? Will the court be soft, because of sympathies with the cause? How will the United States react if Pakistan decides to prosecute instead of extradite? Will this lead to yet another conflict? And what if Pakistan decides to surrender or extradite Bin Laden to the United States? Will he be transferred to Guantanamo Bay? Will the US authorities use 'severe interrogation techniques' to question him? Will he be brought before one of the Military Commissions? Or will there be a jury trial of some kind? And if that would be the case, would it be possible to find jurors who have not convicted him before the trial even started? And most importantly, would the international community have gained an important victory in the struggle against terrorism? Or do we risk severe criticism concerning the fairness of the trial, the lack of impartiality of the court, and the violations of fair trial principles, which will contribute to Bin Laden's martyrdom, and could even function as an inspiration for many people to turn their backs on society?

Now imagine that this trial would take place in an international environment. For me, this certainly draws another picture, and gives me more trust in the fairness of the trial.

After laying out the three different options to prosecute crimes of terrorism on an international level, the question should be raised whether any of these options might be a likely solution to the problem of the legitimacy deficit of the global war on terror that will gather enough international support to become a reality.

True, the problems that the international community in the war on terrorism is facing are severe. In the front row of our bad image campaign team stands the Guantanamo monster, which at the same time plays into the hands of the propaganda team of Osama. With the indefinite nature of the detentions of around 500 people and the procedures before Military Commissions, the United States violates the fundamental principles of not only the international community with regard to fair trial guarantees, but also the ones laid down in the American Justice system. Moreover, it impairs the relations with the US' allies.[50]

The problems with politicized trials in other countries have also been mentioned, as well as the lack of capacity of smaller states and states with unstable governments. There are thus several arguments that would plead in favour of an

[50] Gude, *supra* n. 29.

international tribunal. On the other hand, the impediments that will have to be dealt with in relation to all three options are not to be neglected. The most important question, however, is whether it will be possible to find enough international support to realise the establishment of an international tribunal. Taking into account the persistent objection by the United States to a Special Tribunal or the ICC, one has to wonder whether any solution without the support of the United States would bring the objective of more legitimacy any closer to the struggle against terrorism. An *ad hoc* tribunal established by the Security Council still remains a possibility since, of all the options, this would be the one that the United States can best use to accommodate its own wishes.

As for the rest of the international community, most states are not as outspoken on the matter as the United States. Their fundamental positions vary. Many of the Western states are very ambiguous. Although critical of the shortcomings in procedures in other countries, they do not seem to lead the way in this discussion. As for the procedural choice, in general most states clearly prefer any option that would permit their involvement in the process over the peremptory orders of the Security Council. However, given the predictably long negotiations with regard to a definition of terrorism, most states might settle for the quick solution that can be offered by the Security Council as long as they will be consulted during the drafting procedure. The other advantage would, of course, be that the United States will also be bound by the rules of such an *ad hoc* tribunal.

Leaving aside the ambition to include the United States, amending the subject-matter jurisdiction of the ICC is probably the option that is both attainable as well as respectful with regard to the sovereignty of states, as long as the crimes of terrorism are defined along the lines of the already existing sectoral conventions.

Final remarks

In conclusion, the legitimacy deficit that the international community is facing would certainly benefit from the establishment of an international tribunal that deals with terrorist crimes. Any of the analyzed options would serve that purpose. Taking into account political reality, amending the jurisdiction of the ICC seems to be the most feasible option, even though the possibility of such a success remains limited.

The message, though, is clear. The international community should make a big effort to regain the moral high ground if we want to regain legitimacy in our struggle against terrorism. Variations to the analyzed options would also be worth considering, such as dealing with the Guantanamo detainees outside the

United States (and Cuba) before a military tribunal under international supervision. These options are outside the scope of this chapter, however. But most importantly, the international community should not waste any more time and start working on our credibility as defenders of the rule of law tomorrow. Indeed, 'let's bring them to justice,' as US President Bush remarked in an address to the nation immediately after the 9/11 attacks. But let this justice be true to its word!

EUROPOL AND THE EXTERNAL DIMENSION OF THE EU'S JUSTICE AND HOME AFFAIRS POLICY

Roos Toxopeus & Willy Bruggeman

INTRODUCTION

The external dimension of the policies of the European Union is continually increasing in importance. Events that threaten Europe's internal security often result from causes outside the EU's territory. The EU has several bodies that face these developments. One of those bodies is Europol and in June 2008 the Council of the European Union decided to transform Europol into a fully-fledged EU agency. This transformation opens a range of new possibilities and perspectives for Europol. This chapter discusses the role that Europol currently plays in the external relations of the European Union and the possible changes which the aforementioned Council Decision might bring about here. It will, moreover, try to identify why Europol has become more active in the external dimension of Justice and Home Affairs and what this development means for Europol. The question whether this development is a good thing or whether it hampers Europol in achieving its objectives will be discussed. The chapter concludes with a reflection on possible future developments and prospects regarding Europol and its role in the external dimension of the EU.

EUROPOL TODAY

Europol (short for 'European Police Office') is *the* European Union law enforcement organisation. It handles criminal intelligence and its aim is to improve the effectiveness of and cooperation between the qualified authorities of the Member States in the field of law enforcement.[1] These qualified law en-

[1] Europol supports the law enforcement activities of the Member States against: illicit drug trafficking; illicit migration networks; terrorism; currency forgery; trafficking in human beings; illicit vehicle trafficking; and money laundering. Other priorities for Europol are crimes against persons, financial crime and cyber crime.

J. de Zwaan, E. Bakker and S. van der Meer (eds.), Challenges in a Changing World

forcement authorities include the whole range from police, customs and gendarmerie to immigration services.[2]

The establishment of Europol was agreed upon in the Maastricht Treaty on the European Union in 1992. The first operations, although limited, started in 1994 in the form of the Europol Drugs Unit. Since July 1999 Europol has been fully operational and its mandate has extended to much more than the fight against drugs. The Council Decision taken in June 2008 will put Europol on a par with Eurojust[3] and CEPOL.[4] This Decision shall apply from 1 January 2010.[5] The Decision contains several ambitious possibilities for Europol's future that will be discussed in the final section. Europol's headquarters are based in The Hague.

The organisation of the management and control of Europol, at least until the said Council Decision enters into force in 2010, is as follows. Europol is accountable to the Council of Ministers for Justice and Home Affairs. The Council appoints the Director and Deputy Directors, approves the budget and adopts implementing regulations related to Europol's work. The Council sends a yearly report on Europol to the European Parliament. The Parliament is also consulted if the Europol Convention, or other regulations, has to be amended. Europol has a Management Board which is composed of one representative of each Member State. These members all have one vote each and the European Commission is invited to attend Management Board meetings with a non-vote status. There is a Joint Supervisory Body to monitor the content and use of all personal data held by Europol.

All EU Member States, as well as the non-EU signatories to the Schengen agreement – Iceland, Norway and Switzerland – have liaison officers at Europol.[6] The countries also have a Europol National Unit as a single point of contact on their own territory for both Europol and national authorities. Furthermore,

---

[2] <www.europol.europa.eu>.

[3] The European Union's Judicial Cooperation Unit, which was established in 2002 to enhance the effectiveness of the competent authorities within Member States when they are dealing with the investigation and prosecution of serious cross-border and organised crime. See: <www.eurojust.europa.eu>.

[4] The European Police College was established in 2005 with the aim of bringing together senior police officers from police forces in Europe – essentially to support the development of a network – and to encourage cross-border cooperation in the fight against crime, public security and law and order by organising training activities and research findings. See <www.cepol.europa.eu>.

[5] Council Decision establishing the European Police Office (Europol), Brussels, 24 June 2008, 8706/08.

[6] This is due to the fact that Europol's mandate covers topics that are part of the Schengen acquis related to illegal immigration (illicit immigration networks and trafficking in human beings).

Europol closely cooperates with third countries – such as the United States, Canada and Australia – so closely, in fact, that some of these countries also have liaison officers stationed in The Hague.

There are several ways in which Europol supports the authorities of the participating Member States and non-EU signatories. First of all, it facilitates the exchange of information between the Europol Liaison Officers.[7] Secondly, it provides operational analysis in support of operations and by generating strategic reports and crime analysis on the basis of information and intelligence supplied by Member States or third parties. Besides these reports Europol offers expertise and technical support for investigations and operations carried out within the EU under the supervision and legal responsibility of the Member States concerned. Europol has several systems in which it stores and processes information. There is the Europol Information System, which holds information about individuals and groups suspected of having committed or are likely to commit a crime that falls under Europol's remit. This information is limited to basic identifying characteristics (such as the name, date and place of birth, nationality, sex) as well as information about the crimes committed and suspected membership of criminal organisations. Then there are the Europol Analytical Work Files. These are generated by Europol staff and Europol Liaison Officers dealing with the details of specific offences. The files include the contacts of suspects, potential witnesses and others that could provide relevant information. Access to and the use of information in these work files is limited to the Member States that supplied the data or to a Europol analyst who is authorised according to the Europol Convention.

Besides these Europol systems the organisation has limited access to several other EU information systems, such as the Visa Information System (VIS) and the Schengen Information System (SIS).[8] Through the years new protocols have

---

[7] In accordance with national law, of course.

[8] This limited access means that access is allowed for consultation purposes and limited to certain types of data. In future Europol can possibly acquire full access (including the right to the revision of data introduced by Europol into the system) to these systems. The VIS contains records of visa applications. The SIS (& SIS II) contains data on persons to be refused entry into the Schengen countries as well as wanted persons and it keeps records on stolen vehicles and other types of commodity crime (also stolen passports, etc.). Originally designed as an instrument to ensure effective entry controls at Schengen external borders, it has developed into a general law enforcement instrument in the fight against cross-border crime. SIS is essentially a network system that links national components. The system has its shortcomings, because at the moment it does not allow for any analysis of the data and cannot process crime-relevant data that are not person or object-linked (information on networks of organised crime or terrorism). There is also a difference in the feeding and updating practices of the database by national authorities. Some are more systematic and regular than others and some put in data on categories of persons whereas others do not. SIS II will have new analytical functions. It will become operational in September 2009. These databases can be cross-checked by law-enforcement officials. There have been pro-

been adopted to extend Europol's competences. The list of offences that fall under Europol's authority has been extended and by now includes essentially all forms of cross-border crime. Although Europol has no autonomous investigative powers, it can participate in joint investigative teams and has the right to ask a Member State's law enforcement authorities to start an investigation in the specific cases that fall under Europol's authority.[9] Member States are required to comply with such requests for information or investigation, unless this will 'harm essential national security interests' or 'jeopardise the success of investigations under way or the safety of individuals.' The Europol Convention has been amended to foresee wider access to personal data held in the Europol Information System and the Europol Analytical Work Files.[10]

External dimension to an internal policy area

Europe and the world at large have become very much interconnected in recent decades. As a consequence, there is no internal EU policy area without an external dimension to it. This is no different for the Area of Freedom, Security and Justice, which encompasses the Justice and Home Affairs policy of the European Union. Hence, it is essential for the EU to promote its interests through external relations both in the field of internal security and in that of external or international security. The main difference between these two fields is that the Justice and Home Affairs (JHA) policy has acquired a higher profile in recent years in comparison to the Common Foreign and Security Policy. Developments in the first mentioned area have mainly been pushed by the drive to control illegal immigration, to combat terrorism and to deal with cross-border organised crime. These are issues that directly affect EU citizens and therefore it is of great importance to the EU to show its added value here. Moreover, the EU has used its JHA policy to prescribe to third countries the actions they must take to address cross-border threats. The EU did so in the 1990s through the enlargement process and afterwards through the European Neighbourhood Policy.[11]

The acknowledgement of the necessity of external relations for the effectiveness of the Justice and Home Affairs policy was highlighted in the Presidency

posals to make Eurodac (a database of fingerprints of asylum seekers) accessible by Europol, but as yet Europol cannot access the system.

9 Council Act of 28 November 2002, 2002/C312/01, *Official Journal of the European Union* (16 December 2002).

10 Council Act of 27 November 2003, 2004/C2/01, *Official Journal of the European Union* (6 January 2004).

11 European Neighbourhood Policy: Strategy Paper, Brussels, 12 May 2004, COM (2004) 373 final.

document of November 2005 'A Strategy for the External Dimension of JHA: Global Freedom, Security and Justice'.[12] This document states that 'if the EU is to be effective in doing so [meeting the expectations of citizens in the security domain] it needs to work with countries outside the EU' and that 'the EU should make JHA a central priority in its external relations and ensure a coordinated and coherent approach.' It also says that EU bodies such as Europol should be tasked to enhance operational cooperation with third countries. As debates about security against crime are key in EU Member States, and have been for the past couple of years, ambitions for the role and achievements of EU judicial and police cooperation are still rising.

In recent years several action plans, programmes and strategies have been adopted that aim to strengthen police and judicial cooperation both within the EU as well as between the EU and the outside world. In 2004 the Hague Programme was adopted.[13] This is a five-year programme for closer co-operation in justice and home affairs at the EU level from 2005 to 2010.[14] The Hague Programme was followed up by an action plan, which serves as a road-map to implement the Hague Programme.[15] Since the time frame of the action plan ends in 2010, the initiative has been taken to create an informal group at ministerial level with the objective to consider the future of the European area of Justice, Freedom and Security.[16] The group's official name is the Informal High Level Advisory Group on the Future of European Home Affairs Policy, but is more often referred to as the 'Future Group'. Its findings and recommendations are meant to be an important contribution to the European Commission's proposal for the next multi-annual programme in the field of Justice and Home Affairs. With regard to the exchange of information with third states, the Future Group expresses the opinion that a uniform approach is needed. Furthermore, the Group is very explicit about the importance of the external dimension: 'The

[12] Brussels, 30 November 2005, 14366/3/05 REV 3. The strategy was adopted by the Council after a proposal from the Commission and the Secretary General/High Representative Solana in October 2005, COM (2005) 491 final.

[13] European Council 4-5 November 2004, Presidency Conclusions, Brussels, 5 November 2004, 14292/04 CONCL 3.

[14] The Hague Programme includes some key notions that are – or will become – relevant to Europol: the principle of availability, which means police information is to be available between all EU law enforcement agencies (threats to the security of another EU state must be communicated immediately); and a greater use to be made of Europol and Eurojust.

[15] Commission communication to the Council and the European Parliament, *The Hague Programme: ten priorities for the next five years*, European Commission document COM (2005) 184 final, 10 May 2005, C 236/9, 24.9.2005. The European Council had invited the Commission to present an action plan with proposals for concrete actions in 2005. The action plan was adopted by the Council at its meeting on 2 and 3 June 2005.

[16] Initiative by the German Presidency of the EU, Informal Meeting of Ministers of Justice and Home Affairs, Dresden, 14-16 January 2007.

strengthening of the external security is one of the fundamental elements and prerequisites for the successful assurance of internal security.'[17]

The bottlenecks Europol faces

Europol was originally created as an instrument to be engaged under the internal security policy. As the external dimension of the policy area of Freedom, Security and Justice became more and more important, Europol also became increasingly involved in this external dimension. This may have occurred for various reasons. One of them is that the lack of input from within the European Union has somehow forced Europol to look outside and operate in the external dimension, because there it can be of greater significance. Another reason might be more calculating or deliberate, i.e., that Europol tries to improve its internal position by becoming a more substantial actor in the external dimension.

Let us explain a little more about these incentives for Europol to operate in the external dimension. EU policy should provide added value, that is a primary principle when it comes to the policy areas in the second (Common Foreign and Security Policy) and third pillar (Police and Judicial Cooperation in Criminal Matters) of the Union. In other words, it should supplement the national policies. In the case of Europol it is questionable whether Europol entirely lives up to this principle. Europol was set up as a central hub to collect intelligence from Member States' police forces in order to make links between crimes, suspects and investigations. One could argue that Europol is the obvious institution for EU central collection, handling, dissemination of data and intelligence. Several Member States have even propagated that Europol should become something like a European Intelligence Service. This ambition, however, is still far removed from the current reality. The reason for this is that certain bottlenecks form obstacles to Europol achieving its full potential.

Many authors have touched upon the bottlenecks Europol faces with regard to the fulfilment of its role and in the way it can live up to the expectations of the EU Member States. Europol's existence reflects a catch-22 situation: it has had no competences to gather information autonomously, instead it has been made entirely dependent on Member States to provide input for its analysis. Member States do not cooperate with Europol in an equal manner: some national authorities are much more reluctant than others to provide Europol with data.[18] They prefer to cooperate through traditional bilateral channels or there is a gen-

---

[17] Report of the High Level Advisory Group on the Future of EU Home Affairs Policies, 25-26 January 2008.

[18] Jörg Monar, 'Cooperation in the field of Justice and Home Affairs domain: characteristics, constraints and progress', 28 *Journal of European Integration*, No. 5 (December 2006).

eral lack of awareness about Europol.[19] Cooperation on internal security and more specifically the operational side is still primarily led by Member States and national authorities. The lack of quality intelligence from Member States affects the quality of its analysis work and subsequent reports. Besides this non-cooperation by Member States there is the complicating factor that certain categories of data – especially those from national intelligence services – are centralised and analysed by the Situation Centre (SitCen) and not by Europol. The limited access to SIS data poses a further restriction on the supply side. As a result the added value of Europol reports is questioned and doubts about its effectiveness are raised. The lack of confidence in Europol among the law enforcement bodies of the Member States is acknowledged by several authors.[20] This lack of confidence is due to the fact that Europol is not living up to previous expectations and its added value is perceived to be marginal.

It is often argued that Europol's 'cumbersome' legal framework is preventing it from fulfilling its potential and that therefore this framework needs to be changed.[21] And that Europol needs more powers and a wider mandate to fulfil its potential. The combination of a lack of confidence and awareness on the part of the law enforcement organisations in the Member States and the feeling that Europol does not have the means to perform to its full potential has led to more competences for Europol in external relations as well as in internal affairs.

It has also been said that EU agencies have supported these developments in external relations because they saw an opportunity to enhance their own role by this externalisation process.[22] Europol has been at the forefront of the outreach by the EU towards neighbouring countries and sources of insecurity. Europol has over time accorded its own data-sharing agreements with the United States and has developed its own relationships with Central and East European countries prior to their accession to the EU. But the EU Member States themselves have not always been willing to cooperate with Europol. Some Member States even employ a deliberate policy of starving Europol of information. This of course undermines its effectiveness and is an important explanation as to why Europol is eager to have relationships and agreements with third countries.

---

19 Ben Hayes, 'The Future of Europol – more powers, less regulations, precious little debate' <www.statewatch.org> (August 2006). First published in 84 *Bürgerrechte & Polizei/CILIP*, No. 2 (2006).

20 Wyn Rees, 'Inside Out: the External Face of EU Internal Security Policy', 30 *European Integration*, No. 1 (March 2008); Steve Peers, 'Europol: the final step in the creation of an "Investigative and Operational" European Police Force' <www.statewatch.org> (January 2007).

21 Ibid.

22 Rees, *supra* n. 20.

EUROPOL'S EXTERNAL COMPETENCES

The activities of Europol are a good illustration of the rising external dynamics, since it has quite a few competences in external relations. It may conclude agreements with third states and third bodies on the receipt of information by Europol.[23] The Council determines with which third states and third bodies agreements are to be negotiated and the agreements can only be concluded after unanimous approval by the Council. So the autonomy of Europol is still limited, but autonomy nevertheless exists. The Europol Management Board can determine the EU-related bodies with which agreements are to be negotiated. Of course, these agreements make provisions for the assessment of the reliability of information and its source, of its accuracy and the correction and deletion of information by both Europol and the other party to the agreement. Europol has both operational and strategic agreements with non-EU states, EU bodies and international organisations.[24] The operational agreements include operational cooperation and the exchange of personal data; the strategic agreements are focussed on technical or strategic cooperation. Under these operational agreements Europol can also transmit personal data to third states or bodies.[25] The agreement contains provisions concerning the recipient of data, the type of data and the purposes for which it will be used. The Director of Europol can – in exceptional cases – transmit data without such an agreement when he considers this to be absolutely vital to safeguard the essential interests of Member States. Before any transmission of personal data takes place the law and practice in the area of data protection shall be examined. Transmission is restricted to competent authorities within that third state, and only if it is agreed that they will not communicate those data to other third states or bodies. The agreement also contains provisions on liability in the event of unauthorised or incorrect data processing. Furthermore, Europol can second liaison officers to third states or bodies and receive seconded liaison officers from third states and bodies.[26] The cooperation with non-EU countries and bodies can even take a more direct shape: by

---

[23] Council Act of 3 November 1998, 1999/C26/03, *Official Journal of the European Communities* (30 January1999).

[24] Operational agreements with: Eurojust; Australia; Canada; Croatia; Iceland; Norway; Switzerland; the USA; and Interpol. Strategic agreements with: the European Central Bank; the European Commission; the European Monitoring Centre for Drugs and Drug Addiction; the European Anti-Fraud Office; Frontex; Albania; Bosnia and Herzegovina; Colombia; FYROM; Moldova; Russia; Turkey; the World Customs Organisation; and the UN Office on Drugs and Crime.

[25] Council Act of 12 March 1999, 1999/C88/01, *Official Journal of the European Communities* (30 March 1999), C88/1.

[26] Council Act of 3 November 1998, 1999/C26/04, *Official Journal of the European Communities* (30 January1999), C26/19.

allowing third countries to participate in analysis groups. In such cases experts of third parties are invited to 'be associated with the activities of an analysis group.'[27]

Some examples will better illustrate the current capabilities and needs of Europol's external orientation. Europol has already been tasked to act as the central co-ordinating unit for the sharing and analysis of information relating to the counterfeiting of the Euro, and this involving worldwide cooperation with Interpol through a Joint Initiative.[28] One day the question will arise whether the fact that the exercise of coercive measures is not allowed for Europol members will not hamper an effective fight against Euro counterfeiting. Besides the Joint Initiative, Europol has established cooperation agreements with Interpol. These foresee an exchange of information (operational, strategic and technical); the coordination of activities; and the secondment of liaison officers. Taking into account the external dimension of police cooperation, in the long run a 'security partnership' between Europol and Interpol through mutual information and consultation on working programmes should be envisaged.[29] Even within the framework of Interpol, Europol could be used to bring together the EU Member States' joint positions.

Following the recommendations in the Hague Programme, it is advisable to use the 'experience' which has been acquired with external police operations, with a view to improving the internal security of the European Union.[30] This means that 'experiences' of external police operations will be used for achieving internal security objectives. The Hague Programme does not specify what these 'experiences' are, so they can be freely interpreted to mean intelligence, for instance. This is an interesting development which gives the EU the opportunity to autonomously obtain intelligence from outside its own territory. Terrorism and trafficking in human beings do require a global approach, involving the Member States as well as Europol, Sitcen and Eurojust.

As promised in the Hague Programme Action Plan, the Commission did publish a communication on 'A Strategy on the External Dimension of the Area of Freedom, Security and Justice' on 12 October 2005, a proposal which was adopted by the Council in November 2005.[31] The strategy foresees a number of

---

27 Art. 10.9 of the Europol Convention, consolidated version 16 September 2008.

28 Joint Initiative, November 2001, which provides for arrangements on mutual points of contact; exchange of information; requests for assistance; and the coordination of training and public relations efforts. The Joint Initiative was amended in August 2007 to enhance cooperation.

29 *Freedom, Security, Privacy – European Home Affairs in an open world*, Report of the Informal High Level Advisory Group on the Future of European Home Affairs Policy ('The Future Group'), June 2008 (hereafter: Future Group).

30 Presidency Conclusions, Brussels 5 November 2004, 14292/04.

31 Document COM (2005) 491 final of the Commission of 12 October 2005 and Document 14366/3/05 REV 3.

action-oriented papers covering specific priority countries, regions or themes. The conclusions of these papers should be incorporated into the EU's external relations and will include recommendations for projects or action. The strategy entails that authorities like Europol, Eurojust and CEPOL are expressly involved in the implementation of these projects

The Future Group concurs with the existing awareness of interwoven security issues when it states that it is necessary to cope with the growing interdependence between internal and external security.[32] It follows up on the idea in the Hague Programme of using information gathered during external missions for internal security, when it suggests that greater care should be taken to disseminate the information obtained by external missions and Europol and the Member States should receive this information. Consequently, the possibilities for Europol to obtain information from outside the EU have been significantly extended. If the recommendations of the Future Group are followed it will be possible for Europol to obtain this kind of information without the obligation of a prior agreement with a third party. Together with the Future Group, we think that Frontex[33] must play a central role in maximising the threat analysis, together with Europol. Europol and Frontex have to cooperate closely with the national border forces.[34] Border control is the most prominent example of illustrating the need for an integrated (external and internal security) approach.

As mentioned earlier, the Council Decision establishing the European Police Office as an entity of the European Union will contain several important changes for Europol.[35] First of all, it will change and simplify Europol's legal framework, as it will replace the Europol Convention. Council Decisions are more easily adaptable to changing circumstances and emerging political priorities. Europol will enjoy Community funding and the budget will be increased forthwith. The European Parliament will be more involved, especially when it comes to budgetary control. But there are also new tasks and competences in store for Europol. Its mandate will be extended to cover all forms of serious cross-border crime that do not necessarily need to be forms of organised crime. There will also be new tools and common provisions for information processing. The text states that Europol will make every effort to ensure that its data processing systems are interoperable with those in the Member States and in use by EU bodies with which Europol may establish relations. The text provides for a legal

---

[32] Future Group, *supra* n. 29.

[33] Frontex is the European Agency for the Management of Operational Cooperation at the External Borders and is based in Warsaw. It was created as a specialised and independent body tasked to coordinate the operational cooperation between Member States in the field of border security.

[34] Future Group, *supra* n. 29.

[35] Council Decision establishing the European Police Office (Europol), Brussels, 24 June 2008, 8706/08, EUROPOL 47.

basis for Europol to receive data from private bodies. This is a strikingly new component: the possibility to receive and process information, including personal data, from *private* parties and private persons. The information must come through the Europol National Units or – in case of third states – through the appointed contact point. Europol may not contact private parties or persons directly in order to retrieve information. The possibility to support a Member State in connection with a major international event with a public order policing impact is introduced. National units will have full and direct access to all information available in the Europol Information System. There will be a new post of Data Protection Officer, who will have the task of ensuring compliance with relevant provisions including the protection of all personal data processed by Europol. The decision-making rules in the Europol Management Board will change from unanimity to a two-thirds majority.

In the meantime the European Council has also decided to integrate the provisions on the exchange of information in the Treaty of Prüm into the Union's legal framework.[36] The Treaty of Prüm was an agreement between several EU Member States, but made outside the framework of the EU (in a process similar to that of the Schengen Treaty).[37] Its aim was to step up their cross-border cooperation in order to combat terrorism, cross-border crime and illegal migration more effectively. The ambition was to have provisions of the Treaty integrated into the EU legal framework, and this ambition has been fulfilled. The Council, on this occasion, also indicated that the roles of Europol and Eurojust should be strengthened and that the cooperation between the two agencies should be enhanced. At the same time the Council emphasised the need to strengthen cooperation with third countries and international organisations.

Do Europol's external relations help or hamper the achievement of its objectives?

Europol's vision statement is that it 'will be a world-class centre of excellence to support the EU Member States' fight against all forms of serious international crime and terrorism.'. Its aim is to improve the effectiveness of and cooperation between the qualified authorities of the Member States. To serve this aim it has established relations with third states, with international organisations and in the future it will do so with private companies. However, this chapter has also showed that there is still a serious amount of distrust and a lack of confidence in Europol.

---

[36] European Council on the 19th & 20th of June 2008.

[37] Prüm, 27 May 2005; the seven signatories are Belgium, Germany, Spain, France, Luxembourg, the Netherlands and Austria.

Distrust is identified as a key barrier to fully effective data sharing.[38] Distrust is based on several things, for instance a divergence of policy interests between partners; or a difference in the way in which the counterpart handles intelligence. Questions like: how has it been obtained, how will it be used, analysed and stored, are very important issues. Do partners share similar norms and legislation to govern the treatment of such data? And another big issue is reciprocity: states or other actors are reluctant to regularly share information with partners that have little valuable information to send in return. This accusation has been brought against Europol in the past, which portrays the vicious circle wherein Europol is dependent for its output on the input by others.

If we look at Europol's external relations – with these notions of the cause of trust and distrust in mind – several observations can be made. The third states with whom Europol has operational and strategic agreements do not all share the same interests as the EU Member States. Nor do they share the same norms and legislation to govern the obtaining, use, storage and further dissemination of data. From the perspectives of, for instance, national governments, police forces, privacy watchdogs and civil rights and, of course, EU citizens themselves, this can be a threatening and unhinging perspective. The participation of experts from third states can be an asset to the analysis group. On the other hand, such close involvement by third states can scare off Member States.

Watchdogs like Statewatch argue that Europol will be given more operational leeway without sufficient checks on Europol's investigative and operational competences.[39] They have been very critical about the fact that there has been no in-depth review of Europol's activities so far, nor any objective assessment of its shortcomings and weaknesses.

As we have seen above regarding the bottlenecks which Europol faces, it is an often heard complaint that the current legal framework is hampering Europol from fulfilling its true potential. Europol's new legal framework will make it easier to make amendments: before Europol becomes an agency protocols have to be adopted. This is a lengthy process involving the consent of national parliaments. After 1 January 2010, amendments can be made by the Council of Ministers of Justice and Home Affairs. This will make it possible to respond more flexibly to changing circumstances and emerging political priorities. On the upside, this means that Europol will be more adaptable and can more easily fulfil its ambitions. On the downside, the role of national parliaments will have disappeared. So, the new framework has advantages for the expediency of procedures, but it is not an ideal for the preservation of a feeling of legitimacy. And

---

[38] James Walsh, 'Intelligence-Sharing in the European Union: Institutions Are Not Enough', 44 *Journal of Common Market Studies*, No. 3 (2006).

[39] Peers, *supra* n. 20.

legitimacy is necessary to improve trust and confidence in both Europol itself and in the process of sharing information with it and its external partners.

Then there is the issue of the increased flexibility in relation to trust. Trust is based on security, solidity and rules and regulations: partners to agreements need to be certain as to what they are getting into. When the rules are made more flexible – e.g., if the suggestion of more flexible rules regarding data protection is followed – partners will not be generous in bestowing their trust and hence their cooperation. And because Europol has no autonomous investigative powers as yet, it is desperately dependent on cooperation with its partners –whether these are Member States or third parties – and therefore trust is of the utmost importance. That is why Europol (and the Council being the client, so to speak) should be very careful when entering into actions that may harm the trust that is placed in it.

Besides these more tricky developments, there are a number of developments that will undoubtedly help Europol. The fact that the Europol National Units will have enhanced access to the information in Europol's information system is certain to improve Europol's position. The power to establish new information systems offers another opportunity.

What will the future hold?

The transformation of Europol into a fully-fledged EU agency, on a par with Eurojust and CEPOL, offers new opportunities for Europol's positioning.[40] Three scenarios are possible. The first one is a *status quo* scenario, in which Europol remains as it is at the moment. A second scenario includes the confirmation of a stronger external orientation that forms the basis of decisions within the current framework. This would mean deepening rather than extending. The third scenario comprises a newly fledged external orientation. The third scenario is the most prominent and transparent option subject to the condition that all Member States share this new strategy. External and internal security issues have to be more intrinsically interlinked and the external dimension of Home Affairs policy is vital. This should not only involve Europol, but also Eurojust, CEPOL and OLAF. It also implies a more effective coordination between existing and new European Union initiatives.

As we foresee a future development for Europol in which it can be made the privileged contact for the exchange of information with third countries for aspects that are identified as European criminal phenomena, the rules on Europol's

---

[40] Council Decision establishing the European Police Office (Europol), Brussels, 24 June 2008, 8706/08, EUROPOL 47.

cooperation with third states and agencies have to become more flexible and the individual countries have to accept a stronger Europol positioning. Therefore the Chiefs of Police Task Force[41] should play a more active and energetic role in supporting Europol, also when focussing on its external orientation. A bold suggestion is the creation of an Internal Action Service by 2020 that incorporates all EU bodies active in the field of Justice and Home Affairs.[42] The Future Group is also of the opinion that the technical management of SIS, VIS and Eurodac European files should be grouped within a single specific structure.[43] This would improve efficiency, even more so when also involving other organisations such as Europol, OLAF and CEPOL, based on a comprehensive global approach.

Besides this important Council Decision on Europol, there are other agreements and treaties to be adopted in the near future that can change Europol's prospects. Not only the Lisbon Treaty might offer new opportunities, but especially the programme that will follow up the Hague Programme (which will have to be adopted in 2009 and to which the Future Group has contributed with its recommendations) is an ideal vehicle for reinforcing Europol's positioning as an essential element in a global approach, involving external and internal security in an integrated way. This requires a coherent external concept, especially taking into account the increasing interdependence between internal and external security. Although the Lisbon Treaty might not be ratified in its actual format, this Treaty can guide us in identifying possible future developments.

Concluding remarks

We can conclude that Europol is, and will remain in the future, increasingly involved in the external relations of the European Union. The importance of its role is likely to continue and even grow as is proven by the increase in the possibilities Europol has to conclude agreements with a growing number of parties (third states, international organisations and *private* parties) and to allow third countries to participate in analysis groups. Furthermore, we can see its monopoly in dealing with the counterfeiting of the Euro worldwide. Then there are the ambitions for the future that have not yet been implemented, but that are

---

[41] The European Police Chiefs Task Force (EPCTF) exchanges experiences, best practices and information on current trends in cross-border crime, in cooperation with Europol, and contributes to the planning of operative actions. The EPCTF is not part of the decision-making structures of the EU.

[42] Charles Grant & Tomas Valasek, *Preparing for the multipolar world: European foreign and security policy in 2020* (London, Centre for European Reform, December 2007).

[43] Future Group, *supra* n. 29.

laid down in documents like the Hague Programme or the reports by the Future Group.

At this moment in time it is difficult to tell whether or not this increase in external action is advantageous to Europol's position. It is clear, however, that Europol and its external responsibilities need to be imbedded thoroughly in the broader external security policy. Justice and Home Affairs policy cannot remain a domain entirely separate from the Common Foreign and Security policy. The Lisbon Treaty would foresee more coherence between these policy areas. For this reason it is bad enough that the Lisbon Treaty has been postponed. It is worse that the Hague Programme was designed in anticipation of this reform treaty, so that the failure of the reform treaty hampers the success of other agreements. The provisions that result from the Hague Programme will also work in the current EU framework, but could be more effective when the EU is reformed. The very important task of finding a way out of the impasse caused by the Irish rejection of 'Lisbon' rests on the shoulders of all EU governments and of the institutions in Brussels. All possible solutions will be watched carefully by Europol's Headquarters in The Hague, as it determines the future course of the agency.

ENERGY AND CLIMATE: BRIDGING THE GEOPOLITICAL GAPS

Stephan Slingerland & Stijn van den Heuvel

INTRODUCTION

Climate change is a 'hot' subject as an international political topic, and finding more superlatives about climate change after last year's presentation of Al Gore's *Inconvenient Truths* is difficult. At the 2009 UN Climate Change Conference in Copenhagen a successor has to be found to the present Kyoto Protocol. It is now generally recognized that man-made greenhouse gas emissions have a detrimental effect on the global climate, and emissions seem to increase even more rapidly than when the most pessimistic climate change scenarios are taken into account.[1]

Fossil energy use is mainly responsible for these emissions. However, despite increasing worldwide recognition that climate change is indeed a serious global problem and mounting rhetoric from political leaders, there is still little evidence that the fundamental changes needed to prevent the potential dangers of climate change are being addressed. This chapter argues that there are at least three geopolitical gaps that need to be closed in order to reach an effective agreement in Copenhagen in 2009. The gaps are closely related to the global political and economic structure of energy supply and demand. They concern a divide, firstly between the United States and Europe, secondly between industrialised and developing countries, and thirdly between fossil fuel exporting and importing countries.

---

[1] For the years 2000 to 2006, empirically a CO_2 emission growth rate of 3.3% per year was observed. The most pessimistic IPCC (International Panel on Climate Change) model assumes an emission growth rate of 2.71 % per year over the period 2000-2010. See Raupach et al., *Global and regional drivers of accelerating CO_2 emissions*, Proceedings of the National Academy of Sciences, 2007 <http://www.pnas.org/content/104/24/10288.abstract>.

J. de Zwaan, E. Bakker and S. van der Meer (eds.), Challenges in a Changing World

Policy Gap 1: United States *versus* Europe

A first geopolitical divide concerns two different routes towards a low-carbon economy. One option is to set binding multilateral greenhouse gas emission reduction targets. Another is to reduce emissions in each country on a voluntary basis, primarily concentrating on the development of low-carbon energy technologies. These different routes have gained particular political attention because the first is strongly advocated by the European Union, and the second by the United States.

Both parties have their motives for a respectively more environmentally-driven, and a more security of supply-driven energy policy. The European Union has been one of the most prominent champions of binding emission reduction targets from the 1990s onwards.[2] In 2008 the EU has agreed to reduce its emissions by 20% in 2020, and 30% if an international climate change agreement can be ratified.[3] The EU target in this field is also justified as a contribution to the competitiveness of EU industry: The EU will 'boost growth and create jobs by meeting its climate change commitments,', according to the European Commission.[4] Indeed, since the 1960s in the EU a large nuclear energy industry was built up whose interests are well served with the EU position on climate change. Thirteen out of the twenty-five Member States presently have nuclear reactors, with France generating as much as 80% of its electricity from nuclear energy.[5] In more recent years, European industry has also developed a leading position in several renewable energy technologies, with, for instance, leading wind turbine suppliers in Denmark, Spain and Germany.[6]

The European Commission also uses climate change as a means of demonstrating to the world that the EU can take the lead in an important international policy field. Or, as formulated in a key communication by the Commission: '2007 marked a turning point for the European Union's climate and energy policy. Europe showed itself ready to give global leadership: to tackle climate change, to face up to the challenge of secure, sustainable and competitive energy, and to make the European economy a model for sustainable development in the 21st century.'[7]

---

[2] See, e.g., G. Sjöstedt, 'The EU Negotiates Climate Change', 33 *Cooperation and Conflict*, No. 3 (1998) pp. 227-256.

[3] European Commission, '20 20 by 2020', COM(2008) 13, 16-19 final, Brussels, 23 January 2008.

[4] Ibid.

[5] See World Nuclear Association, 2008 <http://www.world-nuclear.org/>.

[6] REN21, *Renewables, Global Status Report*, 2007 <http://www.ren21.net>.

[7] European Commission, '20 20 by 2020 – Europe's climate change opportunity', COM(2008) 30 final', Brussels, 23 January 2008.

Robust EU climate change policies are furthermore motivated by the fact that, contrary to the United States, the EU is running out of domestic fossil resources. Imports presently account for 82% of the EU oil and 57% of the gas demand.[8] These figures are estimated to increase to 93% and 84% respectively by 2030, giving rise to substantial fears in the EU that it will become vulnerable to the national political interests of gas and oil exporting countries. As the single most important gas supplier to the EU, relations with Russia are in particular under intensified scrutiny. Even more so since the Russian-Ukrainian gas conflict in 2006 demonstrated to many observers in the EU what could happen in the case of a future dispute with Russia.

The United States currently favours a more liberal position towards climate change policy. The main way forward, according to the 2006 *State of the Union* speech by President Bush, should be 'the development of new technologies', such as 'clean coal technology, solar and wind energy and safe nuclear power.'[9] As a consequence, Bush announced a significant increase in domestic energy technology research budgets.[10] No mention was made, however, of binding emission reduction targets. Rather, 'economic growth should be fostered to pay for the necessary investments in low energy technologies.'[11] Politically, therefore, the Bush administration pushes for a partnership with countries that share its view of voluntary technology advancement – in particular the 2006 Asia Pacific Partnership – and for agreements parallel to the UN climate change process, such as the 'Major Economies Meetings' initiated in 2007.

Two underlying energy-related factors in particular contribute to the US position. Per capita energy use in the United States remains much higher than in other industrialised countries.[12] The relatively energy-intensive and car-based society of the United States complicates the realization of emission reductions. Furthermore, the United States still has very important domestic coal and 'unconventional' (less-accessible) gas reserves.[13] Reaping the economic harvests

[8] European Commission, *Energy for a Changing World*, SEC (Brussels, 2007) p. 12. In comparison: oil imports presently account for 60% of the US demand, gas imports for 16%. These figures are foreseen by the US Energy Information Administration (2008) to decline to 54% and 14% in 2030 respectively.

[9] President George W. Bush State of the Union, Speech to the Congress, Washington, DC, 31 January 2006 <http://www.whitehouse.gov/stateoftheunion/2006/>.

[10] The 'Advanced Energy Initiative' announced by President George Bush in 2006 encompasses a 22% increase in energy technology research budgets.

[11] The White House, 'Taking additional action to confront climate change' (2008) <http://www.whitehouse.gov/news/releases/2008/04/20080416-7.html>.

[12] World Resources Institute, 'Earth Trends Statistics, Total Energy Consumption per Capita' <http://earthtrends.wri.org/text/energy-resources/variable-351.html>.

[13] Energy Information Administration (2008). US coal reserves amount to almost a third (29%) of the world's overall coal stock. Unconventional gas reserves are becoming increasingly available because of improved drilling techniques.

of these resources and simultaneously reducing emissions appears to be difficult.

For the future there is some prospect that the gap between the US and EU positions could be closed. In 2008, the Bush administration supported the G-8 Council conclusions that global emission reductions by at least 50% in 2050 would be necessary.[14] President Bush also announced that US greenhouse gas emission growth should be halted by 2025.[15] The two candidates for the US presidential elections support even more far-reaching targets. In his election programme, Obama claims to strive for an 80% greenhouse gas emission reduction by 2050. Similarly, McCain wants an emission reduction of 60% by 2050. If the United States would indeed give up its preference for a purely voluntary and technology-based approach, the debate might be taken one step further. What are, in that case, the right targets to be set, and for whom?

Policy Gap 2: Industrialised *versus* developing countries

A second geopolitical gap regarding climate and energy exists between traditional industrialised countries on the one hand, and developing countries and emerging markets on the other. In the climate discussions, their differing interests have led to a stalemate that has not been resolved so far. Industrialised countries argue that greenhouse gas emissions by developing countries will soon surpass those of industrialised countries, and therefore the former have to start curbing their emissions. Developing countries, on the other hand, stress that the climate change problem originates from high emissions in industrialised countries and consequently these are the ones that will have to show the way forward. In their view, industrialised countries have built their wealth on fossil fuels and now want to prevent developing countries from doing the same.

Both parties are right. Indeed, projections by the International Energy Agency suggest that in 2012 developing countries will overtake OECD countries in terms of absolute greenhouse gas emissions. China has already overtaken the United States as the largest emitter in 2007.[16] But in terms of accumulated greenhouse gas emissions since the beginning of the twentieth century Europe and the United States are still by far the largest emitters.[17] A solution therefore needs to be found that connects these two extremes.

---

[14] Hokkaido Toyako, G8 Summit 2008. For a summary of this summit see <http://www.g8summit.go.jp/eng/news/summary.html>.

[15] The White House, *supra* n. 11.

[16] International Energy Agency (hereafter IEA), *World Energy Outlook 2006* (Paris, 2006) and *World Energy Outlook 2007* (Paris, 2007),.

[17] World Resources Institute (2008) EarthTrends Statistics, Historic CO_2 emissions from fossil fuel combustion 1900-1999 (2008) <http://earthtrends.wri.org/text/climate-atmosphere/map-488.html>.

For overcoming the deadlock a distinction needs to be made between the least-developed countries and emerging markets. In the least-developed countries, of which many can be found in Sub-Sahara Africa and in Asia, often a large part of the population does not take part in the energy market at all. Worldwide there are still 1.6 billion people who do not have access at all to electricity, and 2.5 billion people are still dependent, for their daily energy needs, on traditional forms of biomass, like firewood, dung, charcoal, etc. As much as 1.3 million people per year, mainly women and children, die as a result of diseases induced by indoor air pollution.[18] These figures mean that the least developed countries are, to a large extent, in a phase of pre-commercial energy use: access to 'modern' energy is a key priority for them. Despite many attempts to leapfrog developments and make developing countries enter the renewable energy age in one single step, in developing countries this will inevitably lead to an increased use of fossil fuels – with a corresponding emissions growth.

Whereas access to energy for the poorest is the main energy problem in least-developed countries, in emerging markets like China, India, Brazil or South Africa improving wealth and a developing middle class – although positive from a development perspective – is a serious energy and climate concern. High economic growth rates in these countries in recent years mean that more people in these countries gain access to goods that are already a *sine qua non* in industrialised countries. A prime example is the private car. Before the 1990s private car ownership in China was almost non-existent, but in 2006 some 24 out of every 1,000 citizens owned a car. This number is expected to grow to 42 per 1,000 in 2010.[19] As a comparison: the figures for the United States and the European Union were 765 and 300 respectively in 2002. In India, Tata launched its low-priced 'Nano' in 2008 with the production of 250,000 cars a year for the domestic market, but it soon hopes to expand both domestically as well as to other markets in Latin America, South-East Asia and Africa.[20] All these new cars will be fossil-fuel driven, thus increasing pressure on fossil fuels. And a similar expansion can be seen concerning tv sets, washing machines, air conditioning and other household equipment.[21]

Improving wealth in countries like China and India also means increased pressure on their domestic coal resources. China and India alone account for 45% of the world's coal use and 20% of the world's coal reserves.[22] Energy

---

[18] IEA (2006), *supra* n. 16.

[19] Green Car Congress, 'Per Capita Car Ownership to Climb by 67% in 2010' (2008) <http://www.greencarcongress.com/2006/05/percapita_car_o.html>.

[20] A. O'Connor, 'Tata Nano – World's Cheapest Car is Unveiled in India', *Times Online*, 11 January 2008 <http://driving.timesonline.co.uk/tol/life_and_style/driving/article3164205.ece>.

[21] IEA (2007), *supra* n. 16.

[22] BP, 'Statistical Review of World Energy' (2008) <http://www.bp.com>.

demand in these countries is expected to double by 2030. Combining a rapidly increasing energy demand with reducing the use of domestic coal in these countries therefore seems almost impossible.

For the least-developed countries as well as the emerging markets the need for economic development and improving wealth for their population is the key driving force concerning their position towards climate change. This makes them reluctant to agree to binding emission reduction targets for themselves. For the least-developed countries this does appear to be a proper approach. Emerging markets, on the other hand, might very well be in a position to curb their emissions to some extent and to combine this with economic growth. How this could work is shown by China, where the domestic solar and wind industries and their implementation have shown very high growth rates in recent years.[23]

Policy Gap 3: Fossil-fuel exporting countries *versus* fossil-fuel importing countries

A third political energy and climate gap is that between fossil-fuel exporting countries and fossil-fuel importing countries. The former want to maximise economic benefits from their finite resources, whereas the latter aim to reduce their dependency on these resources. Although these groups partially overlap with those of developing and industrialised countries, the origins of this gap are fundamentally different.

World coal reserves are distributed over a fair number of countries and regions. Oil and gas reserves, on the other hand, are concentrated in just a few countries. Russia, Iran and Qatar account for 60% of the world's gas reserves, whereas oil reserves are predominantly concentrated in the Middle-East.[24] With energy demand rising not only in industrialised countries but also in the developing world this has led to fears in importing countries that exporters with large oil and gas reserves might use their increasing market power in international relations to serve their national economic and political interests only. The large hold of national companies over the world production of oil and gas and the Russian-Ukrainian gas conflict in early 2006 are often, rightly or wrongly, pointed to in this respect.

---

[23] *REN21 news*, July-August 2008 <http://www.ren21.net/newsletter/2008-08/>; and REN21, *supra* n. 6. Chinese wind energy has grown by more than 100% since 2005, and the 5MW implementation goal set by the government for 2010 has already been achieved in 2008. By 2007, there were more than 40 companies aspiring to manufacture wind turbines commercially. The Chinese firm Suntech is the world's fourth largest solar pV cells manufacturer.

[24] IEA (2006), *supra* n. 16.

However, as much as fossil-fuel importing countries need security of supply, the exporting countries need security of demand, i.e., security of income from selling their fossil energy resources. Many OPEC countries derive more than 90% of their export revenues from oil, Russia derives 60% of its export income from oil and gas.[25] Although a rapidly growing population and increased energy prices driven by high economic growth rates in many of these countries will stimulate domestic demand to rise, it will still be in their strategic interest to assure a continued export demand for their resources, either as crude materials or as refined products. Anything that might endanger a continuation of this demand, including a climate agreement, will therefore understandably meet with fierce resistance from these countries for economic reasons – unless the reduction of greenhouse gas emissions can be squared with an ongoing fossil fuel export. Or, as stated by the OPEC Secretary General Dr Alvaro Silva-Calderon in a speech to the UN Climate Conference in 2002, the Kyoto Protocol should be implemented 'in a way that avoids a net detrimental impact on fossil fuel producers.'[26]

Technology as a bridge

Potentially, already many low-carbon technologies exist that can contribute to a future low-carbon energy sector, but all of them run into specific problems that have so far prevented them from becoming a practical alternative to fossil fuels. Apart from economic, technical or environmental restrictions, there is often also an international political component involved.

Hydro and nuclear are the largest low-carbon energy sources presently available. In 2006, they both accounted for 3% of the total final energy consumption.[27] For the electricity sector, large hydro energy is one of the lowest-cost options available, but its use depends on the local availability of rivers that carry sufficient water and that can be dammed without hindering shipping movements and urban settlements. Some of the problems related to large-scale hydro development are the resettlement of the population in dam areas, a reduction of marine biodiversity, the salination of downstream agricultural areas and the spreading of tropical diseases. In particular, the construction of upstream dams in international river basins is politically very sensitive.

---

25 See <http://www.eia.doe.gov/emeu/cabs>.

26 OPEC Statement to the 8th Conference of the Parties to the UN Framework Convention on Climate Change, 23 October-1 November 2002, New Delhi, India <http://www.opec.org/home/environmental%20Issues/statements/cop8.htm>.

27 REN21, 'Renewable Energy Policy Network for the 21st Century' (2008); REN21, *supra* n. 6.

Nuclear energy is currently experiencing a revival. After decades in which hardly any new plants were built due to the 1986 Chernobyl disaster, now 36 reactors are under construction and many more have been announced.[28] However, waste and safety issues surrounding nuclear energy mean that the technology is still controversial, in particular in some European countries. Internationally, the relationship between the production of nuclear energy and nuclear arms proliferation makes the expansion of nuclear energy production particular to countries that presently do not dispose of this technology a delicate issue.

Bioenergy is another energy source that has the potential to contribute significantly to reducing greenhouse gas emissions. This option also finds strong support in the agricultural sector in many countries that sees bioenergy as an interesting new source of income. The loss of biodiversity and deforestation are main potential hurdles to its large-scale implementation. Politically, bioenergy has recently been met with severe international criticism due to its supposed responsibility for high food prices.[29] A second-generation of bioenergy using woody parts of plants might offset these drawbacks in the future, but is still in an early research phase. The latter also holds true for future low-carbon energy sources like tidal and wave energy or nuclear fusion.[30]

Other options for low-carbon energy are wind energy, solar energy and increasing the efficiency of energy production and demand. Wind energy has large potentials but also needs sufficient back-up capacity to compensate for its variable outputs. Where it is applied on land it often meets with resistance from local communities due to its visual impacts, noise and bird killings. Solar energy in many parts of the world is indeed viable, but is very expensive in others. Energy efficiency, involving many different technologies, is in quantitative terms the most important low-carbon option and economically is often the most attractive. However, in practice it encounters a large variety of market imperfections and barriers that hinder its implementation. This is even more so when the efficient use of energy is supposed to involve a change in human behaviour. Despite many attempts to the contrary, this behaviour turns out to be notoriously difficult to influence.

Although all the technologies mentioned can contribute partly to an energy and climate solution and at different time scales, none of them by themselves

[28] World Nuclear Association, 'Information Papers – World Nuclear Power Reactors 2007-08' (2008) <http://www.world-nuclear.org/info/reactors.html>.

[29] FAO, High-level Conference on World Food Security: The Challenges of Climate Change and Food Security, 3-5 June 2008, Rome (2008) <http://www.fao.org/fileadmin/user_upload/foodclimate/HLCdocs/HLC08-inf-1-E.pdf>.

[30] In this context 'hydrogen' is often mentioned as well. However, this is not a primary energy source, but an energy carrier and has to be produced itself from either renewables, fossils or nuclear energy.

provide a readily available answer. It is in particular the combination of the increasing use of low-carbon energy technologies with a long-term decreasing use of fossil fuels that might be difficult to achieve. At the moment that low-carbon energy sources or energy efficiency will effectively and significantly start to replace fossil fuel demand, they will most probably run into serious obstruction from countries with substantial oil, gas and coal reserves: these include not only OPEC and Russia for oil and gas, but also India, China and the United States for coal. Finding a technical solution that combines the continued use of fossil fuels with greenhouse gas emission reductions therefore appears, in international political terms, the easiest route to take.

There is one technology presently investigated that might play an important role here: carbon capture and storage (CCS). If the CO_2 emissions of fossil fuel combustion could be isolated from the other exhaust gases and could be stored underground in impermeable reservoirs, as is the aim of CCS technologies, the use of oil, gas and coal could continue until physical exhaustion – or until alternatives become available in sufficient quantities – and simultaneously greenhouse gas emissions could be reduced. If CCS technology were to be made obligatory worldwide for all fossil fuel plants, this measure alone could contribute to between one fifth and a third of necessary global CO_2 emission reductions by 2050.[31] Such a scenario would reduce the need for substantial reductions in fossil fuel production and could therefore be acceptable to fossil-fuel exporting countries.

However, the special political position that CCS has, as compared to other low-carbon energy technologies, does not mean that it is the 'Silver Bullet' which the energy world is waiting for. Although it appears to offer good perspectives for an international political way of least resistance towards a low-carbon energy sector, it is exactly for this reason also heavily criticised by the advocates of more fundamental changes. CCS in their view can only offer a temporary leeway that might well hinder the development of more structural solutions. Besides, CCS, like many other low-carbon energy technologies, still needs to be proven in practice on an industrial scale, and might not become available as a commercial technology before 2020. To bridge the geopolitical gaps, more is therefore needed than technology development alone.

---

[31] International Energy Agency, *Legal Aspects of Storing CO_2: Update and Recommendations* (Paris; 2006); N. Stern, *The Economics of Climate Change – The Stern Review* (Cabinet Office HM Treasury, Cambridge University Press 2007); P.A. Enkvist, T. Nauclér & J. Rosander, 'A cost curve for greenhouse gas reduction', *The McKinsey Quarterly*, No. 1 (2007).

International cooperation as a bridge

A second pillar crucial to a global energy transition is international cooperation that involves a mutual understanding of national economic and political interests.

With respect to developing countries, international cooperation should be focused on helping these countries with economic growth in a sustainable manner. This is likely to involve far larger financial transfers than presently available from development aid and the Clean Development Mechanism set up as part of the Kyoto Protocol.[32] In 2008 the United States, Japan and the United Kingdom have proposed setting up a multilateral fund involving the World Bank that would help emerging economies to reduce greenhouse gas emissions. With a contribution of 2 billion dollars by the United States and total reserves to be collected aimed at 10 billion dollars, this would only cover part of the estimated 30 billion dollars needed by developing countries to cover the extra costs of clean technologies.[33]

Furthermore, taking into account the need in developing countries for access to energy as well as for economic development, a new agreement should concentrate on stimulating 'development' as an equal goal next to 'climate'. Returning to the 'Environment and Development' title of the 1992 United Nations conference in Rio de Janeiro and far more than a purely cosmetic change, this would reflect a mutual understanding between industrialised and developing countries of the priority order of needs in both groups of countries.

The gap between the voluntary, technology-based approach initially advocated by the United States and the binding emission reductions favoured by Europe, though presently already narrowing, can most likely only be completely closed by an approach that includes both. The United States has repeatedly stated its position of not entering into any binding emission reduction targets without developing countries also taking up obligations.[34] The latter, in turn, will not enter into emission reductions if they will not be financially and technologically compensated for this step. The transfer of technologies on favourable terms from industrialised to developing countries seems to be a way out. It could persuade developing countries to enter into emission reduction efforts,

---

[32] See S. Slingerland, L. van Geuns & C. van der Linde, 'Van zwarte naar groene energie – Geopolitiek van een mondiale energietransitie', 62 *Internationale Spectator*, No. 5 (May 2008) pp. 259-263 [in Dutch].

[33] J. Lovell, 'UN Climate Head Welcomes Marshal Plan Climate Fund', *Reuters News Service* (17 January 2008) <http://www.planetark.org/dailynewsstory.cfm/newsid/46461/story.htm>.

[34] P. Wiseman, 'G-8 Countries Agree to Cut Greenhouse Gases', *USA Today* (9 July 2008) <http://www.usatoday.com/news/world/2008-07-08-bush-g8_N.htm?csp=34>.

which in turn could persuade the United States to accept challenging and binding reduction targets at home as well.

For international climate cooperation between fossil-fuel exporting and importing countries a variety of topics will need to be addressed. Apart from the stimulation of carbon capture and storage technology also greater use should be made of the renewable energy potentials in fossil-fuel exporting countries, since the Middle-East deserts are perfect locations for solar energy and the Russian forests hold ample biomass to be used in a sustainable way. As the technological knowledge for the application of these technologies is predominantly available in the present main fossil-fuel importing countries, technology transfer could help take away part of the resistance to a low-carbon energy transition in exporting countries. However, it is not only technology that needs to be transferred. Fossil-fuel exporting countries often have mono-sectoral economies that are almost completely dependent on gas or oil as their sole export products. For long-term economic progress and social stability it is important that these countries take steps towards the diversification of their economies. Importing countries generally have diverse economies and could therefore, if desired, provide some assistance in helping fossil-fuel exporters to diversify.

Furthermore, trust between exporters and importers could be increased by well-planned interventions in the structure of the global oil and gas markets that ensure the medium-term security of supply for importers and security of demand for exporters, as well as the long-term gradual and structured reduction in the production of fossil fuels instead of a sudden collapse. These interventions could include sharing the risks of much needed investment projects in fossil fuels between producers and consumers and allowing state-owned companies of fossil fuel producers to have access to markets in consuming countries in return for a better dialogue on the short and long-term production quota of exporting countries. It is a positive sign in this respect that at the Jeddah Energy Conference held in June 2008, the first steps were taken towards increased cooperation between the secretariats of OPEC, the International Energy Agency and the International Energy Forum, which together represent most of world's fossil-fuel importing as well as exporting nations.[35]

[35] Jeddah Energy Meeting Joint Statement, June 27, 2008 <http://www.saudi-us-relations.org/articles/2008/ioi/080627-joint-statement.html>. In the meeting it was agreed that the secretariats will start to cooperate to prepare shared analyses of oil market trends and outlook, as well as analyses of the impact of financial markets on the level and volatility of oil prices.

CONCLUSION

Fundamental changes in the global structure of energy supply and demand are profoundly needed to meet the challenges posed by man-made climate change. Technology development and improved international cooperation can jointly contribute to closing the present geopolitical gaps that impede such a global low-carbon energy transition. For that purpose, it should be recognized that countries have different driving forces with respect to energy transition. Environmental motives, security of supply considerations or economic development aspirations are all equally valid driving forces on the path to a global low-carbon energy economy.

Only if these driving forces are properly identified, recognized and mutually respected by all nations is there a chance that a new agreement in Copenhagen in 2009 will bring about more than hot air, nice words by political leaders and a world community that shrugs its shoulders and continues with business as usual.

Turmoil on the International Oil Markets: Getting Used to Production Capacity Constraints

Warner ten Kate & Lucia van Geuns

Introduction

In 2008 the world experienced a prelude to the new realities of the international oil market. These new realities include a tight balance between supply and demand, the rapidly increased cost of the marginal barrel and the extreme price volatility. This price volatility has driven prices up $50 a barrel in the space of 5 months, only to drop $50 in 2 months after the July 14 peak of $147 a barrel when consumers began to seriously drop out of the market and inventories were drawn down. After the extreme downward correction, the crisis on the international capital markets led to dim expectations about economic growth for the rest of the year and 2009, and this also played a role. However, prices are expected to rebound again, reflecting the fundamental upward shift of oil prices from an average of about $70-80 a barrel to about $110-120 a barrel.

This fundamental upward shift is due to a combination of so-called 'underground' and 'above ground' conditions. The 'underground' problems include the size, depth and geological complexities of new oil fields that are driving up the cost per barrel. These complex oil fields need to be taken into production, since 'above ground' problems limit International Oil Companies' (IOCs) ability to access the lower-cost oil in producing countries. The 'above ground' problems slow the pace of development of medium-cost oil in the largest producing countries in the Middle East and Russia. Despite the expectation of a continued demand for oil, oil exporting countries are concerned about the security of demand, and adapt their development plans accordingly.

Moreover, with the increased prices of the last few years and the resulting increase in oil revenues, the management of the monetarised oil wealth has become a concern as well. The value of the dollar has been slipping and oil exporting countries tried to match this depreciation by increasing oil prices. China's rise as an important manufacturer in the world, with the accompanying

J. de Zwaan, E. Bakker and S. van der Meer (eds.), Challenges in a Changing World

surpluses on the balance of trade, has led to a larger Chinese claim on world oil resources. The balance of payment imbalances in the world have increased accordingly, aligning international oil market developments with the overall shift in geo-economic relations.

Although the tensions in the international economic system were also visible in the global capital and goods markets, the impact on world oil markets has elevated oil to the political and strategic agenda of many nations. In this chapter we will focus on the run-up to an oil supply-constrained world and the impact on international relations when oil consuming countries are including the supply constraints in their energy policies.

Run up

Global concerns about the continuous rise in oil prices have been mounting since passing the psychological $100 threshold in January 2008. From the end of January 2008 oil prices continued to rise above the real oil price levels of the early 1980s. The recent price increases started as a result of a surge in demand from in particular China and India, which very quickly implied that the world buffer capacity had to be used to satisfy this new demand whereby the international oil market lost its flexibility to respond to short-term supply interruptions. Therefore international attention moved to the ability to adjust supply to the new demand levels.

The focus on the supply side of the international oil market intensified after the publication of the International Energy Agency's (IEA) *World Energy Outlook 2007* (WEO 2007) that made clear that some serious impediments to increased oil supply exist, which are predominantly 'above ground' issues. For the first time, the annual outlook from the usually upbeat IEA painted a grim short to mid-term outlook for the world oil supply. The WEO 2007 warned that: 'a supply-side crunch in the period to 2015, involving an abrupt escalation in oil prices, cannot be ruled out.'[1]

The IEA's warning struck at the heart of the physical trade in oil. Today, we live in an 86 million barrels per day world of oil supply, matched by about the same amount of oil demand.[2] However, a slowdown or even a reduction in global supply growth could send prices spiralling, since demand under current high oil prices has proven to be resilient, not in the least because the bulk of the oil demand is subsidised. Although high oil prices did impact demand in the United States and other OECD countries, where subsidies are absent, demand continued to grow in other economies.

---

1 International Energy Agency (IEA), *World Energy Outlook 2007* (Paris 2007) p. 43.

2 IEA, *Monthly oil market report* (Paris, 13 May 2008) pp. 5 and 19.

The IEA's *World Energy Outlook 2007* expects that between 2006 and 2015 an additional gross capacity of 37.5 million barrels per day (b/d) will have to come on-stream to supply a continued resilient demand and to offset the natural rate of decline of global oil production.[3] In its reference scenario, the IEA expects global oil demand to be 98.5 million b/d in 2015, up from about 86 million b/d in 2008.[4] Yet, the IEA expects to see an additional 25 million b/d of oil production to come on-stream up until 2015, which could result in a shortfall in oil supply of about 12.5 million b/d in 2015: hence a possible future *supply-side crunch*. These expectations exclude the impact of the current economic downturn on both supply and demand expectations, which, depending on the severity, could push the run-up to a possible crunch-back in time.

Converging demand and supply, diverging investment

The IEA's expectations of a crunch have been echoed by captains of industry from major IOCs. In October 2007, Total's CEO Christophe de Margerie put the world highest possible oil output at 100 million b/d overall, much below the IEA's expected level of 116 million b/d. He stated that the industry: '[have] been, all of us, too optimistic about the geology. Not in terms of reserves but in terms of how to develop those reserves: how much time it takes, how much realistically you need.'[5] In addition Jeroen van der Veer, CEO of Royal Dutch Shell, expected severe constraints in oil and gas supply within seven years when he stated in 2008: 'Shell estimates that after 2015 supplies of easy-to-access oil and gas will no longer keep up with demand.'[6]

Up until recently the IEA expected that global demand would be matched by an equal amount of production that will increasingly have to come from countries in the Middle East and North Africa (commonly referred to as MENA countries[7]).[8] However, these demand-based forecasts of the global oil supply have come under increased scrutiny. In response to these criticisms, the IEA's chief economist, Fatih Birol, indicated that the IEA will have to adjust the (WEO 2007) reference scenario of world oil output of 116 million b/d in 2030, to a more modest maximum output of 100 million b/d in 2030.[9] In addition, the IEA

---

[3] IEA, *supra* n. 1, p. 84.

[4] Ibid., p. 80.

[5] Ed Crooks, 'Total chief warns on oil output', *The Financial Times* (31 October 2007).

[6] Carl Mortished, 'Shell chief fears oil shortage in seven years', *Times Online* (25 January 2008).

[7] Most important producers from the MENA countries are: Iran, Iraq, Kuwait, Qatar, Saudi Arabia, United Arab Emirates, Algeria, Egypt and Libya.

[8] IEA, *World Energy Outlook 2005* (Paris 2005) p. 53.

[9] Neil King JR. & Peter Fritsch, 'Energy watchdog warns oil-production crunch', *The Wall Street Journal* (22 May 2008).

embarked on a study for the *World Energy Outlook 2008* (WEO 2008) that aims to formulate a supply-based scenario.[10] This scenario would bring the IEA scenarios more into line with global industry expectations (as mentioned above), and international criticism of the IEA's demand-based models.[11]

The outlook of a continued tight oil market is largely due to a slow response from the international oil industry (national [NOCs] as well as international oil companies [IOCs]) to bring sufficient supplies on-stream to compensate for declining oil-producing mature fields.[12] When discussing why future oil supply would be limited to 100 million b/d, Mr de Margerie stated that this limit was not because of a lack of oil in the ground, but that: 'the industry had also "misunderstood" that resource-rich countries would want to preserve some of their best oil fields for the future, while offering smaller and more difficult fields to foreign investors.'[13] This statement gives an insight into one of the fundamental flaws in the global oil market: even though the oil market is increasingly global in terms of consumption, it is increasingly fragmented in terms of investment.[14]

Despite the large amount of criticism directed at the IEA and its scenarios, the central role of MENA countries in our future oil supply is universally undisputed. This central role of the MENA countries has everything to do with their abundant hydrocarbon endowment. The MENA countries possess 61% of the known world oil reserves and 50% of the known gas reserves.[15] Apart from plentiful MENA reserves, they are also relatively easy (cheap) to develop. MENA countries could therefore, in theory, expediently supply the medium-cost oil which the market needs. Yet, the MENA reserves are usually developed by NOCs from the respective MENA countries, and have different priorities when it comes to the pace of developing such resources. Not only do the investments in the oil industry compete with other sectors of the economy, but these investments are also increasingly balanced against the performance of surplus oil funds.

As a consequence IOCs are destined to develop production portfolios that are increasingly dominated by high-cost barrels, and the IOCs consequently require substantial global oil prices to recoup these costs. In a response to the drop in oil prices since July 2008, Mr de Margerie stated that major high-cost

---

[10] IEA, *supra* n. 1, p. 84.

[11] King & Fritsch, *supra* n. 9.

[12] Coby van der Linde, Wilbur Perlot & Femke Hoogeveen, 'Tomorrow's mores: The future geopolitical system and the structure of the international oil market', *Politica Exterior* (Madrid 2006) p. 1.

[13] Crooks, *supra* n. 5.

[14] 'Energy Watch', Goldman Sachs (20 February 2008).

[15] IEA, *supra* n. 8, p. 56.

oil projects were at risk when the oil price would drop beneath the $90 mark.[16] As a result global capital markets can only invest (via IOCs) in high-end expensive oil projects that will carry a great risk premium to develop under continued volatile market conditions. International capital will not have access to develop the more lucrative medium-cost oil that can provide considerable relief to world markets and ensures a rate of return on investment even if markets remain volatile.

The current oil price is determined by the marginal cost of supply (e.g., the cost of the last barrel that can be produced profitably, which is about $80 for high-cost oil developed by IOCs), while supply and demand fundamentals, a short-term risk premium and long-term scarcity considerations account for the remainder of the oil price.[17] The continued volatility in the oil price will find its origin in supply-demand fundamentals and short-term risk premiums, while long-term scarcity could drive up prices in the long run. Below we will discuss the geopolitics of medium-cost oil to alleviate supply constraints, while we will then continue to discuss other sources of volatility, i.e., short-term risk premiums.

Geopolitics of medium-cost oil

With international capital increasingly locked out of medium-cost oil investment opportunities (leaving them exposed to the current volatile price conditions) NOCs will become increasingly responsible for investment in substantial medium-cost oil production capacity to satisfy world oil demand. In the past, some of these companies have been responsible for managing spare capacity, notably Saudi Arabia, the United Arab Emirates and until 1990 Kuwait, thus providing the market with crucial flexibility. This flexibility could return temporarily in the face of a global economic downturn, but it is unlikely that these NOCs will willingly create an excess capacity in the future.

NOCs from the major producer countries do not necessarily share the economic goals of the consumer countries (lower energy prices to foster economic growth in the centres of energy consumption), nor can they always afford to create excess capacity that helps to balance world markets. Some member countries of the Organization of Petroleum Exporting Countries (OPEC) are experi-

---

16 Carola Hoyos, 'Oil price fall puts projects at risk', *The Financial Times* (12 September 2008).

17 Jan Hein Jesse & Coby van der Linde, *Oil turbulence in the next decade: an essay on high oil prices in a supply constrained world* (The Hague, Clingendael International Energy Programme 2008).

encing difficulties in maintaining production levels, such as Venezuela and Nigeria. Only a country such as Iraq can expand its production capacity substantially due to past underutilization. Other countries are becoming more interested in conservation. As a prime example of resource holders preserving their finite resources for the future is considered the recent declaration by the King of Saudi Arabia, in which he stated that any new found reserves will be preserved for future generations.[18]

Although NOCs differ according to size, function, organization, competence and relationship to the state, NOCs are dominant in global oil production with more than 77% of world oil reserves under their direct control.[19] IOCs have direct access to about 7% of world oil reserves, while they had access to about 85% in the 1970s.[20] NOCs from MENA producer countries are instrumental for their national governments in achieving their domestic political and economic goals, and they are therefore often vital for domestic regime legitimacy.[21] Hence NOCs' decision-making and the resulting investment in oil production reflects an effort to balance social and political objectives with commercial imperatives, as opposed to IOCs where commercial imperatives dominate decision-making.[22] Therefore despite high oil prices NOCs will not necessarily increase oil output, or invest more in future exploration and production, because their priorities are with their countries' long-term gradual economic development.

In addition, the main MENA producers are also members of the OPEC that tries to coordinate global oil supply.[23] The exploration of resources and especially the production of resources for the world market are capped for OPEC member states, that have to limit production to their respective quotas. These individual quotas result in a small amount of spare capacity currently estimated to be 2.5 million b/d (mostly held by Saudi Arabia and the United Arab Emirates). The spare production capacity available is usually comprised of very heavy grades of crude oil that are difficult to process (due to refining constraints) and

---

[18] Carola Hoyos, 'Saudis put oil capacity rise on hold', *The Financial Times* (21 April 2008).

[19] 'The changing role of National Oil Companies in international energy markets', *Baker Institute Policy Report 35* (Houston 2007) p. 1.

[20] 'Report of IOCs' demise greatly exaggerated', 47 *Petroleum Intelligence Weekly*, No. 8 (25 February 2008).

[21] Joe Barnes & Matthew E. Chen, *NOCs and U.S. foreign policy* (Houston, The James A. Baker III Institute for Public Policy 2007) p. 3.

[22] Ibid.

[23] In addition to the major MENA producing countries, Saudi Arabia, Iraq, Iran, Kuwait, the United Arab Emirates, Qatar, Libya, and Algeria, OPEC members also include the major producing countries of Venezuela, Nigeria, Angola, Ecuador and Indonesia (although Indonesia is a net importer of petroleum and will leave OPEC in 2008) together controlling nearly 75% of global proven oil reserves.

are therefore less in demand on the world market.[24] The IEA expects OPEC's spare capacity to erode to minimal levels by 2012.[25]

Although the current high oil prices have increased international political pressure on OPEC to release more oil on the market, OPEC members have so far been reluctant to do so when oil prices were approaching $100 per barrel once more. Only Saudi Arabia increased its production in July 2008 to calm the markets but in the September 2008 OPEC meeting it was decided to adhere to the original production quota once again. OPEC members argued that supply was meeting demand, and that the rise in prices was partly a consequence of speculation and a lack of refining capacity, not of market fundamentals.[26]

OPEC has been very cautious in reading the market signals in order to avoid the mistake made in 1997 when the cartel released 2.5 million b/d to mitigate rising oil prices just as the Asian financial crisis surfaced. The Asia crisis slowed global economic growth which resulted in a drop in the oil price to $10.[27] The current credit crisis and the expected impact on world demand are feeding the oil producing countries' reluctance to increase supply. In addition, the climate agenda that has recently gained considerable traction in OECD economies, most notably the EU, is further feeding reluctance to invest in oil production. This 'insecurity of demand' is currently withholding investment for a possible 8-10 million b/d of future medium-cost oil production in major resource-holder states.[28] Moreover, the OPEC member states are content with price levels at around $100 a barrel, partly because some of the more vocal members, most notably Venezuela, need a fairly high oil price in 2008 and 2009 to maintain their external balance.[29]

The output of major reserve holders in the MENA and OPEC countries will continue to be a complex balance between their state's, NOCs' and OPEC's objectives.[30] These different social and political objectives from different interconnected actors are making the amount of investment in medium-cost oil production capacity, and the eventual oil delivered to market, very uncertain. In any event, the delay between investment decisions and actual oil production will continue to constrain production growth beyond 2015. It is therefore very

---

24 Grant Smith, 'IEA Says Lower OPEC Capacity to Keep Market "Tight"', *Bloomberg* (1 July 2008).

25 King & Fritsch, *supra* n. 9.

26 'Interview Opec's Abdullah al-Badri', 47 *Petroleum Intelligence Weekly*, No. 19 (12 May 2008).

27 Jad Mouawad, 'OPEC to lift output modestly', *The New York Times* (12 September 2008).

28 Jesse & Van der Linde, *supra* n. 17, p. 10.

29 'The Floor Price for OPEC States', *Goliath* (17 March 2008). Available at: <http://goliath.ecnext.com/>.

30 Barnes & Chen, *supra* n. 21, p. 7.

likely that under continued (subsidized) demand growth, and the decline rates of current oil fields, the global oil market will continue to be a 'sellers' market with very limited spare capacity to compensate for sudden supply disruptions. In addition, price volatility will also increase, which could further accentuate existing geopolitical tensions about the security of supply and demand.

Short-term risk premiums and price volatility

As a result of the continued tightness in the international oil market and a lack of spare capacity, the international oil price will be susceptible to relatively minor incidents that can have a large effect on oil prices and therefore on the consuming economies. Although the causes of disruptions in global oil supply could be as various as the locations where they occur, from natural causes, to maintenance, to violence, the tight market circumstances increase the vulnerability to risks related to producer and transit government (domestic and regional) policies. Also non-political short-term risks related to 'force majeure' incidents could trigger volatile prices and increase the insecurity of supply in global oil markets.

Force majeure: stuff can go wrong…

Force majeure is a common clause in contracts that essentially frees both parties from liability or obligations when an extraordinary event or circumstance beyond the control of the parties to the contract occurs. Oil companies can invoke 'force majeure' when accidents occur that are triggered by weather-related incidents, rebel attacks or industrial unrest. These 'force majeure' events have contributed to several of the major supply disruptions in recent history. The most recent ones are related to the rebel attacks and other problems on oil installations in Nigeria or the Nigerian offshore, reducing supplies by up to 1 million barrels per day since 2005.[31] The impact of a supply disruption is determined by the level of inventories in consuming countries, the duration of the disruption and the spare capacity that is available on the world market.[32] At the presentation of the *2007 Oil Security Report*, the IEA stated that member states held 4.1 billion barrels (or 122 days worth of imports) in oil stocks.[33]

---

31 Peter Richter, 'Nigeria attacks disrupt oil flow', *Los Angeles Times* (29 June 2008).

32 IEA, *Oil supply security: emergency response of IEA countries 2007* (Paris 2007) p. 18.

33 Ibid. p. 12.

Table 1. **Major oil supply disruptions**[34]

Year	**Incident**	**Supply loss (mb/d)**
2008	Hurricane Gustav/Ike	0.7
2005-2008	Nigerian Delta Crisis	0.7 – 1.0
2005	Hurricane Katrina/Rita	1.5
2003	War in Iraq	2.3
2002-2003	Venezuelan Strike	2.6
2001	Iraqi oil export suspension	2.1
1991	Iraqi invasion of Kuwait	4.3
1981	Outbreak of Iran-Iraq war	4.1
1979	Iranian Revolution	5.6
1973-1974	Arab-Israeli war and Arab oil embargo	4.3
1967	Six-day war	2.0
1957	Suez crisis	2.0

As OPEC's spare capacity has dwindled from its historic peak of nearly 5 million b/d in 2000 or 4.6% of world demand to current levels of about 2.3 million b/d (2-3% of world demand), smaller and quite localised incidents in producing regions can have disproportionate consequences for the world economy. Generally speaking, three 'force majeure' incidents come to the forefront that have plagued global oil supply in recent years (see Table 1). First of all, hurricane Katrina that struck the southern coast of the United States in 2005; apart from a shut-down in crude oil production, Katrina also wreaked havoc on refining capacity on the US Gulf coast, which caused a release of product stock to compensate for refinery outages. In response, the IEA member countries released a total of 59.5 million barrels of crude oil and products from their strategic stocks on the world market.[35] In 2008, the impact of hurricanes Ike and Gustav is almost as large, with 700,000 barrels of production shut in (or about half of the production in that region) and three refineries, with a capacity of about 700,000 b/d, that are still closed.[36]

---

34 Ibid., p. 19; and CIEP analysis.

35 Ibid., p. 28.

36 U.S. Energy Information Administration Website: <http://tonto.eia.doe.gov/oog/special/hurricanes/gustav.html?featureclicked=1&>.

Another 'force majeure' situation is the continued unrest in the Niger Delta where rebel attacks and sabotage have severely hindered onshore oil production. Despite a rise in offshore supplies to compensate for the onshore fall in production, strikes by oil field workers have further limited production, causing a total shut-in of production of about 1 million b/d for the foreseeable future.[37] Strikes by oil industry employees have had dire consequences for global oil supply in the past, the prime example being the strike at Venezuela's state oil company PDVSA in 2002-2003. Not only did the strike (aimed at the Chavez government) result in the temporary loss of about 2.6 million b/d on the world oil market, it also resulted in the laying off of about 11,000 of its experienced employees which continues to hinder the development of Venezuela's oil production.[38]

As shown in Table 1, most of the large supply disruptions on the global oil market were due to circumstances beyond the control of oil companies. Except for natural disasters, other 'force majeure' disruptions (rebel attacks, labour strikes) are all intimately related to host government policies that could cause or prevent any future supply disruptions. Especially resource-holder government domestic policies are an important factor (albeit interdependent with other factors) that limit or stimulate world oil supply.

Who owns what?: host government policies to strengthen public ownership of resources

Although host government policies can influence the development of resources through a broad range of policies (or a lack thereof, since unrest in Nigeria can be contributed to a lack of wealth distribution policies from the central government), three specific issues come to the fore when considering the opportunity for oil companies to invest in oil production in resource-holding states.

Firstly, access restrictions for oil companies to develop reserves. Currently, about 75% of proven conventional oil reserves are outside the realm of foreign direct investments. After 1991 access to global reserves temporarily increased due to the collapse of the Soviet Union and the chaotic privatization that ensued in the Russian Federation. However, as the developed OECD economies expected that states from the Former Soviet Union (FSU) would integrate into the liberalized world economy with a well functioning open and transparent oil market, they were in for an unpleasant surprise.[39] Since 2003, the Russian gov-

---

[37] Richter, *supra* n. 31.

[38] David R. Mares & Nelson Altamirano, *Venezuela's PDVSA and world energy markets; corporate strategies, its behaviour and influence* (Houston, The James A. Baker III Institute for Public Policy 2007) p. 6.

[39] Van der Linde, Perlot & Hoogeveen, *supra* n. 12, p. 1.

ernment has initiated a crackdown on foreign-owned oil projects in Russia, in order to establish state energy giants that could further develop the Russian economy and society.[40] In the first months of 2008, Russian oil production has not grown for the first time since Vladimir Putin became president. Therefore, doubts have arisen as to the sustainability of oil production in Russia in the coming years. Experts point at the unwillingness of the remaining private oil companies to invest, as they build up war chests and pay out dividends to shareholders in anticipation of the government's next move. In addition, the large state oil producers are also building up war chests to fund further takeovers and are paying off debts created by takeovers in the past. Under these circumstances no funds for investment in oil production are available, especially since the government has also increased its windfall profit tax to boost its own coffers.

The uncertainty that resource nationalism has created for further investment is in the Russian case fuelled by increased taxes on oil revenues. The continued and relentless rise in global oil prices makes governments eager to increase their share of the oil revenues.[41] Venezuela serves as a prime example of a major producing country that is trying to increase oil revenues despite a decline in oil production. The national assembly in Venezuela has recently imposed a new tax on the export of oil which should boost government revenues to about $9 billion.[42] In addition, other producing countries (like Kazakhstan) have strengthened their tax regime in order to increase the government's share of petroleum revenues.

The rising oil prices have also affected tax regimes in the upstream sectors in major consuming countries. Most notably in the United States where a fierce debate has erupted as to whether IOCs are entitled to manufacturing tax credits in the face of substantially higher oil prices. Democrats in the US Congress have started efforts to reduce these tax credits by some $18 billion, arguing that these are no longer necessary since oil prices have risen nearly ten fold since the legislation was developed in the 1990s. Industry executives have stated that a shift in tax legislation could discourage further investment in US oil production, limiting future oil output.[43] The underlining message was that businesses will invest in (high-cost) oil production when they have a long-term viable busi-

---

40 Harley Balzer, 'Vladimir Putin on Russian energy policy', *The National Interest* (November 2005). Available at: <http://www.nationalinterest.org/Article.aspx?id=10884>.

41 Alex Forbes, 'Scramble for assets goes global', *Petroleum Economist* (February 2008) p. 4.

42 Venezuela strengthened its export tax to about 50% levy when the Brent benchmark is at an 70 USD average, and a 60% levy when Brent prices hit an 100 USD monthly average. *Petroleum Intelligence Weekly* (21 April 2008).

43 Stephen Hargreaves, 'Congress, critical of tax breaks, lays into oil execs', CNNmoney.com (1 April 2008).

ness case and a long-term predictable tax regime to match. Fiscal stability continues to be of great importance for future oil output, especially in mature producing regions where the marginal cost of an extra barrel of oil is substantially higher.

Recently producer countries have focussed on environmental policies either to minimize the environmental impact of oil production or to pursue alternative political agendas. Government policies to mitigate environmental impacts of oil production can prohibit the development of resources, or substantially increase costs to develop resources. At the same time environmental laws can be used to break up existing agreements (most notably Production Sharing Agreements). The Shakalin II example is a case in point. The lead operator in the development company, Royal Dutch Shell, was effectively forced by the Russian government to hand over its controlling share, after months of discussions over environmental 'infractions'. However, as soon as the handover had occurred, the Russian government's environmental concerns seem to have disappeared. In short: environmental legislation can obstruct, delay or increase the costs of investments in global oil production.

Mitigating volatility: rising prices

Short-term supply disruptions are increasingly caused by either 'force majeure' incidents or producer countries' government policies. The only volatility mitigating strategies for consumer nations that could be adopted on the supply side is an even further expansion of high-cost oil production, since medium-cost oil continues to be off-limits. This will involve investments in output in reasonably stable political environments, such as tar-sand development in Canada, the Outer Continental Shelf (OCS) development in the United States, deep offshore in Brazil, or extensive (and expensive) usage of Enhanced Oil Recovery (EOR) techniques in currently producing regions such as the North Sea. However, in doing so oil companies will continue to run into a large array of interdependent factors that will facilitate or prohibit investments to increase global output. These 'above ground' investment risks might not affect IOCs and NOCs equally, but the aggregated global impact on the industry will be the same, i.e., higher costs, increased delays and lower global output.

Industry cycle: investing in future output, while mitigating a constrained past

To expand future oil production the petroleum industry has to gear up across the board, not only to increase drilling capacity, but also to be able to transport and refine and to eventually sell petroleum to consumers. Since considerable time is needed to address the overall shortages in the petroleum industry, soaring costs for the use of existing equipment and expertise are a direct consequence. Most notably a lack of drilling capacity has sent prices for drilling rigs through the roof. Since 2002 the monthly rates for deepwater rigs have gone up from $125,000 to $600,000 for long-term contracts.[44]

Despite the current high oil prices that have developed over the past few years, the global oil industry still needs to adapt after years of underinvestment, to increase global oil production. Alleviating shortages in equipment, expertise and raw materials is hampered by rising cost inflation that will continue to obstruct an expedient build-up of industry capacity. Cost inflation has risen due to the fact that the raw materials, equipment and expertise needed for the expansion of the industry's capacity are bought on an international market where the petroleum industry has to compete with other industries that need these resources as well. For example: although 75 ultra deepwater rigs have been ordered (to be delivered between 2008 and 2011), the shipbuilding industry is suffering from the same shortages in raw materials, personnel and energy that plague the construction sector as a whole. In response prices for new drilling vessels have risen from about $100 million to about $500 million in the last year.[45]

Due to the large restructuring of the oil industries in the 1990s, an entire generation of petro-professionals was lost when they were forced to pursue carriers in other sectors. To make matters worse, the number of academic departments in petro-technical areas has shrunk, reducing the number of available academic professionals even further. As a result, the current petro-workforce is ageing and in need of replacement as over half are to retire within a decade.[46] In response to the increased demand for expertise and the lack of supply thereof, global wages have increased in the petroleum industry. Currently in the United States a petroleum engineer will have a higher starting salary than an Ivy League graduate going to Wall Street (although that is under today's financial market conditions perhaps not such a big feat).[47] The global shortage in petroleum engineers has called on those countries with a surplus in graduates (i.e., China and Indonesia) to offset the need for engineers. Although engineers from other sectors are also recruited, the petroleum industry's public image is also an ob-

---

44 Jad Mouawad & Martin Fackler, 'Dearth of ship delays drilling of offshore oil', *The New York Times* (19 July 2008).

45 Ibid.

46 Mark Anderson & Hilary Dayton, 'Human resources', Working Document of the NPC Global Oil and Gas Study (Washington D.C. 2007) p. 2. Available at: <http://downloadcenter.connectlive.com/events/npc071807/pdf-downloads/Study_Topic_Papers/23-TTG-Human-Resources.pdf>.

47 Daniel Yergin, 'Oil has reached a turning point', *The Financial Times* (27 May 2008).

stacle to alleviate the labour shortages.[48] As a result labour costs within the petroleum industry will remain high in the future, thereby exacerbating the overall cost inflation for petroleum development.

Another contributing factor to rising cost inflation in the petroleum industry is the so-called 'credit squeeze' following the US sub prime mortgage crisis. As a result the international cost of investment capital has increased due to banks' reduced willingness to extend credit. Although this reduced willingness has not influenced the availability of credit for petroleum industries, banks do want a higher return on their capital. The international financial markets are thereby contributing to the cost inflation in the petroleum industry. As a consequence of these capacity constraints in raw material, labour and financial markets inflationary pressure on resource development will remain high for the oil industry as a whole (both NOCs and IOCs).

Pipeline infrastructure constraints: how to get oil to markets?

As a result of soaring costs, oil pipelines are also turning out to be more expensive than expected. The construction of a pipeline is a complex and capital-intensive process. The construction is undertaken by international consortia of multinational companies that finance, construct and operate the pipeline. A pipeline is capital intensive, has low flexibility (once constructed the flow of oil is unchangeable) and requires a large scale of operations.[49] In some particular cases this complexity directly obstructs the development of oil reserves, especially when combined with unwilling transit countries that seek to increase their share revenues from oil flowing through their countries.

As a prime example of continued complexity surrounding the development of oil pipelines and the consequences for oil development in a potential oil province is the CPC pipeline (operated by the Caspian Pipeline Consortium). The development of the Caspian oil basin, long touted as an important alternative for OPEC oil production on the world market, has been severely hindered by a lack of capacity to deliver oil to the world market. Despite the development of extra pipeline capacity via China and Turkey, the expansion of the main export route via Russia has remained cumbersome. The CPC pipeline that has to deliver Kazakh oil to the world market is run by a consortium, half of which consists of governments and the other half of IOCs.[50]

---

48 Anderson & Dayton, *supra* n. 46.

49 R.H. Dekmeijan & H.H. Simonian, *Troubled waters: The geopolitics of the Caspian region* (London 2001) p. 34.

50 Governments: Russia (24%), Kazakhstan (19%), Oman (7%); Private Companies: Chevron (15%), ExxonMobil (7.5%), Lucarco (12.5%), Rosneft-Shell (7.5%), AGIP (2%), BG (2%), Orix (1.75%), and Kazakhstan pipeline ventures (1.75%). The Omani government has recently

The pipeline's capacity reached the targeted 560,000 b/d in 2005. An agreed increase in capacity would then expand capacity to 1,350,000–1,600,000 b/d by 2015.[51] However, negotiations on the expansion of the CPC pipeline have been stalled by the Russian government. This has led the TengizChevroil consortium to postpone the additional investments to ramp up production in the Kazakh Tengiz oil field until 2008-2009.[52] Despite some recent progress on the expansion of the CPC pipeline, the lack of export capacity has forced Kazakhstan to seek exports via the Caspian Sea into the BTC Pipeline.[53] These investments will take many years to materialize into export capacity and additional oil supply to world markets. The lack of infrastructure capacity and their slow development can therefore severely limit world oil supply.

Sector maturity: approaching the limits of possibilities?

The rise in oil prices has been accompanied by a steep increase in development costs. In order to manage costs increasing pressure is being exerted on existing energy infrastructure. Increasing oil prices make investments in further oil field development with additional Enhanced Oil Recovery (EOR) techniques profitable, which causes drilling platforms, pipelines and other infrastructure to be utilised for longer than they were originally designed for. As a result outages in infrastructure may more frequently hamper global oil production. The shut-down of a pipeline at BP's Prudhoe Bay oil fields in August 2006 initially resulted in the loss of about 400,000 b/d of oil supply to world markets (approx. 8% of US total oil production). Although the shut-down was overcome fairly quickly (resulting in an average loss of 27,000 b/d for the third quarter that year), it did result in BP's commitment to replace all pipelines to ensure future operations.[54] To mitigate the effects of wear and tear on supply, additional investments will have to be made to keep infrastructure running; this will increase the costs of oil production in addition to general cost inflation.

A second result of increased oil prices in conjunction with rising resource nationalism in major producing countries is the opening up of increasingly re-

---

announced that it would sell its share to the Russian government, increasing Russian influence but keeping the balance between public and private.

51 *CPC-brochure*, Caspian Pipeline Consortium (5 June 2007). Available at: <http://www.cpc.ru/_press/documents/cpc_a4_0303_en.pdf>.

52 'Kazakhstan oil output and export data dramatize need for Trans-Caspian outlets'; online: <http://www.kogiguk.com/News/Archive/2007/Jan/Article3044.htm> (13 February 2007).

53 47 *Petroleum Intelligence Weekly*, No. 24 (16 June 2008) p. 7.

54 'BP 2006 results' Press conference, 24 October 2006. Available at: <http://www.bp.com/liveassets/bp_internet/globalbp/STAGING/global_assets/downloads/B/bp_third_quarter_2006_press_briefing_transcript_q_and_a.pdf>.

mote regions (like the Arctic) to oil exploration and production by IOCs and NOCs. An example is the development of the huge (an estimated 13 billion barrels of recoverable reserves) Kashagan oil field in the Caspian Sea that must face some of the most inhospitable conditions in the world. The IOCs developing Kashagan have to face extreme offshore conditions in a landlocked sea with shifting ice, and temperatures of –35°C in the winter (and 40°C in the summer), while the reservoir itself is under extreme pressure (about 500 times the surface pressure) and filled with noxious hydrogen sulphide gas.[55] As a result of these extreme weather, geological and geographical conditions the costs of full development have recently been revised upwards to $136 billion from $57 billion.[56] As a result of this cost explosion the Kazakh government has increased its share in the development consortium, thereby increasing its oil revenues from an earlier stage onwards.[57] Kashagan is expected to reach a peak production of 1.5 million b/d in 2019, with early oil in 2013.

As Kashagan was discovered in 2000 and peak production will not be reached until 19 years later, it shows that the speedy development of these major reserves in difficult conditions can be extremely costly and requires considerable time-spans. The recently discovered ultra-deep offshore Tupi oilfield off the coast of Brazil was heralded as a major find. Tupi is considered to contain between 5 and 8 billion barrels of oil and part of a sub-salt complex in the Santos basin.[58] The field was discovered nearly 5,000 meters below the ocean floor in about 2,100 meters of water which makes for a total exploration depth of more than 7,000 metres. In addition, considerable finds have been announced in the Jupiter section of the Santos basin, at equal depths. Although the Brazilian NOC Petrobras considers early oil from the Tupi field to be possible by 2011, it will take considerable time to bring both fields into full production.[59]

The incredible depths at which these new resources are located, the very low temperatures and the extreme pressure mean that development is made extremely difficult and expensive. The Tupi oilfield is estimated to cost anything between

---

[55] Guy Chazan, 'In Caspian, big oil fights ice, fumes, Kazakhs', *Dow Jones Newswire* (28 August 2007).

[56] Isabel Gorst, 'Caspian lesson for oil giants', *The Financial Times* (3 September 2007).

[57] The Kashagan Production Sharing Agreement stipulates that companies are allowed to recoup their investments before any revenue goes to the host government; hence the Kazakh government wanted to increase its share in the developing consortium to ensure more speedy revenues from oil production.

[58] 'What lies beneath: is there really an ocean of oil off Brazil?', *The Economist* (18 April 2008). Available at: <http://www.economist.com/daily/news/PrinterFriendly.cfm?story_id=11043022>.

[59] Izundu Uchenna, 'Petrobras to start Tupi oil development by 2011', *Oil & Gas Journal* (17 January 2008). Available at: <http://www.redorbit.com/news/business/1218926/petrobras_to_start_tupi_oil_development_by_2011/index.html#>.

$100 and $200 billion to develop.[60] The total sub-salt off-shore Campos basin development is expected to cost anything between $600 billion and $1 trillion.[61] However, even these broad estimates are very preliminary and subject to considerable change as cost inflation might continue to rise.

As oil companies will venture into deeper and more inhospitable terrain, the technology and skills necessary to extract resources will continue to be put to the test. This will require huge-scale investment projects with multiple partners that are increasingly difficult to manage, due to their sheer size and project complexities, as is clearly exemplified in the case of Kashagan. As the petroleum industry is looking to increase world oil production it runs into a large array of obstacles that increase the price of the last barrel produced. This will raise the floor of the oil price even further, increasing the long-term oil price, but hopefully mitigating its volatility.

Conclusion

The various industrial, geopolitical, and financial factors described above continue to dominate, to a large extent, the availability of oil on the world market. As the 'above ground' turmoil continues to be very diverse and geographically widespread, supply is likely to remain tight for the years to come. The global oil market and economy will continue to feel the spill-over effects of local and regional short-term risks (e.g., high and volatile prices for energy and oil in particular). Due to the small, various and local nature of these crises they are very difficult to predict and to avoid.

Any serious attempt by the developed economies and other net oil consumers around the world to mitigate these risks will be futile unless spare capacity is created to make the world oil market more resilient to short-term disruptions. The available medium-cost oil needs to be unlocked and made available for the international market. To achieve this, the oil producing countries' claim for security of demand will need to be addressed. In addition, the expansion of oil production capacity can only be realized by increasing high-cost oil production, but this would also require the confidence that the oil price stays above the inflated cost levels. Of course the current crisis in the international capital markets could cause the global economy to slow down, thereby reducing the immediate pressure on oil supplies. When the resource-holding states and their NOCs

---

60 Anna Driver, 'Brazil's Tupi seen a bonanza for oil service companies', *Reuters* (11 March 2008).

61 'Petrobras in need of a capital idea', 47 *Petroleum Intelligence Weekly*, No. 39 (29 September 2008) p. 3.

look at the current slowdown of the world economy their reluctance to invest might increase. All we can hope for is that the recession can buy us time to prevent an oil crunch and that this time will be wisely used.

Fragile States: State Building is not Enough

Louise Anten

Introduction: why the increased interest?

The recent international interest in so-called 'fragile states' is partly caused by the awareness that global security is increasingly linked to conditions of conflict, political instability and the lack of development anywhere in the world. The terrorist attacks of 11 September 2001 were an eye-opener in this respect. The linkages between global security and a number of interrelated threats and trends are explored, for example, in the 2004 Report of the UN High Level Panel on Threats, Challenges and Change[1] and at the September 2005 UN World Summit.

Another source of interest originates within the development community and its aim to realise the Millennium Development Goals by 2015. Although steady progress towards these goals is being made in many parts of the world, it became clear that fragile states lag seriously behind.

In both trains of thought, it is increasingly thought that a functioning state is crucial to reduce fragility and facilitate development. This explains the focus on state building in policies dealing with fragile countries.

This chapter will explore the reasons for the increased international interest, what fragile states are and why they are likely to remain on the international agenda. It will discuss global and in-country factors and trends, concluding that these will probably lead to an increase in state fragility in the coming decades. It will then turn to the policy implications, arguing that a limited focus on state building in these countries is unlikely to solve the issues. The industrialised states will have to effectively address factors leading to fragility that they themselves are largely responsible for.

---

[1] See <http://www.un.org/secureworld/>.

J. de Zwaan, E. Bakker and S. van der Meer (eds.), Challenges in a Changing World

What are fragile states?

There is no internationally accepted definition or listing of fragile states. This is partly so because the term is used for a very heterogeneous group of countries struggling with problems of governance, security and/or development. State fragility is not a clear-cut condition; rather there is a continuum from collapsed states to well-functioning states. Politically, the term is felt to be stigmatising by the countries concerned, which hinders acceptance of the concept. Various other terms are in use, like 'failing states', 'failed states' or 'collapsed states', indicating a scale of increasingly problematic situations.

The Failed States Index, which is published annually since 2005 by the Fund for Peace, is one of the more transparent efforts to rank states on indicators of state failure (defined as internal conflict and state collapse).[2] The Index uses 12 indicators. Four indicators cover social aspects (e.g., mounting demographic pressures), two are economic indicators (e.g., sharp and/or severe economic decline) and six political indicators (e.g., criminalisation and/or delegitimisation of the state). Of the 177 countries ranked in 2008, 35 were in the (most serious) alert zone and 92 in the warning zone. The top 5 are Somalia, Sudan, Zimbabwe, Chad and Iraq. An overwhelming majority of alert states are in Africa (Central, Horn and West) and to a lesser extent in Central Asia (e.g., Afghanistan, Pakistan and Bangladesh).

Many development aid donors stress that failures of good governance lie at the heart of state fragility. The governance systems in fragile states are seen as lacking in resilience, in strong interaction between state and society and in a dynamic social contract between the two. Fragile states are defined as states where the government cannot or will not deliver the core functions to its population. These core functions are generally seen to consist of security and the rule of law, the delivery of basic public goods and services, political legitimacy and development.[3] The development analysis of fragile states limits itself to low-income countries.

Other actors, e.g., in the domains of foreign policy and defence, rightly place emphasis on external threats and shocks that can put pressure on the capacity and resilience of countries and their governments.[4] The models developed are very helpful to illustrate the complexity of state fragility, and the large number of possible causes or triggers, as well as internal and external stabilising factors.

---

[2] See <http://www.fundforpeace.org>.

[3] ODI – JICA, 'Donors and the "Fragile States" Agenda: A Survey of Current Thinking and Practice', 2006 <http://www.odi.org.uk/events/horizons_nov06/15dec/JICA%20Report.pdf>.

[4] E.g., the UK Foreign and Commonwealth Office, see <http://www.strategy.gov.uk/work_areas/countries_at_risk/index.asp>.

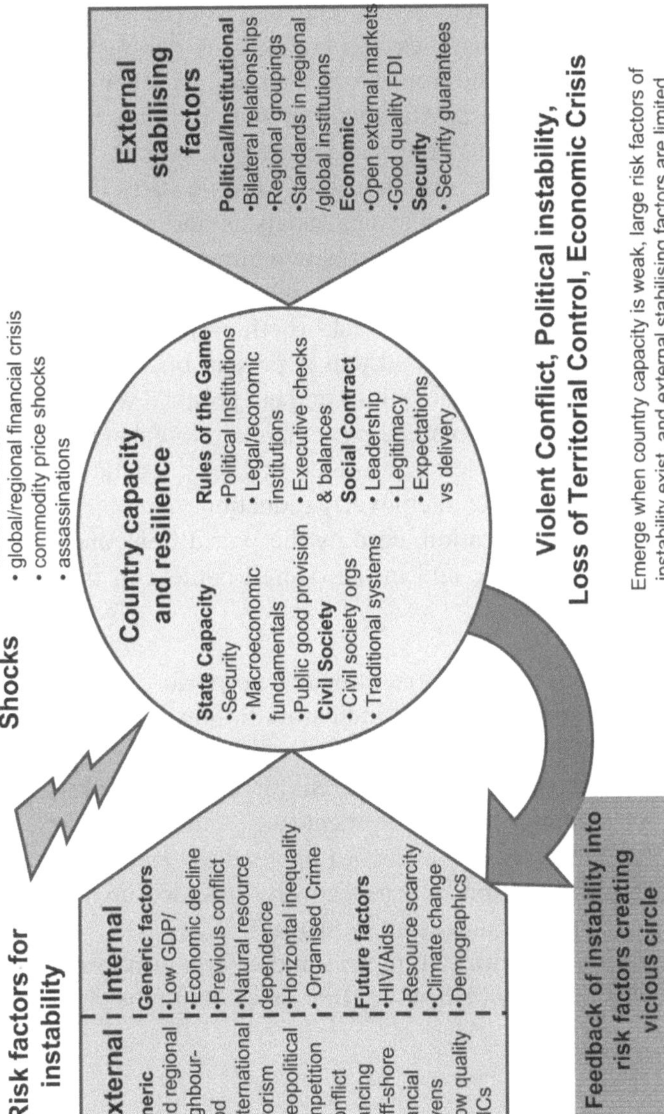

Figure 1. **The Instability Framework**

Figure 1 is the model developed by the United Kingdom Prime Minister's Strategy Unit.[5]

Fragility (in the form of violent conflict, political instability, and/or economic crisis) emerges when country resilience is weak, internal but also external risk factors and/or shocks for instability are high and external stabilising factors are insufficient. Instability feeds back and strengthens risk factors of instability, creating a vicious circle. The framework (see Fig. 1) retains the capacity and resilience of the state as the central factor of state fragility, but it creates more balance between internal and external causes and remedies.

Various efforts have been made to classify fragile states into more homogeneous sub-categories which would help analysis and policy development. A simple classification used by DFID takes two dimensions of governance (government capacity and political will) as defining characteristics and distinguishes three types of fragile states: 'weak-weak' (both political will and capacity are weak), 'weak but willing' (political will is present but capacity is weak) and 'strong but unresponsive' (capacity is strong but political willingness for development is weak; these states may be repressive).[6] Note that the latter category of 'strong' states is nevertheless considered fragile, since the states in question do not deliver core functions like poverty reduction.

Another helpful classification, used by the World Bank among others, tries to add trends in governance and in the overall context of the countries concerned, and distinguishes:[7]

- Deterioration: capacity and/or willingness to perform core state functions in decline, economic and social indicators falling (e.g., Zimbabwe, Papua New Guinea);
- Arrested development, prolonged crisis or impasse: lack of willingness, failure to use authority for development (e.g., Guinea-Conakry, Fiji);
- Post-conflict transition: peace accord opens the window of opportunity to work with government on reform, capacity low, willingness may be high or low (e.g., Liberia, Afghanistan, Sudan);
- Early recovery or reform: willingness and efforts to improve performance but uneven results, may be post-conflict or not (e.g., Sierra Leone).

---

[5] Ibid.

[6] DFID, 'Why we need to work more effectively in fragile states', London, January 2005.

[7] Cf. World Bank, 'Fragile States – Good practice in country assistance strategies', Washington, December 2005; and Brinkerhoff, 'Capacity Development in Fragile States', Maastricht, ECDPM, May 2007.

A third classification ranks conflict-affected fragile states according to the conflict phase, distinguishing states at risk of conflict (e.g., Nigeria), states in the midst of war (e.g., Democratic Republic of Congo) and post-conflict states emerging (or trying to emerge) from external or civil war.[8] A further sub-classification of post-conflict states is helpful for operational purposes, distinguishing the three phases of stabilisation, reorganisation plus institution building, and consolidation, together covering a period of some ten years.[9]

In all classifications the assignment of countries to sub-classes remains a hazardous job since this will necessarily involve an amount of subjective assessment of the country context. Moreover, fragile situations may change very quickly, with states moving between sub-classes.

Past and future trends in state fragility

Systematic attention to fragile states with various actors is of recent interest (2002-2005), so past trends have not been much analysed from this perspective. But if one takes the number of internal armed conflicts (civil wars) as a proxy indicator, the findings show a decline since 1990. The number of armed conflicts has steadily decreased from a peak of 51 in 1992 to 31 at the end of 2005. Practically all of these conflicts were (or are) civil wars. Since the number of states has increased in the same period (from 159 to 192) the number of countries affected has decreased even more. While in 1990 almost one in four countries was directly affected by armed conflict on its territory, in 2005 only slightly above one in nine was.[10] At the same time, the number of UN peacekeeping missions has been growing in this period, from 10 in 1990 to the current 19 peace missions directed and supported by the UN Department for Peacekeeping Operations.[11] It would seem that this trend reflects the increasing concern over the global negative effects of local conflicts and fragile states.

Can we extrapolate this decline in armed conflicts to future trends of state fragility? The answer is probably not. One reason is that the decline in armed conflict need not be durable. An International Peace Academy study notes: 'If we head into a period in which proxy war (against terrorists or groups described as such) comes back into style, or prospects of cooperation between major international players diminish, there is a risk that this trend will be shorter-lived

---

[8] Larry Diamond, 'Promoting Democracy in Post-Conflict and Failed States, Lessons and Challenges', 2 *Taiwan Journal of Democracy*, No. 2 (2006) pp. 93-116.

[9] See Deutsche Gesellschaft für Technische Zusammenarbeit (GTZ), 2005.

[10] 'Towards a more peaceful world' Oslo, IPRI, September 2006, see: <http://www.prio.no/files/file48260_prio_uppsala_eng_press_release_020906.pdf>.

[11] See <http://www.un.org/Depts/dpko/dpko/bnote.htm>.

than hoped.'[12] The conflict zones where IPI[13] can imagine future wars are broadly the alert zones of the Failed States Index cited above.

Another reason is that trends in some of the global threats that likely affect fragile states are not positive. The Instability Framework (see Fig. 1) points, e.g., to the role of climate change, global economic crises, scarcities, terrorism, etc. Current negative trends in these factors might very well aggravate state fragility in the world.

Climate change may increase the risk of 'natural' shocks'[14] and tends to reinforce existing tensions within and between countries. Impacts to be expected are the loss of infrastructure, resource scarcity and mass displacement of peoples, while security consequences are expected in the form of civil unrest, inter-communal violence and international instability.[15]

Water shortages create tensions, especially in regions where several countries rely on the same water sources – e.g., the river Nile in North Africa, the river Jordan in the Middle East and several rivers in South-East and Central Asia. Access and distribution issues could contribute to internal or regional conflicts.

Scarcities of energy, especially oil, pose another potentially destabilising factor. China's quest for oil in Africa already has serious implications for the world's policies towards fragile states, e.g., in the case of Sudan and its Darfur region. The conflicts in the Middle East present another well known energy-linked example.

Economic crises, when they occur, strongly and negatively affect fragile states. The sudden severe decline of economic growth is one of the proven predictors of conflict and instability. Scarcities and price increases for commodities and especially food are closely linked to this risk factor. Food riots, as they have occurred this year in various countries like, e.g., Haïti where they threatened the succes of the peacekeeping mission, have a proven potential to destabilise countries.

But predicting future trends of state stability or fragility remains a precarious challenge, as illustrated by Donald Steinberg, the International Crisis Group's Deputy President. Steinberg recalls how 'in 1995, as the US President's Special Assistant for Africa, I suggested Nigeria, Côte d'Ivoire, Zimbabwe, Ethiopia

---

[12] Charles T. Call & Elizabeth M. Cousens, *Ending wars and building peace, Coping with crisis* (New York, IPA, March 2007).

[13] The International Peace Academy has since changed its name to the International Peace Institute (IPI).

[14] Cf. 'Climate Change and International Security, Paper from the High Representative and the European Commission to the European Council', S113/08, 14 March 2008.

[15] Chris Abbott, 'An uncertain future: law enforcement, national security and climate change', FRIDE, 2008.

and Kenya as anchors for the promotion of democracy, good governance, poverty reduction, military demobilization, debt relief and improvements in health, education and other social indicators. With large populations, vibrant economies, democratizing regimes, and internal stability, these countries could serve as entrepots, sources of energy and transport infrastructures, channels of trade and investment, sources of negotiators and peacekeeping forces, models of proper behavior, and havens for refugees.'[16]

In 2007 all of these countries are in the alert category of the Failed States Index, and that was even before the 2008 events in Kenya. Incidentally, this shows that there certainly were early warning signals for Kenya.

General policy implications of state fragility trends

Fragile states will probably continue to affect world security and development. But the reverse is also true: global developments will continue to affect the more fragile states in the world. Curbing state fragility definitely requires international support for state building in these countries, and it is now on the agenda of most development actors (bilateral donors, multilateral organisations). However, just as important is that the more powerful international actors address the external risk factors of instability for which they largely bear responsibility. The most relevant ones would be: interference in fragile states for geopolitical reasons (proxy war against real or perceived terrorists, competition for oil or other scarce resources, control over zones of influence), management of global economic crises and management of climate change.

Addressing these issues, or at least incorporating the risks and costs of increased state fragility into the various policy considerations, would also shift fragile states policies from a curative to a more preventive approach. It would offer a better solution than the unsustainable burden of stabilisation operations that at present are undertaken to restore stability in states.

As Larry Diamond points out: 'Stabilising a country is costly. And it is not only a question of money, for deployable military force is a far more finite resource than money alone. With more than 60,000 UN peacekeepers deployed, the world is running out of available forces for peacekeeping.'[17]

However, such approaches would require a thorough remake of the global architecture for the mobilisation and coordination of efforts towards fragile states. Deep divisions between the UN member states have hindered effective international intervention, as was spelled out at the September 2005 UN World Sum-

---

16 See <http://www.crisisgroup.org/home/index.cfm?id=5303&l=1>.

17 Diamond, *supra* n. 8, pp. 93-116.

mit. Efforts are being undertaken to improve matters, e.g., through the Peace Building Commission (PBC) created at the summit. But although the PBC is beginning to show its effectiveness, its focus is not on the global factors that are so decisive as contributing factors of state fragility.

If, indeed, the world is 'moving inexorably from an order centred on a single super-power towards one of several competing poles'[18] the deep divisions are likely to stay. The challenge will then be that the geopolitical competition is not fought out and in countries that are too fragile to withstand such interference.

A stable global economic order, while evidently of interest to the industrialised world, is also an important potential stabilising factor for state fragility. But, as Call and Cousens rightly observe,

> 'missing from virtually any analysis of international peacebuilding [...] is discussion of economic policy instruments that could have a powerful effect in combating state fragility and reversion to war, such as terms of trade, monetary policy, management of currency fluctuation, and so on. Over the longer term, these and other more systemic issues may exert a greater effect on the vulnerability of states to war or state weakness.'[19]

To these instruments could be added effective management of economic crises like the current food and credit crises.

Lastly, the area of climate management offers an area where the interests of the industrialised world and fragile states could coincide. The wish to curb state fragility could act as an additional incentive for the industrialised world to effectively address climate change issues.

Policy implications for the Netherlands

The Netherlands has a history of strongly supporting international order. Also in the domain of fragile states it is set to take its responsibility and address the policy implications mentioned above. The current government has committed itself to intensify its fragile states policy, and a policy paper detailing the approaches is being prepared. Part of the policy is to strengthen the international architecture for security and development, through the UN, EU, NATO, the World Bank and regional organisations.

---

[18] Mark Leonard foresees, in addition to the United States, as emerging poles China, Russia, the EU and the Middle East, in: Mark Leonard, 'Divided world, the struggle for primacy in 2020', Centre for European Reform, January 2007.

[19] Call & Cousens, *supra* n. 12.

In dealing with the problem of fragile states the Netherlands uses an integrated approach of security, governance and development interventions. Experiences in several post-conflict countries are promising, but have nevertheless shown that many questions remain as to how integrated approaches can be made to work effectively.

Some questions centre around the balance to be kept, in each specific country, between the military, political and development interventions. How could the military effort be tailored to support the political and development processes that would strengthen the states concerned, and *vice versa*? Other questions have to do with the capacity dilemma: both quick visible results and the engagement of local stakeholders are needed to retain the positive momentum of a peace process, but local stakeholders' capacities are generally too weak to deliver quickly. If external intervention is chosen as the way out of this dilemma it will have to walk the tightrope in choosing the scale and nature of the intervention. The intervention would be tailored to strengthen local drivers of change, and enhance (or at least not reduce) incentives for local government, civil society and private entrepreneurs to take their development into their own hands. In all of this the Netherlands fully appreciates that support for fragile states in their state-building effort is a highly political process, since it affects the fundamentals of the relations between elites and society. The central challenge may be to support the governments and societies in fragile states in getting the political solutions right.

Like other countries, the Netherlands still has to integrate policies on global threats into its fragile states policies. These new perspectives have to be added, on the one hand, to fragile states' policies and, on the other, to current policies for climate change, energy security, scarcities, terrorism, etc. Since the scale, urgency and nature of the interlinkages are not yet clear, it would be logical to start by researching these issues.

Implications for research institutions

The international policies on fragile states, although converging towards a fairly broad consensus, remain premised on comparatively shaky empirical evidence, mostly from the domain of security and development. For example, while there has been a considerable deepening of analysis about conflict trends in recent years, both the data on and the analysis of war recurrence remain surprisingly limited.[20]

---

[20] Ibid.

Consequently, all of the areas of policy development indicated above need to be supported by a substantial research effort. For the development of integrated approaches, for example, research needs to work out for each of the tracks (security, governance and development) what works in which situations and how the tracks support or undermine each other. Questions of how to prioritise, coordinate and sequence activities in each of the tracks, and continuously calibrate the decisions in the light of changing circumstances remain to be solved. A crucial element is how to reinforce state-society interaction by involving the population, including women, as the drivers of reform.

In addition to the topics presented by the policy implications, two areas stand out to be taken up by research institutions. One is the issue of early warning, the second is the monitoring and evaluation of fragile states policies. A number of efforts in early warning are ongoing.[21] Further development seems to be needed to extend the timeline of the projections, to integrate global threats and to link early warning systems to early action. A range of systems to serve various policy timeframes, e.g., early warning indexes (0-1 year), medium-term structural assessment (1-5 years) and long-term risk trends would have to be developed and linked to policy-making processes.[22] The second topic of monitoring and evaluation is self-evident. Now that more and more international interventions are taking place in fragile states it is important to monitor and evaluate from the start the approaches and their results, to draw lessons to be learned and to build up further the body of knowledge. The OECD-DAC has taken up the challenge to lead policy development in the monitoring and evaluation of fragile states policies. But also here, additional work is needed to integrate the global risk factors and stabilising interventions into the monitoring and evaluation systems.

Concluding remarks

The increased interest in fragile states stems from different concerns (national interests as well as development concerns) and masks different and sometimes opposing objectives in combating state fragility. Development concerns tend to limit themselves to internal causes and remedies for fragile states. National interest approaches tend to focus on the stabilisation of the security situation in fragile states. Both approaches tend to neglect the impact of external factors in creating and maintaining state fragility. The highly developed countries of this

[21] E.g., the Failed States Index of the Fund for Peace, the Country Indicators for Foreign Policy of Carleton University in Canada, the work of the UK Prime-Minister's Strategy Unit on Countries at Risk of Instability, and the EU Initiative for Peace project.

[22] Recommendation of the UK FCO Countries at Risk of Instability Programme.

world are best placed to mitigate these factors. This is not to say that dealing with external factors is easy. It is saying that more focused intervention to mitigate external factors and their effects on state fragility could tip the scales of current fragile states policies towards success: to reduce fragility and facilitate security and development.

How Rogue States Play the Game: The Case of North Korea's Nuclear Programme

Sico van der Meer

Introduction

One of the difficult issues in the field of international relations is the question of how to deal with so-called 'Rogue States'. Rogue Regimes, by definition, do not play the 'game' of international politics according to the international and legal 'rules'. So far, it has proven rather difficult for the international community to deal with these kinds of states and to put a stop to their 'rogue' activities. This chapter will try to analyze the ways in which Rogue States play the game of international politics. Understanding how Rogue States act may be vital to improve the international strategies towards them.

After discussing the term Rogue State, this chapter will use North Korea as case study. This country is probably the clearest example of a Rogue State and also one of the oldest Rogue States of these times as it has already frustrated the international community for some sixty years. The case study will especially focus on the clandestine nuclear programme of North Korea. This programme has been the main 'rogue activity' of the regime in Pyongyang during the past 15 years, and as such attracted the most international attention and activity in order to halt it in this period. How has North Korea acted in reaction of this international pressure? After analyzing the North Korean case, the chapter focuses at the existing 'basic strategies' towards Rogue States, comparing them to the North Korean situation. The chapter ends with some concluding remarks on dealing with Rogue States.

Rogue States: definitions and problems

There exists no internationally accepted definition or listing of Rogue States, and the term is not uncontroversial either. The term Rogue State became fashionable especially during the 1990s, but these kinds of states are also known as

J. de Zwaan, E. Bakker and S. van der Meer (eds.), Challenges in a Changing World

'Pariah States', 'Outlaw States' or 'Renegade Regimes'.[1] States that are labelled as a Rogue State often have authoritarian rule, restrict human rights, carry out or support terrorist activities, attempt to acquire or proliferate weapons of mass destruction, and/or are involved in large-scale criminal activities like illegal weapons and drugs trafficking, money laundering or counterfeiting activities. More generally, they can be characterized as 'flouting established international rules and norms.'[2]

Rogue States are nothing new in history. The twentieth century is full of examples of states that could be earmarked as a Rogue State – from Germany under Adolf Hitler to Libya under Muammar Gaddafi and from Uganda under Idi Amin to Iraq under Saddam Hussein. Nevertheless, the international community still struggles with the question: how does one deal with this kind of state?

Rogue States have been actors in the past and will also be so in the future, threatening other states in whatever way. Today, countries that are often labelled as Rogue States are North Korea, Iran, Syria and Sudan. In addition, some states are not a Rogue State at this moment, but are seen as a potential future one. Examples are states like Venezuela, Saudi Arabia and Russia. Some authors also consider the United States to be a Rogue State.[3] When talking about the threat of Rogue States in the near future, especially North Korea and Iran are frequently named, mostly because of their nuclear programmes. Their quest for weapons of mass destruction threatens the security of other international actors. The threat becomes even greater when weapons of mass destruction are proliferating from these Rogue States to other states, or even worse: to non-state actors like terrorist organisations.

Given the differences between the countries mentioned above, it may be clear that every Rogue State is a case apart. Hence talking about general policies towards Rogue States is difficult. It is possible, however, to learn from case studies. These can be positive cases, because there are some instances to be found in recent history in which the international community had surprising success in dealing with Rogue States. The sudden change, some years ago, of the Libyan regime of Muammar Gaddafi from 'rogue' to 'best friend' may be the best example. It proves that, although there are many difficulties along the way, Rogue States may be effectively persuaded to change. It may also be possible, however, to learn from cases in which the international community has

[1] Christopher Preble, 'The Bush Doctrine and "Rogue" States', *Foreign Service Journal* (October 2005) pp. 25-30; Miroslav Nincic, *Renegade Regimes. Confronting deviant behavior in world politics* (New York, Columbia University Press 2005).

[2] Preble, *supra* n. 1, p. 26.

[3] William Blum, *Rogue State. A guide to the world's only Superpower* (Monroe, Common Courage Press 2001 (second edition)).

failed in effectively dealing with Rogue Regimes. The ultimate case in this regard might be North Korea.

This chapter will analyze the case of North Korea, especially with regard to its nuclear programme. Although North Korea is only one of the Rogue States that can be distinguished nowadays, the regime in Pyongyang may be described as one of the most obvious members of this category of states – presumably, the regime is even proud of its reputation, given the way it exploits the international fear about its nuclear programme. Being some sort of Rogue State since coming into existence in the 1940s, North Korea may also be labelled as probably today's oldest Rogue State. How has it managed to survive six decades without being influenced by the international community to end its rogue activities?

The perfect Rogue State?

North Korea may be depicted as an almost perfect example of the classic 'Rogue State'. Not especially because of the somewhat lunatic, Cold War type of regime that is often portrayed in the Western media,[4] but more because of the astonishing capability of this regime to play the game of international politics in a 'rogue' way without being overthrown by its far more powerful opponents. The regime in Pyongyang, first led by Kim Il Sung and after his death in 1994 by his son Kim Jong Il, has a long record of 'rogue activities'. Even without mentioning the invasion of South Korea in 1950, that started the Korean War, the rogue activities during the 1960s, 1970s and 1980s were multiple. Infamous are the various terrorist attacks on South Korean politicians and citizens, the dropping of spies on South Korean territory and the abduction of Japanese citizens to use them as language trainers for North Korean spies.[5]

Since the 1990s, however, the terrorist activities, in particular, seem to have ceased. The efforts in the field of other rogue activities, on the contrary, have increased. The North Korean state is still involved in large-scale international criminality, such as drugs and weapons trafficking, counterfeiting and illegal gambling activities. In addition, North Korea has increased its efforts in running a clandestine nuclear weapons programme and has been involved in nuclear proliferation activities. In particular these nuclear activities have attracted the most international attention during the 1990s and the current decade and they therefore show how difficult it is to deal with a Rogue State.

---

[4] Hugh Gusterson, 'Paranoid, potbellied Stalinist gets nuclear weapons. How the U.S. print media cover North Korea', 15 *Non Proliferation Review*, No. 1 (March 2008) pp. 21-42.

[5] E.g., Andrew Scobell, *North Korea's strategic intentions* (Carlisle, Strategic Studies Institute 2005) p. 23.

Background to North Korea's nuclear policy

To understand the background of the North Korean nuclear programme, at least to some extent, it is necessary to look into the ideology of the regime that has shaped the (political) culture in North Korea since the establishment of the state in the 1940s. The essence of the so-called Juche ideology is often summarized as 'self-determination' or 'self-reliance'.[6] After a long history of suppression by the neighbouring states of China and Japan, North Korea's main goal is complete independence in all respects. All the policies of the North Korean regime are based upon this ideology.

The foreign policy of North Korea can be described by the terms 'fear' and 'distrust'. The strong belief in Juche ideology is that other states will never accept a completely independent North Korea; every (regional) power will always try to influence and to make use of the North Korean people, just as they did in the past. After Chinese and Japanese rule, now the United States is considered to be the main threat: after arriving on the Korean peninsula during the Second World War, the Americans never left and made half of the Korean nation (read: South Korea) a 'vassal state' where troops and weapons are stationed to conquer the independent North as soon as they will see a possibility. These ideas are the source of North Korea's aim to become a military power to be reckoned with, even by superpowers like the United States, China and Russia. Military strength is considered necessary to guarantee self-determination. Next to its large conventional forces – North Korea has the largest army in the world when counting the military as a percentage of the population – acquiring weapons of mass destruction has always received a great deal of attention. North Korea possesses large amounts of chemical and biological weapons, and the nuclear programme is just another step along the road to 'self-defence'. Nuclear weapons are seen as necessary to deter all (possible) enemies that are often nuclear powers themselves.[7]

In the field of economic policy, the self-reliance of the Juche ideology is also important. The problem is that economic self-reliance is almost impossible in North Korea. The agricultural conditions are quite unfavourable, while the country does not possess many raw materials either. That the North Korean economy has already survived for some sixty years has only been possible because this economic self-reliance has not been taken to the extreme. During the Cold War the North Korean regime proved very skilled in playing off the communist ri-

[6] For an interesting overview of the Juche ideology see: Kongdan Oh & Ralph C. Hassig, *North Korea through the looking glass* (Washington D.C., Brookings Institution Press 2000).

[7] Andrew Scobell & John M. Stanford, *North Korea's military threat. Pyongyang's conventional forces, weapons of mass destruction and ballistic missiles* (Carlisle, Strategic Studies Institute 2007).

vals China and the Soviet Union against each other, receiving extensive economic support from both. When the Cold War ended, however, the assistance from its main supporter at that time, the Soviet Union, also stopped. This resulted in a major (and still ongoing) economic crisis. Famine became a returning catastrophe for the population; estimates of famine victims during the past fifteen years vary between one hundred thousand and several million.

Although North Korea still receives economic support from China, and to a lesser extent from South Korea and Russia, the country has a structural lack of almost anything, especially food and energy. Rather than pursuing economic reforms, the North Korean regime seems to prefer to rely on foreign aid, in the same way the regime has survived during the last six decades. This 'aid-seeking policy' is an important part of the explanation for North Korea's nuclear programme and the way the regime deals with the international negotiations on this subject. Seen from an economic point of view, the nuclear programme has a so-called 'blackmail function' to extract aid from other states. Pyongyang wants to be paid for every step it takes on this issue, even for coming to the negotiation table at all.[8]

Aims and strategies of North Korea's nuclear policy

The aims of the North Korean nuclear programme are multiple. Nuclear deterrence against supposed enemies is the most important goal. Next to that, there is the economic goal of using the nuclear programme as an instrument for 'blackmailing' in order to extract foreign aid. In exchange for North Korean concessions on this programme, many concessions from the other side of the negotiation table are expected. A third aim that should be mentioned, although it partly overlaps with the first two aims, is that North Korea wants to be taken seriously, to be dealt with like a state that matters. This is one of the reasons why North Korea always urges the United States to engage in unilateral talks; the world's biggest superpower has to recognize that North Korea is an equal partner.

Especially the non-security aims make the North Korean case special when compared to other states with clandestine nuclear weapons programmes. Normally, these states try to develop their nuclear weapons in secret to prevent any interference from outside. The North Korean regime, on the contrary, openly acknowledges its endeavours to become a nuclear weapons state – some observers characterize the North Korean behaviour as 'atomic exhibitionism'.[9]

---

8 E.g., ibid., p. 22.

9 William J. Broad, 'North Korea's nuclear intentions, out there for all to see', *New York Times* (8 October 2006).

By showing how dangerous North Korea is, the regime expects to extract more concessions from the international community.

In the meantime, the North Korean leadership takes into account that military intervention is not highly likely at this moment in time. First of all, there is no unity among its opponents. The United States seems to be the only state eventually willing to intervene militarily, but it will not do so without the consent of its most important partners in the region, South Korea and Japan. Those states are fearful of North Korean violence towards their own territory and will probably refuse any support for military action. Especially South Korea is not in favour of military options for various reasons, one of them being the fact that the South Korean capital, Seoul, is very close to the border and might be destroyed in the first hours of any war because North Korea considers the South to be a vassal state of the United States. China and Russia, in turn, are not at all in favour of US involvement in what they consider to be their area of influence. An even more important reason for North Korea to assume that international military action is highly unlikely is the fear, shared by all parties involved, of the chaos that would arise in case the regime in Pyongyang were to collapse. Because of a lack of political opposition in North Korea, a collapsing regime will not be easily replaced by new leaders in the short term, so anarchy and chaos will spread through the country – and beyond its borders. The neighbouring states of China, Russia and South Korea fear large flows of hungry refugees, as well as the spread of weapons (including weapons of mass destruction).[10] Chaos and instability in North Korea may influence the whole region in a negative sense and the costs of stabilisation and the development of the ruined country will be enormous.[11] North Korea not only recognizes these international fears, but also makes use of them, playing 'the instability card' at the negotiation table to attract more concessions from its counterparts.[12]

Next to the strategy of playing the instability card, the North Korean regime uses the strategy of constantly slowing down all negotiation processes. Every possible detail is used to delay negotiations. One example of many is the Banco Delta Asia affair. In 2005 the United States declared that the North Korean accounts at this bank in Macau had been 'infected' because they had been used for illegal activities. The bank accounts were consequently frozen. North Ko-

---

[10] Robert D. Kaplan, 'When North Korea falls', *The Atlantic Monthly* (October 2006) pp. 64-74.

[11] Charles Woolf Jr. & Kamil Akramov, *North Korean paradoxes. Circumstances, costs, and consequences of Korean unification* (Santa Monica, RAND Corporation 2005). Estimates concerning the costs of developing North Korea toward a level comparable to South Korea vary between 290 billion and 3.2 trillion US dollars (Ibid., p. 49).

[12] Bruce Bennett, 'Commentary: North Korea policy options', *United Press International* (28 November 2006).

rea, in turn, refused to negotiate any further on anything as long as this relatively small problem was not resolved.[13] Time is on the North Korean side, or so seems to be the idea in Pyongyang. As long as negotiations are possible, military action against the regime is highly unlikely, while at the same time rogue activities may continue. And as long as negotiations are dragging along, aid requests due to floods and other disasters – that sometimes seem to be exaggerated to extract more support – are more likely to result in concrete deliveries by the international community. After all, nobody wants to see the regime in Pyongyang collapsing because of popular unrest as long as there could be nuclear devices available in the chaos that will arise, so food and energy supplies will surely follow such aid requests.

North Korea has been rather successful in dealing with pressure by the international community. As will be explained next, the international activities to end the nuclear programme of Pyongyang have been continuously thwarted and slowed down during the last 15 years.

International strategies towards North Korea

During the 1990s, when the world found out about the North Korean clandestine nuclear programme, the international efforts to end this 'rogue activity' started. The international community, led by the US administration of President Bill Clinton, tried to stimulate Pyongyang to change its behaviour by diplomatic negotiations combined with imposing economic and political sanctions. These international efforts led to the 1994 Agreed Framework, in which North Korea agreed to freeze its nuclear programme in exchange for energy assistance (oil supplies and the construction of energy plants).

Soon, however, controversy arose about the requirements of the agreement. North Korea claimed that not all the promised assistance and the lifting of sanctions were being delivered. The United States, backed by other Western states, stated that North Korea did not completely fulfil the inspection and verification requirements of the Agreed Framework. In the end, it was Pyongyang that dealt the last blow to the agreement in 2002 by revealing that its nuclear activities had not been halted at all. North Korea expelled all verification experts, withdrew from the Non Proliferation Treaty and openly restarted its nuclear reactors. In the meantime, President George W. Bush had taken office in the White House and described North Korea as one of the states of the 'Axis of Evil'.

The international strategy towards North Korea did not change, however. Diplomatic negotiations, combined with pressure through sanctions, were still

---

13 International Crisis Group, *North Korea-Russia relations. A strained friendship*, Asia Briefing No. 71 (Seoul/Brussels 2007) p. 8.

seen as the best instrument to deal with North Korea. This is why in 2003 the so-called Six Party Talks were started, i.e., diplomatic negotiations in which North Korea, the United States, China, Russia, South Korea and Japan are participating. The main goal of the negotiations is 'the verifiable denuclearization of the Korean Peninsula in a peaceful manner.'[14] The Six Party Talks are still continuing at the time of writing, five years later.

Negotiating within the Six Party Talks

To learn how North Korea plays the game of international politics, it is important to analyze the North Korean negotiation strategy within the Six Party Talks. This strategy can be described as follows: slowing down the negotiations as much as possible, not only by causing problems concerning as many details as possible, but also by making the negotiations as complicated as possible. This is why Pyongyang does not want to negotiate on the nuclear programme as an isolated subject, but also wants to include other themes, like relations with South Korea and the United States, energy deals, economic and security arrangements, and so on. The Japanese insistence on including the abduction case in the negotiations in this sense favours the North Korean strategy, making the negotiations even more diffuse. By making the negotiation process as complicated as possible, it is easier to slow it down or to sabotage parts of it.

Although the North Korean negotiation strategy is sometimes simply earmarked as rude and unwilling by the Western media, it is important to acknowledge that indeed this sometimes rude and seemingly unwilling behaviour is not meant to completely end the negotiations. On the contrary, North Korea has nothing to gain by ending the international negotiations.[15] The non-cooperative behaviour that North Korean diplomats often demonstrate at the Six Party Talks is only meant to slow the negotiations down, not to let them fail completely. From the North Korean perspective, the negotiations should preferably go on forever – negotiations avoid conflict, offer possibilities to obtain foreign aid, and do not seriously restrict the regime's room to manoeuvre.

Nevertheless, the Six Party Talks have had a positive outcome for the international community. Although the negotiations seemed to have completely failed when in October 2006 North Korea conducted its first nuclear test explosion, only some months later, in February 2007, an agreement was reached. According to this agreement, North Korea would dismantle its nuclear programme and

---

[14] 'Joint Statement of the Fourth Round of the Six Party Talks', Beijing, 19 September 2005', see <www.state.gov>.

[15] James A. Foley, 'Fail-safe: North Korea's stability paradox', *Jane's Intelligence Review* (October 2007) pp. 30-37.

give complete openness about all past nuclear activities in exchange for economic (mainly energy) assistance and the normalisation of international relations, among other things by lifting the US anti-terrorism sanctions. Although the February 2007 Agreement resembles the failed 1994 Agreed Framework, on this occasion North Korea seemed to be more serious. Nuclear installations were indeed closed down and documents on past nuclear activities were handed over. True, the North Koreans did miss all the agreed deadlines, but in the end they apparently did what they had agreed to do. When, in August 2008, the United States missed a deadline to remove North Korea from the list of state sponsors of terrorism, however, North Korea immediately ended all cooperation and threatened to restart its nuclear programme. The United States, in turn, mentioned the inadequate information received from Pyongyang as the reason for the delay in sanction lifting.[16] What these developments mean for the process as a whole is still to be seen.

Considering the North Korean aims with its nuclear weapons programme, one may question Pyongyang's willingness to fulfil all promises it has made. Some observers can simply not believe that North Korea would ever completely surrender its nuclear weapons programme, because it is Pyongyang's only real bargaining chip concerning the international community.[17] They may have a point there. But in spite of the image of the North Korean regime in the Western press, Pyongyang is not at all irrational, but is very capable in playing the game of international politics. When the North Korean leadership made the calculation that dismantling the nuclear programme is the most profitable action at this moment, it may be serious. The outcomes of this kind of North Korean calculation are unfortunately not known outside a select group of people in Pyongyang. And this rather mysterious way of acting is exactly the problem when dealing with Rogue States: they do not always act like 'normal' states would do, and their reactions to international strategies to influence them are thus difficult to predict. It is this unpredictability that makes it difficult to formulate successful international strategies to deal with Rogue States. This can be illustrated by comparing the existing basic strategies to the North Korean case.

How North Korea evades international pressure

The case of North Korea's nuclear programme effectively shows how difficult it is for the international community to deal with a Rogue State. Considering the

---

16 'N Korean nuclear disablement falters in dispute over terror list', *Financial Times* (27 August 2008).

17 E.g., Andrei Lankov, 'Staying alive. Why North Korea will not change', 87 *Foreign Affairs*, No. 2 (March/April 2008) pp. 9-16.

five 'basic strategies' towards Rogue States that are described by the American researcher Colin Dueck;[18] none of them have proved very effective in ending these 'rogue activities' of Pyongyang. All five strategies, appeasement, engagement, containment, rollback, and non-entanglement, will hereafter be projected in case of North Korea.

The strategy of *appeasement*, to start with, does not seem that illogical when one considers the background to North Korea's nuclear programme. One of the reasons for developing nuclear weapons is the perceived insecurity of the regime; it feels threatened and especially fears an American attack in the future to reunite the North with the 'American vassal state' South Korea. Appeasement could be an appropriate method to decrease this feeling of insecurity in Pyongyang. But even when neglecting the ideology of the North Koran regime that is built upon a fear of 'the world outside', there is a problem with the appeasement strategy. Next to the security background, the nuclear programme has economic aims; it functions as a so-called 'blackmailing tool' to extract economic support from the international community. Appeasement will not easily be able to solve this part of the problem.

At first glance, *engagement* may also seem a promising strategy. North Korea suffers from severe economic problems, so when negotiating, the international community certainly has something to offer. And even without negotiating, economic and diplomatic contacts may open the door to modernisation, liberalisation and democratisation, which in the long term may change the (foreign policy of the) regime so that it no longer sees any need for its nuclear policy. But this also appears unrealistic. North Korea's state ideology is not aiming to achieve 'Western-style' contacts and negotiations. Instead, because of the fundamentally paranoid and authoritarian nature of the North Korean state ideology, every engagement strategy that will give Pyongyang the impression of being encapsulated into international structures will fail. The experiences with engagement strategies towards North Korea indicate that Pyongyang will wring whatever concessions it can from the other party, without changing any policy or ambition.[19]

Containment is actually the strategy that has been mostly used by the Western part of the international community since the North Korean state came into being – during the Cold War North Korea belonged to the communist bloc and China and Russia were allies of Pyongyang to some extent (and to a lesser extent, they still are). Even more so, North Korea stimulated its own containment by the policy of self-reliance and the conscious lack of international con-

---

[18] Colin Dueck, 'Strategies for managing Rogue States', 50 *Orbis* (Spring 2006) pp. 223-241.

[19] Ibid., p. 235.

tacts. Even after the end of the Cold War, when almost all observers predicted a collapse of the Stalinist regime in Pyongyang, no signs of any crumbling of power have been signalled. North Korea's isolationalism makes it more or less immune to containment strategies. Although, economically, Pyongyang certainly needs assistance from the outside, only a few countries that are willing to support the regime even to a lesser extent (China, South Korea, Russia) are enough to survive.

Rollback is no option either at this moment. As described above, almost no one wishes to see a sudden regime change in Pyongyang. A regime change, in whatever way, will most likely result in a power vacuum and thus cause enormous chaos by which the whole region of North East Asia may be negatively influenced. Pyongyang even makes use of this fear by playing the 'instability card' at the negotiation table.

Non-entanglement, finally, seems to be no option either. Sooner or later Pyongyang will reach the status of nuclear weapons state, and, even worse, may sell these weapons or manufacturing techniques to whoever will pay. Most world powers understand that something has to be done to stop the 'rogue activities' of the regime in Pyongyang.

What strategy might then be useful to deal with North Korea? A combination of engagement and rollback strategies seems to be an imperfect, but at this moment the best option available. It is important, however, to be aware of the North Korean strategies to make the international policies towards it less effective. Although the behaviour of the regime in Pyongyang may be difficult to predict, it is not irrational. More research into the way North Korea plays the 'game' of international politics could be very helpful.

Concluding remarks

While the threat of Rogue States to the international community might be increasing – think of the current concerns about the proliferation of nuclear weapons – it has so far proven rather difficult to stop the 'rogue activities' of these kinds of states. In this chapter the case of North Korea's clandestine nuclear programme was analysed to describe the difficulties in dealing with rogue regimes. North Korea has been able to move on with its rogue activities without being seriously hindered by international efforts to stop them. Because North Korea is not adhering, like all Rogue States, to the general international and legal norms and rules, the international community has little leverage concerning the regime in Pyongyang. North Korea has so far been able to thwart and slow down all international initiatives to stop its rogue activities.

Rogue States do not always act like 'normal' states would do, and their reactions to international strategies to influence them are thus difficult to predict.

It is this unpredictability that makes it difficult to formulate successful international strategies to deal with Rogue States. This chapter showed that a combination of engagement and rollback strategies seems to be an imperfect, but at this moment the best available way to deal with Rogue States. To improve the effectiveness of the international policies, a better understanding of the counter-strategies that Rogue States use is vital. Although all Rogue States differ and there is no single way to deal with them, much can be learned from studying their behaviour. As long as no better strategies towards them will be found, Rogue States will remain an international problem.

IRAN AND THE EUROPEAN PREDICAMENT

Alfred Pijpers

INTRODUCTION

In the run-up to the American presidential elections of November 2008 both candidates have spoken repeatedly about the Iranian nuclear danger. In an interview with a *Fox* reporter Barack Obama said: 'Iran is a major threat; I would never hesitate to use our military force in order to protect homeland, US interests.'[1] Obama indicated that he would be prepared to direct talks with the Iranian leaders, but considered 'any action against them legitimate, if they show no willingness to change their nuclear policy.' He also said that he would make the Iranian nuclear issue 'a top priority for him as president.'[2] His opponent, John McCain, was against direct negotiations, and was even more than Obama in favour of military measures if Iran does not change its course. Most famously he has claimed that 'the only thing worse than a war with Iran would be a nuclear Iran.'[3]

Such warnings do not fall on fertile soil in the European Union. It is true that the Iranian nuclear programme has been a permanent point on the European diplomatic agenda since 2003, but most European politicians would rather not prefer to formulate the danger in the wording of US leaders. In the EU it is not a real foreign policy priority. The issue is largely absent in the media and the public debate. Other major conflicts in the Middle East, Afghanistan, or the Caucasus, humanitarian and natural disasters in the world, climate change, or the financial crisis are considered much more important. Barack Obama was undoubtedly the favourite candidate among broad segments of the European population, but his foreign policy priorities were not really understood or appreciated.

[1] Quoted by NetNews.com (9 May 2008).

[2] *Haaretz* (31 July 2008).

[3] See Richard Holbrooke, 'The next president: mastering a daunting agenda', 87 *Foreign Affairs*, No. 5 (September/October 2008) p. 16.

J. de Zwaan, E. Bakker and S. van der Meer (eds.), Challenges in a Changing World

The purpose of this chapter is to slightly redress this European misjudgment, and to push the Iranian nuclear danger more into the heart of the European foreign policy debate. What are the risks of the Iranian nuclear activities? What are the principal options left for the international community and the EU? We shall argue that Israel in particular has much reason to worry, and the EU should become more aware of a possible Israeli preventive strike.

Early EU involvement

Although today the dangers of Iran's nuclear programme are less salient in Europe than in the United States or Israel, it was surprisingly the EU that, five years ago, opened the negotiations with the Iranian authorities about this matter. In October 2003, the French, British and German Ministers of Foreign Affairs (the EU3) went to Tehran, and signed a document in which the Iranian government agreed to suspend its nuclear enrichment activities.[4] Tehran also agreed to sign the Additional Protocol of the Non-Proliferation Treaty (NPT). For the EU a nice windfall after the frustrating European discord over Iraq earlier that year.[5] Now Europe could show the world a bit more unity and the benefits of civilian instruments over saber rattling. Shortly before, the EU had already presented its views on non-proliferation and in December 2003 it even launched its own 'security strategy'.

With their involvement in the Iranian nuclear *imbroglio* the EU assumed a sharper foreign policy profile, also by using openly the EU3 formula as the best way forward in a Union of 25 and more member states. The High Representative of the Common Foreign and Security Policy (CFSP), Javier Solana, would gradually become the principal coordinator for the talks with Iran, also on behalf of the five permanent members of the UN Security Council plus Germany (P6 or '3 + 3 group'). Washington refused direct negotiations with a regime it had not recognized since the Islamic revolution of 1979, and it was also fully preoccupied by the wars in Afghanistan and Iraq.[6] But from the beginning the Bush administration urged for sanctions by the Security Council, and has exerted constant pressure on the European diplomatic efforts in this regard.

---

[4] This programme, revealed in 2002 by an Iranian resistance group, had been kept hidden during twenty years from inspectors of the International Atomic Energy Agency (IAEA), and was largely illegal under the rules of the Non-Proliferation Treaty (NPT).

[5] Initially, the EU3 did not officially speak for all EU member states. This changed when in 2004 the High Representative of the CFSP, Javier Solana, became associated with the talks on behalf of the EU. See Tom Sauer, *Coercive Diplomacy by the EU: the Case of Iran,* Discussion Papers Diplomacy (The Hague, Clingendael Institute 2007).

[6] Recently, however, Washington has shifted its position in this regard. William Burns, Under-Ssecretary for Political Affairs at the State Department, was present at the Geneva summit of the P6 and Iran on 19 July 2008.

The hour of Europe, however, was only granted a short life. Tehran revoked the agreement with the EU3 as early as June 2004 and resumed the construction for uranium conversion and probably also its enrichment activities.[7] In Paris, later that year, the EU3 convinced the Iranian government again to comply with the regulations of the NPT. However, this agreement was immediately nullified after the election of President Mahmoud Ahmadinejad in August 2005, who made it clear that Iran would never give up the right to fully control the nuclear fuel cycle.[8] The Additional Protocol, with its stronger provisions for inspections and safeguards, was not ratified. This despite the fact that even the United States held out the prospect of economic incentives, such as the supply of spare parts for the aging Iranian airlines, and Iran's accession to the World Trade Organization (WTO). In September 2005 the board of governors of the International Atomic Energy Agency (IAEA) concluded that Iran no longer complied with the rules of the NPT. In February 2006 the case was brought to the UN Security Council, which has adopted three resolutions since that time, imposing a number of economic and financial sanctions against Iran. [9] EU diplomacy has undoubtedly contributed to foster a significant multilateral coalition against Iran, with Russia and China on board for (not too strong) economic sanctions, and it has perhaps prevented Washington from taking risky unilateral steps, but the main purpose, to stop Iran's illegal nuclear programme, has not been achieved.

The Iranian nuclear capacity

On the contrary. Iran has used the past years to considerably expand its nuclear installations and today it most likely has the capacity to enrich uranium to a weapons-grade level without any further technical, material, or personnel assistance from abroad. The Iranian government denies categorically that it has this military ambition. For years on end it has argued that its nuclear efforts are exclusively meant for civilian energy. But few people believe this. The mere size of the complexes in Isfahan and Natanz, for instance, can only be explained from the perspective of military objectives. Their capacity for uranium enrichment and related processing activities is far above the necessary scale for the peaceful application of nuclear energy, quite apart from the argument that Iran already possesses the largest reservoirs of oil and gas in the world. The heavy

[7] Emily B. Landau & Ephraim Asculi, 'Iran's Nuclear Program and Negotiations with the EU3', 8 *Strategic Assessment* (Tel Aviv), No. 3 (November 2005).

[8] *Disarmament Diplomacy*, No. 80 (August 2005).

[9] SC Res. 1737 in December 2006, SC Res. 1747 in March 2007, and SC Res. 1803 in March 2008. Cf. Dick Leurdijk, *De Veiligheidsraad en de nucleaire programma's van Noord-Korea en Iran* (The Hague, Clingendael Institute 2007).

water reactor in Arak is constructed for the production of plutonium, fuel only needed for nuclear weapons. For a strictly civilian nuclear programme Iran might very well manage with fuel provided by Russia or the EU, as has been suggested by the EU on a couple of occasions. Despite its proclaimed need for nuclear energy and many years of work, Iran has, apart from the reactor in Bushehr, failed to develop a single nuclear power plant for the generation of electricity. If the Iranian programme were indeed that peaceful, there would, of course, be no need to conceal it from IAEA inspections for a period of twenty years. Tehran is on record for repeated violations of the NPT rules; it has breached the agreements with the EU3, and since 2006 it has defied, and continues to defy, the binding sanctions of the Security Council under Chapter VII of the UN Charter.

The latest periodic report of the IAEA Director General, Mohamed ElBaradei, on the implementation of the NPT Safeguards Agreement by Iran, published in September 2008, gives reason for serious alarm.[10] According to Israeli experts Iran has 'stepped up both the rate of uranium enrichment and the development of more advanced types of gas centrifuges that in turn would increase the rate of enrichment further. If all goes well for Iran, it would be able to amass a sufficient quantity of low-enriched uranium to enable it to further enrich it and produce a quantity of military grade uranium by the turn of the decade, sufficient for the production of a single nuclear explosive device.'[11] A few months earlier ElBaradei had already warned that 'in a period of six months up to one year' Iran might be able to produce a nuclear explosive.[12]

Many analists and officials take a similar view.[13] It is true that the celebrated 2007 'National Intelligence Estimate' (NIE) of the joint American intelligence services concluded that Iran stopped building nuclear weapons in the autumn of 2003, but this does not detract from the fact that its current nuclear efforts could irrevocably lead to a nuclear weapons potential once again. Just a few months are needed for the conversion of low-enriched uranium into weapons-grade uranium.[14] With a sufficient amount of high-enriched uranium, combined with a suitable detonator, the actual manufacturing of a nuclear weapon may be quickly

---

[10] *Implementation of the NPT Safeguards Agreement and relevant provisions of Security Council resolutions 1737 (2006), 1747 (2007), and 1803 (2008) in the Islamic Republic of Iran*, Vienna, IAEA board of governors, GOV/2008/38, 15 September 2008.

[11] Ephraim Asculai, *The Latest IAEA Report on Iran and the Options Facing the International Community*, Tel Aviv, Institute for National Security Studies (INSS), *INSS Insight*, No. 73 (22 September 2008).

[12] MEMRI, Special Dispatch Series No. 1967 (23 June 2008).

[13] See for a survey: Daan de Wit, *De volgende oorlog. De aanval op Iran: een voorbeschouwing* (Rotterdam, Lemniscaat 2008).

[14] 'Iran's nuclear program', New York, Council of Foreign Relations (online) (17 July 2008).

realized. The NIE 2007 report judges that 'with moderate confidence Iran probably would be technically capable of producing enough high-enriched uranium for a weapon sometime during the 2010 – 2015 time frame.'[15] The Director of the National Intelligence Council in Washington DC, Michael McConnell, has in his Annual Threat Assessment of February 2008 supplemented this concern by pointing to the growing missile capability of Iran.[16]

Israeli experts share these assessments, and it is not hard to imagine that they remain rather on the pessimistic side of the estimates.[17] There is a broad consensus among leading Israeli politicians like former Prime Minister Ehud Olmert, Defence Minister Ehud Barak, or the new leader of the Kadima party (and possibly the next prime minister), Foreign Minister Tzipi Livni, that Iran will very soon be able to produce nuclear weapons. In their view the point of no return will be reached by 2010.[18] Thereafter, the actual production of weapons is only a matter of time. 'It is a race against time and time is winning,' declared deputy Prime Minister Shaul Mofaz on a visit to Washington DC in August 2008.[19]

Delivery vehicles like the mid-range *Shahab*-3 ballistic missiles (i.e., for targets in the Middle East) have already been developed. These are partly based on Russian technology, and not very advanced or precise, but they certainly do work, as Saddam Hussein famously showed during the Gulf War in 1991. With similar renovated Russian *Scud* missiles (though without a charge of mass destruction) he was able to hit nearly forty targets in Israel. Provided with a nuclear warhead, such missiles do not need to be very precise to have catastrophic consequences. The widely mediatized launch of the three-stage *Safir* rocket on 17 August 2008 above northern Iran was probably a failure, but it indicates that the Iranian space programme is rapidly speeding up.[20]

The risks of an Iranian nuclear weapon

The security implications of an Iranian nuclear weapon are well known. All states in the Middle East and around the Gulf are widely exposed to the risks.

---

[15] Quoted by Eich Follath, Cordula Meyer &Christoph Schult, 'Intelligence Agencies put brakes on Bush's Iran Plans', *Der Spiegel* (online) (12 October 2007).

[16] De Wit, *supra* n. 13, p. 45.

[17] See, e.g., Ephraim Kam, ed., *Israel and a Nuclear Iran: Implications for Arms Control, Deterrence, and Defense*, Tel Aviv, Institute for National Security Studies (INSS), Memorandum No. 94 (July 2008). Cf. Yossi Melman & Meir Javedanfar, *The Nuclear Sphinx of Tehran. Mahmoud Ahmadinejad and the State of Iran* (New York, Carroll & Graf Publishers 2007) pp. 151-170.

[18] Cf. the CNN interview by Wolf Blitzer with Tzipi Livni on 3 August 2008, available on <www.mfa.gov.il>

[19] 'Israel warns on Iran nuclear arms', *BBC News* (2 August 2008).

[20] See Michael Persson, 'Een pruttelende V-2 uit Iran', *De Volkskrant* (23 August 2008).

Iran would become the undisputed hegemon of the region, and its nuclear status might very well encourage Egypt and Saudi Arabia to develop their own nuclear arms. That would be a fatal blow to the NPT. Iranian missiles could easily hit the many American bases and troops in the region, or aggravate local crises in Lebanon and the Gaza strip. Nuclear material can also be maliciously turned over to terrorist organizations. It is not inconceivable that nuclear explosives might be assembled at secret locations in Egypt or Lebanon, to be subsequently transported in container trucks into Israel. In the United States, both the White House and the Congress have declared on many occasions that an Iranian nuclear weapon is 'unacceptable', and that to prevent this perspective 'not a single option' should be excluded. This viewpoint is shared by the two presidential candidates, as we have seen. Yet an Iranian nuclear weapon does not in itself pose a direct threat to the American homeland given, among other things, the insufficient range of the Iranian missiles. The EU, too, considers an Iranian nuclear weapon to be unacceptable, and for France in particular it has already been a more or less open point of concern in its defence policy for a number of years, the White Paper of 2008 included. 'Iran' was also the initial argument to set up American anti-missile shields in Poland and the Czech Republic. But the EU as such sees the Iranian nuclear dossier primarily as a diplomatic issue, not as a military one.

For Israel the situation is entirely different. Here an Iranian nuclear arsenal is widely perceived as an existential threat. Just one hit by a nuclear loaded *Shahab*-3 near Tel Aviv would cause hundreds of thousands of victims and massive destruction. President Ahmadinejad has repeatedly called for the annihilation of the Zionist entity, or suggested that the Jewish state should be wiped from the face of the earth, or removed from the 'pages of history.'[21] Other Iranian leaders have joined this chorus, and calls for the fight against the Jews are a standard feature in the Friday sermons of the Iranian clergy. This is combined with the denial of the Holocaust and other flagrant forms of anti-Semitism. In the Iranian media the Protocols of the Elders of Zion are often seen as serious proof of the Jewish conspiracy for world domination.[22] Moreover, Tehran puts deeds into words, and openly provides terrorist movements such as Hamas, Hezbollah or the Islamic Jihad with advanced weaponry and instructors, as was shown, for instance, during the Lebanon war in July 2006. Not surprisingly, Jerusalem considers Iran as a bigger threat to the security of Israel than the Palestinians.

The persistent Iranian nuclear efforts leave the international community essentially with three sets of options.

---

[21] Melman & Javedanfar, *supra* n. 17, p. 53.

[22] MEMRI, Special Dispatch Series No.1975 (2 July 2008).

Further economic sanctions and incentives

By far the best option, preferred by nearly everybody, particularly the EU, would be mounting diplomatic pressure, combined with economic sanctions and incentives, in the hope that these will eventually lead to Iranian compliance with the demands of the IAEA and the UN. This perspective, however, is rather bleak for various reasons.

First, Iran considers its nuclear programme as the inalienable right of a sovereign state. As we have seen, the government denies that it is pursuing military objectives, and it argues – in itself correctly – that the NPT gives ample scope for the development of nuclear energy. The programme already started under the Shah, and apart from a temporary freeze after the revolution in 1979, it has taken the Islamic Republic, after many years of work, to a point where it is approaching control over the complete nuclear fuel cycle. These huge investments will not be easily given up.

Moreover, the regime feels itself seriously threatened by the many American military bases and troops in the surrounding countries, and it has not forgotten the attack from Iraq in 1980 and the ensuing war, which was partly fought with weapons of mass destruction, and caused hundreds of thousands of casualties. And, of course, Israel is a nuclear power as well, even without being a party to the NPT.[23] The Iranian population, opposition groups included, by and large supports the atomic programme, so a regime change does not offer a solution, quite apart from the question of how such a change could be engineered from abroad.

The sanctions by the international community do not leave the leadership in Tehran entirely unaffected – Iran considers itself to be a prominent Muslim state, not a pariah – but so far these have only incurred some minor economic incoveniences. Economic sanctions can easily be bypassed, and Russia, China, and the EU still conduct, on a large scale, trade and investment relations with Iran. For instance, earlier this year the federal bureau for export controls in Berlin has given permission for a major German investment in the Iranian gas industry, despite protests from Jerusalem.[24] Research has shown that even severe economic sanctions seldomly lead to the desired outcome if the highest national interests are at stake.[25]

---

[23] See for a recent analysis: *Nuclear Programmes in the Middle East. In the shadow of Iran* (London, International Institute for Strategic Studies 2008) pp. 119-140.

[24] *Der Spiegel* (online) (8 January 2008). Cf. Sico van der Meer, 'Economische sancties tegen Iran: successen en tegenvallers', 62 *Internationale Spectator*, No. 9 (September 2008) pp. 451-453.

[25] For an assessment see Ted Galen Carpenter, 'Iran's Nuclear Program. America's Policy Options', *Policy Analysis*, No. 578 (20 September 2006) pp. 4-5.

The fact that Tehran in June 2008 once more turned down a lucrative offer from the '3+ 3' team – large-scale economic cooperation in exchange for suspending enrichment – indicates clearly that economic costs and benefits are not of decisive importance for the strategic considerations of the ayatollahs.[26] It is therefore by no means certain that the additional sanctions which the EU set up in July 2008 will have the intended effect. Nor is it very likely that China and Russia, which already have great difficulty with the current set of sanctions, will agree to military means of coercion. China is very dependent on Iranian oil deliveries, while Vladimir Putin – still President at that time – said quite unambiguously during his visit to Tehran in April 2008 that he would not support a military option. As a result of the recent tensions between the West and Russia with regard to the crisis over Georgia it is not to be expected that Moscow has become more accommodating in this matter. Moscow in any case cancelled a meeting of the '3+3' group in New York in September 2008, which was supposed to plan a fourth set of UN sanctions against Iran in reply to the latest findings of the IAEA.[27]

Reconciliation with an Iranian nuclear force

If further economic sanctions fail, and Iran continues its nuclear programme, essentially two options remain for the international community: it may either accept the new reality and try to come to terms with it, or it may apply military measures. The first possibility has many negative consequences, but compared with the perspective of yet another war in the Middle East, it might nevertheless be the second-best outcome for the EU, and certainly for Russia or China. A potential large-scale conflict in and over Iran would be a great disaster for the whole world, and therefore the international community will undoubtedly try, through containment, deterrence and whatever other means to accommodate the Iranian nuclear threat.[28]

Even for the United States this might be the second-best outcome. Though many senior politicians and officials in the Bush/Cheney administration have

---

[26] The Ministers of Foreign Affairs of the United States, Russia, China, France, the United Kingdom and Germany (the '3+3') have made this offer in their joint letter of 12 June 2008, that was presented in Tehran by Solana to the Iranian Minister of Foreign Affairs, Manuchehr Mottaki, a few days later. For Solana's press conference on this occasion, see: Council of the European Union, Spokesperson of the High Representative for the CFSP, S211/08, 14 June 2008.

[27] 'Russia scuttles meeting with US on Iran', *International Herald Tribune* (25 September 2008).

[28] The preferred approach of the German analist Christoph Bertram in his paper: 'Rethinking Iran: From confrontation to cooperation', *Chaillot Paper No 110* (Paris, Institute for Security Studies of the European Union, August 2008).

repeatedly called for a US military strike against the nuclear facilities in Iran, it seems that in the latter days of his presidency, Bush has recoiled from the consequences of such unilateral and preventive measures. By 2008 a number of neoconservative diehards had left the administration. Everybody is haunted by another 'intelligence failure'. The wars in Iraq and Afghanistan have already stretched US military forces to the very limits. The rising national debts in the wake of the financial crisis make additional overseas military commitments nearly impossible. According to press reports President Bush would also have withheld American support for a possible Israeli strike in the summer of 2008.[29]

But what about Israel itself, after all it does find itself first in the firing line? Despite the very real threat to the state (and the people) of Israel posed by an Iranian nuclear force, Jerusalem could nevertheless decide to live with the danger, and avert it by means of deterrence. In theory this is not impossible, given the nuclear status of Israel itself. Should Iran consider a nuclear attack, massive Israeli retaliation will follow, even if Iran succeeds in delivering the first blow. Hence, the two Middle East powers might together create a balance of terror, along the same lines as the American-Russian nuclear balance during the Cold War. Both parties, according to this reasoning, will refrain from nuclear brinkmanship because of the mutual destruction that would be assured.

Nevertheless, this scenario has some serious flaws.[30] First of all, Tehran does not meet the precondition of rationality, required for a credible deterrence. That presupposes that both parties want to prevent a nuclear war at all costs, in order to stave off their own destruction. The question is whether similar calculations are made by the ayatollahs. Anti-Jewish martyrdom is a cherished part of their fundamentalist ideology. And self-sacrifice is not an alien feature for a regime that sent huge waves of young Iranian soldiers to their certain deaths towards the Iraqi lines during the Iran-Iraq war. The former Iranian President, Ayatollah Rafsanjani, known as a moderate, already observed in 2001 that one single atomic bomb might destroy Israel, while a retaliatory attack on Iran would inflict only limited damage to the Muslim world as a whole.[31]

Successful mutual deterrence also requires reliable channels of communication, very clear hierarchies of control and command in both states, and at least a recognition of Israel's right of existence. An idea that is completely taboo among politicians for whom the liberation of holy Muslim territory in all of the former Palestine lands is a fundamental religious duty. Successive Israeli governments

---

29 'Israel asked US for green light to bomb nuclear sites in Iran', *The Guardian* (25 September 2008).

30 See Yair Evron, "An Israel-Iran Balance of Nuclear Deterrence: Seeds of Instability", in: Kam, ed., *supra* n. 17, at pp. 47-64.

31 Efraim Inbar, 'The need to block a nuclear Iran', 10 *Middle East Review of International Affairs*, No. 1 (March 2006).

of all stripes and colours, therefore, have come to the conclusion that they cannot live with this option. Even American security guarantees present no *panacea* to Jerusalem. Such guarantees mainly offer subsequent retaliation, and no solid physical protection against incoming Iranian ballistic missiles. This also holds true for the anti-missile shield that Israel is currently constructing with the help of *Arrow* systems provided by the United States. Undoubtedly a useful additional defence measure, but not the watertight protection needed by a people still haunted by the memory of the Holocaust. Israeli experts have also advised against building nuclear shelters in order not to give the population a false impression of safety.[32]

Military intervention by Israel

This automatically leads us to the third distinct possibility: Israel kills off the Iranian nuclear programme by means of military force, without waiting for American approval or military assistance – probably the best prepared option in Israel's military history. The Israeli air force is familiar with risky operations far beyond its borders (Entebbe, Tunis, Osirak), and underlined this capacity in September 2007 by unexpectedly eliminating a presumed research reactor in the North of Syria.[33] The next possible assignment, however, is a lot more difficult. The Iranian nuclear installations are located much farther from Israel than the reactors in Iraq and Syria, and they are scattered over the whole country. Furthermore, they are fairly well-defended, and largely built in deep underground, heavily armoured spaces. Iran is also engaged in the purchase of a new generation of Russian anti-aircraft defence missiles, making it more difficult for Israeli aircraft to reach their goals. Yet, according to military experts, it can be done.[34] The Israeli air force has advanced F-15 and F-16 aircraft that are especially adapted to long-distance operations and, equipped with 'bunker busters', they are able to hit targets deep under the ground with great precision. And not all nuclear installations need to be eliminated. A few attacks directed at the key complexes of Isfahan or Natanz will probably do the job, at least for a couple of years. In the spring of 2008 the Israeli air force held extensive military exercises in and above the Mediterranean sea to practice the complications of long-distance flights.

---

[32] See David Klein, 'A Nuclear Defense Policy for Israel without shelters', in Kam, ed., *supra* n. 17, pp. 83-96.

[33] Strangely enough without much fuss in the Arab world; possibly the presumed reactor was some sort of a dummy to test the Israeli readiness to attack.

[34] See Whitney Raas & Austin Long, 'Osirak Redux? Assessing Israeli Capabilities to Destroy Iranian Nuclear Facilities', 31 *International Security*, No. 4 (Spring 2007) pp. 7-33.

At the same time rumours about an imminent Israeli strike have increased.[35] Even European politicians have become alarmed. The former German Foreign Minister, Joschka Fischer, for instance – who participated in the initial EU3 contacts with Tehran in 2003 and has closely followed the developments since – has said that the main question is not 'if' Israel will strike, but 'when'.[36] The French President Nicolas Sarkozy, partly in his capacity as the EU chair during the second half of 2008, has also warned Iran of an approaching Israeli strike.[37] He tried to convince Syria, an ally of Iran, to take the message home to Tehran.[38]

But a great deal of uncertainty remains. Many factors come into play for the Israeli decision makers: the composition of a new Israeli cabinet, the perspective of further sanctions by the United Nations, the possible implications for the Palestinian-Israeli peace talks, and most importantly also the new American President. Though at the end of the day the government in Jerusalem retains the option to make up its own mind, it seems very unlikely that it would prefer to proceed without at least the silent consent of Washington.

At this point a new administration may complicate matters. President Bush had already refused, as we have seen, to give the green light to the military plans of Ehud Olmert, and it is most unlikely that the new American President will allow his term to begin with yet another military conflict in the Middle East. Barack Obama, for example, does not rule out military options against Iran, but if he is elected, he also wants to open direct negotiations with Tehran, without setting impossible prior preconditions. As long as these bilateral talks last, Israel obviously cannot resort to military action, while Tehran will do everything to delay the start and the proceedings of those talks. The new president is sworn in at the end of January 2009, and it may take many months before serious contacts will be made. Obama may also decide to wait for the next presidential elections in Iran, which will probably take place in June 2009, hoping that a more moderate candidate than Mahmoud Ahmadinejad will be elected. Either way, Israel has to wait as well.

And what will happen if Iran makes far-reaching concessions related to another American ambition: the Annapolis process? The Iranian leaders might prod their friends in Damascus to conclude peace with Israel, to diminish their support for Hezbollah or Hamas, and even to make moves to recognize Israel, without at the same time renouncing their nuclear programme. They could re-

[35] 'Israeli ministers mull plans for military strike against Iran', *Der Spiegel* (online) (16 June 2008); 'It's later than you think', *The Economist* (26 June 2008); 'Fear over Israel's threat to strike Iran', *Financial Times* (2 July 2008); 'Israel asked US for green light to bomb nuclear sites in Iran', *The Guardian* (25 September 2008).

[36] In an op-ed article for the Lebanese newspaper *Daily Star* (30 May 2008).

[37] 'Sarkozy warns Iran it risks attack by Israel', *Financial Times* (4 September 2008).

[38] MEMRI, Special Dispatch No. 2039 (3 September 2008).

play the 'grand bargain' of 2003, when – in vain – the Bush administration was offered a series of political concessions (but not on the nuclear programme) in return for the normalization of the bilateral relationship. This would pose an awful dilemma for the Israeli government. On the one hand, it would gain a serious perspective on peace and stability in the Palestinian territories and with their neighbours. But, on the other hand, the nuclear threat of Iran would remain. An Israeli military strike against Iran under such circumstances would, however, encounter huge resistance from the international community at large, the United States included. Even John McCain would probably not prefer to spoil the possibility to end the Palestinian-Israeli conflict with threats about bombing Iran. If, with the help of Tehran, the Annapolis process leads to a satisfactory outcome, diplomatic pressure would switch very soon from Iran to Israel. Some have pleaded, therefore, to strike still during Bush's time in office.[39]

Final remark

Needless to say, any military intervention by either Israel and/or the United States will have far-reaching consequences for the world at large, Europe included. Iran could counter-attack American bases across the Gulf, stir up civil war in Iraq, let loose Hezbollah and Hamas in Lebanon and the Palestinian territories, or resort to a variety of energy sanctions, including the closing of the Strait of Hormuz.[40] One does not need to share the doomsday feelings of IAEA chief ElBaradei ('an attack will simply create a ball of fire which will ricochet everywhere, every part of the world'), without admitting the huge effects for vital European security and economic interets.[41]

Against this backdrop the European Union and its Member States should become more aware of the urgency of the matter. European politicians and their public should wonder whether their favourite approach of diplomatic pressure, combined with economic sanctions and incentives, is indeed the best way forward. For the EU not much has been left from its early diplomatic role. The civilian instruments of the EU are practically exhausted. It is highly doubtful

---

[39] Like the Israeli historian Benny Morris, 'Using bombs to stave off war', *The New York Times* (18 July 2008). This viewpoint was shared by the former American ambassador to the UN, John Bolton, in the *Daily Telegraph* (24 June 2008).

[40] See Patrick Clawson & Michael Eisenstadt, *The Last Resort. Consequences of Preventive Military Action against Iran* (Washington DC, The Washington Institute for Near East Policy (WINEP) 2008).

[41] Quote of ElBaradei in: 'IAEA chief: Iran on path to build nukes', *Jerusalem Post* (26 September 2008).

whether tougher economic sanctions, within or outside the UN framewok, will do the job. Tehran has essentially used the negotiations with the EU and the '3+ 3'group to gain time. Javier Solana has succeeded in keeping EU Member States together on this dossier, but that was partly because military options were left out of consideration. As usual, the EU Member States are divided over the use of force. Nicolas Sarkozy stated, shortly after taking office as President, that military measures cannot be excluded. Germany, however, is extremely reluctant to discuss this option, although Chancellor Angela Merkel declared during her visit to Jerusalem in May 2008 that the security of Israel is also the security of Germany. The crisis over Georgia in August 2008 and the resulting tensions with Russia have overshadowed the Iranian issue. The 'new cold war' is for most EU countries (and NATO) a more immediate concern than Iran. But the clock is ticking. It is not completely unthinkable that eventually Tehran will come round under imminent military pressure. To this effect close transatlantic cooperation is required in the months ahead, and a Western consensus on the possible use of military force by either Israel or the United States, if other measures fail. The EU should in any case become much more aware of the fact that playing the good cop only works if there is also a bad cop in the wings.[42] Or that the case of Iran deserves even two bad cops.

---

42 Cf. Dalia Dassa Kaye, 'Time for Arms Talks? Iran, Israel, and the Middle East Arms Control', *Arms Control Today* (November 2004) p. 7.

THE NETHERLANDS ARMED FORCES PROMOTING THE INTERNATIONAL RULE OF LAW AND STABILITY: MATCHING AMBITIONS, STRUCTURES AND FUNDS

Edwin Bakker & Kees Homan

INTRODUCTION

One of the three main tasks of the Netherlands Armed Forces is to promote the international rule of law and international stability. The other two are protecting the integrity of national and Alliance territory – including the Netherlands Antilles and Aruba – thereby supporting civil authorities in upholding the law, and providing disaster relief and humanitarian assistance, both nationally and internationally.[1] This chapter focuses on the capabilities and approaches of the Netherlands Armed Forces in fulfilling the 'international task' in a constantly changing political and military environment. These issues are at the core of the current debate on the future of the armed forces that has been organized by the Dutch government. This debate is channelled through the 'Future Policy Survey' – a joint project of the ministries of Defence, Foreign Affairs, the Interior and Justice – which should result in 'a sound judgment on the armed forces and the level of defence expenditure associated with it.'[2] This chapter aims to contribute to this debate by analyzing the problem of the enormous challenges posed by high political ambitions, limited means and new requirements. In addition it discusses various choices that need to be made to make sure that the Netherlands Armed Forces can continue to fulfil their international task in the years to come. Basically, a decision has to be made between the so-called 'Venus option' – structuring the armed forces for peace operations – and the 'Mars option' – which means focusing on expeditionary capacities to participate in combat operations.

[1] Ministry of Defence of the Netherlands (hereafter: Ministry of Defence), *Facts and figures about the armed forces*, October 2007.

[2] Ministry of Defence, *Future Policy Survey. A foundation for the armed forces of 2020*, Summer 2008.

J. de Zwaan, E. Bakker and S. van der Meer (eds.), Challenges in a Changing World

DUTCH FOREIGN AND SECURITY POLICY

After the end of the Cold War there was a brief feeling of euphoria around the world. The then United States President, George H.W. Bush, spoke of a 'new world order', an era in which worldwide peace and prosperity seemed closer than ever. However, very soon the situation in Somalia and the civil war in the former Yugoslavia brought an end to this optimism. The Cold War situation, in which the major threats to security were relatively clear, changed into a situation characterized by uncertainty. Open hostility between (blocs of) states made way for an increase in intrastate conflicts in failing and fragile states, and a wide range of risks and threats posed by non-state actors: terrorism, international organized crime and piracy. Some of the most life-threatening Cold War challenges remained, such as the proliferation of weapons of mass destruction. In addition, ongoing globalization made the world more vulnerable to economic disruption. Collapsing stock markets, a dollar crisis, or rising food prices may ultimately have unpredictable consequences for international security. And finally, climate change may cause floods and pandemics may claim hundreds of thousands of victims. In other words, the overall international security landscape has become more complex and less predictable.

What position does the Netherlands take in this uncertain and unstable world? Despite its small size, the Netherlands is an important economic power. As one of the top ten exporting countries in the world it has economic and political interests worldwide. Due to its geographical location, the Netherlands also plays an important role in international trade as the main port of Europe. As a consequence, the prosperity and security of the Netherlands is strongly linked to stability elsewhere in the world.

In accordance with its position in the world and a dependence on what is happening outside its borders, Article 90 of the Constitution of the Netherlands states that the government should promote the international legal order. As a consequence Dutch foreign and security policy takes a very proactive stance when the international legal order and international stability are threatened. This implies a general willingness to intervene at an early stage in crisis situations in other parts of the world, preferably under the auspices of the United Nations.

However, self-interest is not the only reason why the Netherlands promotes the international legal order and contributes to international stability. The rule of law and peace are also very important values that are anchored in Dutch culture and traditions. The same holds true for democracy and human rights.

THE ROLE OF THE NETHERLANDS ARMED FORCES

In line with the Netherlands foreign and security policy, the Netherlands Armed Forces actively contribute to stability and freedom in the world. This is expressed in one of its three main tasks, which is 'promoting the international rule of law and international stability.' The two other main tasks are 'protection of the integrity of national and Alliance territory, including the Netherlands Antilles and Aruba,', and 'supporting civil authorities in upholding the law, providing disaster relief and humanitarian assistance, both nationally and internationally.' In this chapter, however, we focus on the first-mentioned task.

Every year, thousands of Dutch military personnel are deployed for peace support operations abroad, or contribute on a rotational basis to (NATO and EU) rapid response forces. Currently, more than one hundred of them contribute to peace and stability in the Balkans, mainly in Bosnia Herzegovina. In the Middle East, the navy patrols the coast of Lebanon and the army participates in the NATO Training Mission in Iraq. And already for decades Dutch armed forces provide observers to the UN Truce Supervision Organisation in Israel, Syria and Lebanon (UNTSO). Most of the Dutch military personnel that are currently deployed abroad are based in Afghanistan. About 1,650 of them are part of the International Security Assistance Force (ISAF) and Operation Enduring Freedom (OEF). In early 2008, the Netherlands Council of Ministers decided to take part in the EU operation in Chad and the Central African Republic (EUFOR Chad/RCA). The Netherlands Armed Forces have deployed a marine reconnaissance unit of approximately sixty troops. In the Democratic Republic of Congo some forty Dutch military personnel serve in the EU mission. Smaller groups of observers and advisors are seconded to the International Military Advisory Team (IMAT) and the UN mission in Sudan (UNMIS), as well as the UN mission in Eastern Congo (MONUC).[3]

The number of missions and that of military personnel express a strong commitment by the Netherlands to international security and international organizations (UN, NATO, EU). The figures also indicate a heavy workload for the Netherlands Armed Forces. Set against the background of the new and ever changing security environment, trying to successfully contribute to these missions has become an increasingly difficult task. It requires armed forces capable of working in a complex political environment, working together with traditional and new allies, and operating in hostile and difficult geographical environments. The question is to what extent the armed forces possess the capabilities and the right approaches to effectively fulfil their task.

---

[3] Ministry of Defence, *supra* n. 1.

Capabilities

The capabilities needed to operate in the current security environment are very different from those during the Cold War. In today's security environment, the Netherlands Armed Forces must be quickly deployable, flexible and able to react swiftly to unexpected developments and threats, in different parts of the world. Increasingly, this includes conflict and crises areas located in far-away places; such as Chad, Eritrea or Afghanistan. As a consequence, the armed forces must be equipped to deal with lines of supply that are very much longer. Also the operational areas are much larger. Compare, for instance, the Srebrenica enclave in Bosnia with the province of Uruzgan in Afghanistan. In addition, the Netherlands Armed Forces have to be capable of operating within larger, international contingents that are composed of not only the traditional (NATO) allies, but also new partners, some of them with quite a different cultural background. At the same time, the Netherlands Armed Forces are increasingly deployed for national tasks. In particular the terrorist threat and nature-related incidents have made the third main task of the armed forces, 'supporting civil authorities in upholding the law, providing disaster relief and humanitarian assistance,' much more relevant.

These new circumstances and developments require a Defence organization that is flexible and that has enough capacity to fulfil a wide range of tasks. How are the Netherlands Armed Forces currently doing in this respect?

Matériel

In the field of *matériel*, the Netherlands Armed Forces are implementing an ambitious programme. In the coming years the armed forces will see the introduction of the NH-90 helicopter, additional Chinook transport helicopters, ocean-going patrol vessels, and new infantry combat vehicles. Other improvements include equipping the mechanized howitzer with precision ammunition, modifications to the deck guns of the Air Defence and Command Frigates, and equipping the F-16 fighter aircraft with new target designation assets. Owing to these measures, the Netherlands Armed Forces will continue to be one of the most modern ones in the world.

However, due to current budgetary constraints and the unexpectedly high expenditure incurred by the Uruzgan Task Force as part of ISAF, in 2007 the Ministry of Defence had to take additional financial measures by reducing a number of operational capabilities. These included the sale of 28 of the current 88 Leopard II main battle tanks; 12 out of 36 self-propelled howitzers and 18 out of 90 F-16 fighter aircraft.[4] In addition, the Netherlands decided to with-

4 Ministry of Defence, Policy Letter to Parliament 'Service worldwide', 18 September 2007, p. 29.

draw from NATO's Alliance Ground Surveillance project, which consists of a mix of manned and unmanned airborne radar platforms that can look down on the ground and relay data to commanders. The Ministry of Defence also scrapped plans to acquire tactical Tomahawk cruise missiles for its frigates as well as medium-altitude long-endurance unmanned aerial vehicles. Some of these projects and *matériel* would be very welcome in Uruzgan and other areas of operation. This particularly holds true for the extra sets of 'eyes in the sky'.

The limited budget and the mission in Afghanistan make it difficult to do something about a number of *matériel* shortcomings. One of them is the shortage of strategic transport, especially in the air. This is an important bottleneck in logistics, especially now that the Netherlands Armed Forces increasingly operate in far-away places such as Afghanistan and Chad. The alternative to acquiring one's *own matériel* is leasing, hiring or outsourcing. Another solution is the pooling of means and tools. NATO's Strategic Airlift Capability C-17 initiative is an example of this. NATO will buy three C-17s Globemaster heavy transport aircraft as NATO-pooled assets with multinational crews. The Netherlands Ministry of Defence and of Foreign Affairs will invest • 130 million in this project. Participating countries will receive allocated flight hours relative to their participation. The Dutch Minister of Defence has signed a Memorandum of Understanding and will participate to the extent of 500 flying hours per year.[5]

The most important project on which the government has to decide is without doubt the replacement of the F-16 fighter aircraft. The Netherlands has taken part in the development of the Joint Strike Fighter (JSF) since 2002. In the next few years a number of intermediate steps need to be taken before a definitive decision can be made to procure the aircraft. The final (formal) decision-making phase on the replacement of the F-16 is planned for 2010, but all intermediate steps seem to indicate a choice (at a very early stage) for the JSF. Of course, the JSF is a controversial project, both in the United States and the Netherlands, as it is very costly and it can be argued that there are other, more pressing needs than replacing the – regularly modernized – F-16 fighter aircraft that are still militarily superior in all the areas in which they operate.

One of the more pressing needs is the further enhancement of the expeditionary capabilities of the Netherlands Armed Forces. This is the chief priority of the Ministry of Defence. According to the Minister, Eimert van Middelkoop:

> 'First of all, operational capabilities need to be improved. It is not just a matter of the number of troops or weapons systems, but of finding the right balance between all key capabilities, including intelligence, command and control or logistics. While we are quite advanced in terms of the expeditionary capability of our armed

[5] Ministry of Defence, Letter to Parliament, 6 June 2008.

forces, we also note that the effectiveness of expeditionary operations increasingly depends on those support capabilities.'[6]

Personnel

People are the core of the Netherlands Armed Forces. In order to fulfil its tasks, the Netherlands Armed Forces employ about 50,000 military men and women. According to the Defence Plan 2008-2017, the total personnel strength should grow slightly in the coming years to 51,000 in 2012.[7] However, recruiting new personnel seems increasingly difficult. Currently the armed forces cannot fill about 7,000 vacancies.[8] Explanations include better opportunities for youngsters elsewhere, as the Dutch economy is doing rather well, and the fact that serving in military missions abroad is not attractive to all youngsters. The latter particularly holds true for people with young families. Also the more than twenty serious injuries and the more than a dozen fatalities in the Uruzgan mission have a negative impact on recruitment.

A personnel problem of a different kind is attracting enough highly qualified persons. More than ever, the armed forces rely on high-tech transportation and weapons systems. In general there is a shortage in the Netherlands of people with technical expertise and therefore the armed forces have to compete with companies that can pay much higher salaries.

In an attempt to deal with these challenges, the Netherlands Armed Forces are, increasingly, making use of civilian service providers. They do so at home and in operational areas. Examples include leasing ships and aircraft, as well as contracting local business for various services, some of which may even involve the use of 'private' forces. Civilian services are becoming increasingly important as the Netherlands Armed Forces engage in more and more operations, which are increasingly long term and complex in nature. However, the activities of an uncontrolled or poorly regulated private security industry can act as an obstacle to peace building, good governance and sustainable development. One principal question that has to be answered for the near future is what services may be outsourced and what preconditions should the Dutch government observe when doing so?[9]

---

[6] Interview in: 45 *Jane's Defence Weekly*, Issue 5 (30 January 2008) p. 34.

[7] Ministry of Defence, *supra* n. 1.

[8] 'Defensie heeft tekort van 7.000 militairen', *NRC Handelsblad* (29 August 2008)

[9] For the current discussion, see: Advisory Council on International Affairs, 'Employing Private Military Companies, A Question of Responsibility', December 2007, and the response of the government, Ministry of Defence, 25 April 2008.

Approaches

3D

In the attempt to contribute to international stability, the Netherlands Armed Forces are involved in stabilization operations in which peace, security and development are more interconnected than ever before. As a consequence, one of the cornerstones of the current Dutch foreign and security policy is the implementation of a comprehensive approach. Different labels are in use to indicate more or less the same. The one that is used most often is the 'diplomacy, defence and development approach', or '3D approach'. The then Minister of Foreign Affairs of the Netherlands, Bernhard Bot, stressed that security is a precondition for development and that development contributes to lasting peace and security. At a conference of the Society for International Development and the National Commission for Sustainable Development he stated that

> '[...] to achieve success, we will have to make sure that we establish an overall framework in which our political, military and development instruments can be put to good use in a logical and coherent manner. That is why I spoke today of the trinity of politics, security and development, which we should treat as an inseparable trinity. [...] When the trinity of politics, security and development is broken, the work of soldiers, police officers, diplomats and development workers will lack direction, lack coherence and lack impact, and, at worst, will become counterproductive.'[10]

'Hearts and minds'

The success of integrated approaches in stabilization operations not only depends on the cooperation between the 3 'Ds' but also on the involvement of the local population. It is very difficult to 'win' a military mission without a successful 'hearts and minds' campaign: aimed at gaining and maintaining the support of the population in order to isolate the insurgents. For instance, in Afghanistan, the insurgency by the Taliban is not only a military problem, but a social and political problem as well. Although NATO military power may be far superior, political considerations make it less desirable to use all the available destructive power. The military must understand the relative value of using force and how easily excessive force, even when apparently justified, can undermine popular support. This requires the ability to use force in an aimed, subtle and implicit way, which will often not be massive or aimed at other armed forces.

---

[10] Speech delivered by Dr Ben Bot at a conference of the Society for International Development and the National Commission for Sustainable Development, 7 April 2006.

The military are therefore faced with the necessity to think less in terms of 'combat' and to focus their attention on the political 'effects' of their operations. The military must be able to see issues and actions from the perspective of the domestic population. In other words, in addition to the skills of the diplomats and development workers, they also need social and political skills in order to be successful.

Consequences

The implementation of the idea that military deployment can only be successful as part of a larger and integrated approach to security and stability, involving a wide range of partners, has very much widened the scope of the work of the Netherlands Armed Forces. As a consequence, military deployment, in day-to-day practice, involves a great deal more than the deployment of military units. Moreover, the military operations are more complex than ever. Often, the armed forces fulfil several military tasks within the same region – sometimes under different mandates. As a result, peace support operations have evolved into complex stabilization operations, being a mix of the following elements:

- Classic peacekeeping
- Peace enforcement
- Police tasks
- Counterterrorism and counterinsurgency operations
- Rebuilding and reconstruction, and
- Disarmament, demobilization and reintegration.

In addition, the operations not only involve managing certain acute crises, but also projects aimed at addressing some of the root causes of security problems. Security Sector Reform (SSR) is a good example of the increasing array of tasks for the armed forces. SSR refers to the development of democratic, professional and effective security structures so as to enable civilians to live their lives in security and freedom, and to resolve internal conflicts within the form of government without resorting to force.[11] The aim is to establish a well-functioning security sector under political control. The Netherlands Armed Forces show an increased interest in this field, contributing to the reform of the security sector in fragile states such as Afghanistan and various African countries. However, the total personnel involved remains limited.

---

[11] Ministry of Defence, *supra* n. 2, p. 9.

CHOICES NEEDED

At least the nominal range of activities and competences of the Netherlands Armed Forces has become enormous. As a consequence, the defence organization as a whole is facing the problem of becoming overstretched. The military men and women have to be able to fulfil many different tasks: to assist civil authorities in evacuation operations or counterterrorism activities, to fight around the world together with allies in the highest spectrum of violence, and to be able or to work together with aid workers and local leaders in the reconstruction of post-war regions, just to mention a few. Moreover, they have to be able to participate in sustained operations with (too) limited means. In the medium and long run, this challenge is simply too much to ask for, especially against the background of the gradually declining defence budget. Basically, there are two answers to the questions posed by this challenge: either one spends more money on defence, or one has to decrease the number of tasks and to lower ambitions.

To the military, the most favourable of the two answers is to pour in more money. They point at the (informal) NATO standard of two percent of the gross domestic product (GDP) to be spent on defence. According to the State Budget 2007, the Netherlands expends less than 1.5 percent. This standard, and especially the large amount of tasks given to the military, have been presented as compelling arguments to demand a higher budget. However, political reality is that the budget has declined for almost two decades under post-Cold War governments, whatever political colour. It decreased from three percent of the GDP in the late 1980s to the above-mentioned figure of about 1.5 percent. Within the same time period, the political ambitions have never been 'decreased' by the same rate, thus creating a growing gap between capabilities, on the one hand, and demands and expectations, on the other.

High political ambition level

The Defence Priorities White Paper of 1993 introduced the concept of 'political ambition level'. The contribution to crisis management operations was set at one battalion or its equivalent (an F-16 fighter squadron, two frigates). The capabilities would have to enable Dutch participation in four simultaneous operations that could be sustained for a specific period. In previous years, this ambition level was only adjusted once. Due to budgetary limitations the government decided to reduce it from four to three simultaneous military operations.

In practice Dutch military contributions are generally composed on the basis of the specific demands of the mission in question. For instance, the current contribution to ISAF, including the Air Task Force, consisting of F-16 fighter aircraft and helicopters, is seen by the government as three contributions with a task force of battalion size or the equivalent. At the same time, the Netherlands Armed Forces are also involved in other missions, such as the naval contribution to UNIFIL and the naval protection of food transportations near Somalia. In other words, the Netherlands Armed Forces are still organized in such a way as to be able to cope with 'any' kind of conflict. This sounds 'robust', but in practice it is not. The government can always say 'yes' to requests and contribute to missions in a rather political and 'symbolic' way instead of a concrete way. In operations such as in Iraq or Afghanistan, the armed forces run the risk of missing the mark, because the capabilities have thinned out to the extent that a robust operation has become impossible.

As mentioned above, the 'simple' answer to this risk is to pour in more money. However, it is highly unlikely a political majority may be found, now or in the near future, that would support such an answer. In fact, one must expect a further decrease in the budget for defence. Therefore, the military, the Ministry of Defence and politicians should start considering to abandon the idea of armed forces that are able to cope with 'any' situation.

This will not be easy, as it requires having to say 'no' to certain requests. Moreover, it requires making difficult choices: On what tasks should the Netherlands Armed Forces concentrate as part of its obligation to promote the international rule of law and international stability? On what particular operations and concrete tasks will the future Netherlands Armed Forces specialize? Basically there are roughly two different options that could be labelled as the 'Venus option' and the 'Mars option', with a different set of political ambitions and different structures for the armed forces.

The Venus option

According to the Venus option the Netherlands Armed Forces will be fully structured for peace operations (including reconstruction and rebuilding) in relatively stable environments. A second task would be to support humanitarian operations. The Venus option emphasizes the use of military capabilities to support civilian authorities, private parties and nongovernmental organizations (NGOs). The often protracted deployment in this option is aimed at achieving a state of law and order as well as offering a 'security umbrella'. A sustained presence in a country or region would allow the armed forces 'to finish the job', instead of being a temporary pawn in a larger game in which it is a minor player.

Regarding combat capacities and operations, the armed forces will be able to perform such tasks only to a very limited degree. In the case of the Venus option, this capacity is primarily earmarked for self-defence in case the strategic environment proves less stable than expected or cases where the distinction between operations at the higher and lower ends of the conflict spectrum are less clear.

The Venus option allows substantial reductions of major weapons systems. The battalion will become the basic unit in the Army and Marine Corps. Regarding the other key task of the Netherlands Armed Forces, protecting the homeland, it requires close cooperation with the armed forces of Germany. The Venus option also demands a substantial capability for supporting civil tasks, for instance a 'CIMIC battalion' and a battalion-size 'riot and crowd' unit. This option also envisages a bigger role for the fourth entity of the Netherlands Armed Forces, the Marechaussee (Gendarmerie).[12]

As this option focuses on peace operations and post-conflict reconstruction, the armed forces will need to closely cooperate with the other two 'Ds', diplomats and development experts. This requires additional investments in training and exercises between these actors. It may even necessitate joint staffs at the ministries in The Hague as well as joint headquarters in the field.

The Mars option

Choosing for the Mars option means specializing the Netherlands Armed Forces into an 'expeditionary force' that can participate alongside major allies in combat operations. The core task of the armed forces is to protect national interests and that of our closest partners, through NATO, EU, UN or *ad hoc* coalitions of the willing. They have to be able to operate in extremely violent situations, also against well-equipped military opponents. Post-conflict peace-building missions or the support of civilian authorities are not neglected in this option, but these tasks are not leading when the decisions are made on the capabilities that will have to be developed.

For the armed forces as a whole, the first criterion of this option is the power of force projection. In other words, they have to be able to project stability to protect and enforce the international rule of law. The means and tools the armed forces will use must be modern and of high quality. They also have to be interoperable with the main military partners, as the Netherlands Armed Forces are not in a position to independently carry out larger operations. In other words, they have to become 'complementary' armed forces, offering a 'credible contribution' to international coalitions. Modularity and multi-readiness at the level of both the unit and the organization are important factors in that respect. A further increase of strategic (air or sea) lift capabilities will be necessary in

[12] Many elements of the Venus option can be found in the defence plans of the Dutch Social democrats as formulated in, e.g., *In dienst van Nederland, in dienst van de wereld', Een plan voor een actieve en doelmatige krijgsmacht*, PvdA Tweede Kamerfractie, Den Haag, November 2007.

order to improve the mobility of the force, which requires additional investments in assets of the Air Force and, to a lesser extent, the Navy.

The contribution of the Netherlands could be a range of tasks, but should preferably fill in lacunas in NATO's operational capacity (as part of NATO's Response Force [NRF]), or that of the Battle Groups of the EU). The final consideration regarding the Mars option concerns the coherence and balance of the toolbox as a whole, with a view towards military effectiveness. This is determined by the entire collection of weapons systems, sensor, communication and information systems, intelligence and logistics support.[13]

Concluding remarks

One of the main obligations of the Netherlands Armed Forces is to promote the international rule of law and international stability. Given the 'challenges' in the field of *matériel* and personnel and the need to participate in more and more comprehensive approaches to security, this task is an increasingly difficult one. Add to that today's complex and ever-changing security environment and we may have to speak of a sheer impossible task.

This means that in order to be able to effectively contribute to the international rule of law and international stability the Netherlands Armed Forces should focus on certain tasks and abandon or disregard others. This requires a fundamental choice with regard to the Netherlands defence policy and the future shape and orientation of its armed forces.

The *Venus option* with its focus on peace operations contributes to the goal of promoting the international rule of law and international stability as part of a more 'reactive security policy'. The Netherlands Armed Forces are mainly used in peace operations, with an emphasis on reconstruction and rebuilding. This option is more or less equivalent with the defence profiles of countries like Ireland and Austria.

The *Mars option*, with its focus on combat operations, is part of a more 'proactive security policy'. It requires building up an expeditionary military organization that can be deployed worldwide to participate in combat operations. The Mars option allows substantial reductions of some major weapons systems – such as submarines – but requires more budget than the Venus option.

In our opinion the expeditionary armed forces are better equipped to deal with and operate in the new international security environment. Therefore the

[13] Many elements of the Mars option can be found in the defence plans of the Dutch Christian democrats as formulated in, e.g., 'Zo ver de wereld strekt. Ambities voor de Nederlandse krijgsmacht in een veranderende internationale omgeving', Rapport Wetenschappelijk Instituut voor het CDA, Den Haag, May 2007.

Mars option should be preferred if one considers promoting the international rule of law and stability the prime task of the Netherlands Armed Forces. This option also underlines the principles of 'solidarity' and 'sharing risks', which are the cornerstone of a well functioning NATO and European Security and Defence policy.

Looking at the political ambitions of the government as well as at the current defence plans and investments, it seems that both the government and the Netherlands Armed Forces favour expeditionary armed forces. While in the Defence White Paper 2000 the words 'expeditionary force' had still been explicitly avoided, in the text accompanying the State Budget 2003, the 'Expeditionary Force' became the *Leitmotiv* of plans and investments. Also the recent letter to Parliament in which the government unfolds its plans regarding the transformation of the Netherlands Armed Forces considers strengthening expeditionary capacities as a priority.[14]

A majority in Parliament probably shares this position, as politicians like to have a well-assorted military toolbox at their disposal from which – depending on the situation – the right tools may be selected for either a peace mission or a combat one. At the same time, however, it is highly unlikely that a majority in Parliament, as well as a majority among the general public, are willing to pay for what such armed forces need. Breaking this deadlock requires more political courage than was available in the last decade or so. Perhaps a bit more daring will emerge from the current 'Future Policy Survey' on future ambitions, the structure of the armed forces, and the defence budget, which will produce its findings in 2009.[15] For the time being, the gap between capabilities and expectations and demands will continue to exist. Unfortunately, this carries serious risks, for the missions in Afghanistan and elsewhere, and for the armed forces as a whole. It is therefore high time that Government and Parliament find the courage needed to let go of the idea that the Netherlands Armed Forces can participate in 'any' kind of conflict and all types of operations. And next, they have to decide on what the armed forces will focus; on peace operations or on combat operations. The latter are more expensive and less safe than the former. However, given the new security environment, a focus on combat operations, the so-called Mars option, seems to be the most appropriate one.

---

[14] Ministry of Defence, *supra* n.2, pp. 22-27.

[15] Ibid., *Project Verkenningen* (April 2008), 'Verslag startconferentie verkenningen' <www.yourdefence.nl/file.php/1/Verslag_startconferentie.pdf>.

SPRINGER NATURE

GPSR Compliance

The European Union's (EU) General Product Safety Regulation (GPSR) is a set of rules that requires consumer products to be safe and our obligations to ensure this.

If you have any concerns about our products, you can contact us on ProductSafety@springernature.com

In case Publisher is established outside the EU, the EU authorized representative is:

Springer Nature Customer Service Center GmbH
Europaplatz 3
69115 Heidelberg, Germany

FSC
www.fsc.org
MIX
Papier | Fördert gute Waldnutzung
FSC® C083411

Kolibri 360 GmbH
Ferdinand-Jühlke-Straße 7
99095 Erfurt, Deutschland
produktsicherheit@kolibri360.de